THE LETTERS OF
PAULINE PALMER

For Louisa and Mike — lovers and sharers of a wonderful history — with love from Rée (Dwight)
August 2006

ALSO BY ELEANOR DWIGHT

Edith Wharton: An Extraordinary Life

The Gilded Age: Edith Wharton and Her Contemporaries

Diana Vreeland

THE LETTERS OF
PAULINE PALMER

A GREAT LADY OF CHICAGO'S FIRST FAMILY

EDITED BY ELEANOR DWIGHT

M.T.TRAIN/SCALA BOOKS

BOOK DESIGN
ELIZABETH PAUL AVEDON AND LAURA WHITE
www.elizabethavedon.com

———————

PUBLISHED BY M.T.TRAIN/SCALA BOOKS
DISTRIBUTED BY ANTIQUE COLLECTOR'S CLUB, EASTHAMPTON, MA. USA
PRINTED BY ZONES, MILANO

———————

THE LETTERS OF PAULINE PALMER COPYRIGHT ©2005 ELEANOR DWIGHT
ALL RIGHTS RESERVED
No part of this book may be reproduced or transmitted in any form
without written permission except in the case
of brief quotations embodied in critical articles and reviews.
EDITORIAL ASSISTANT: SANDRA ROLDAN

FIRST EDITION

ISBN 1851494979
Library of Congress Control Number 2005927128

"One of the great ladies without trying to be."
—Obituary in *Chicago American*, 1956

CONTENTS

EDITOR'S NOTE

It was a pleasure for me to edit the letters of Pauline Kohlsaat Palmer for readers of the twenty-first century. They were written almost one hundred years ago, starting in 1908, when a young bride set off on a honeymoon trip to Europe with her husband. They are enthusiastic and full of detail as Pauline wants to bring her mother Mabel Kohlsaat along with her—telling her all her impressions and many of her feelings on first leaving home. The last letters in the collection are written almost twenty years later in 1926, when Pauline is an accomplished mother of four, a contributor to the Art Institute, the chatelaine of "the Castle," a concerned world citizen who helped the French after the World War, and the successful wife of the now patriarch of Chicago's first family. She has grown older but has lost none of her enthusiasm or wonder for life. The world as she sees it has changed, and with the Great Depression, the Palmers' era will end.

My mother and grandmother knew the Palmer family, and I remember going to dinner at the Palmers' summer house in Bar Harbor when I was a child. I observed the stately Pauline Palmer at the head of her table. Graceful and ladylike, she had enormous blue eyes, striking white hair, and a regal but thoughtful manner. She wore light shades of gray and blue, as she was still in mourning for her husband, who had died in the mid-'40s.

Pauline's letters were kept in a black-and-white marbleized cardboard box, fastened by rubber bands into twelve packets. They were found by her granddaughter, Charlotte Bordeaux, in the house of her mother, Bertha Palmer Thorne, after Bertha, who appears in the letters as a baby and little girl, died in the 1970s. I thought they would make a good book, showing as they do the life of an early twentieth-century woman, and making it possible to weave her impressions of a very different world in the past into our lives in the present.

I have made a few changes for clarity, but there are mysteries in the letters I cannot solve. For example, she writes her mother from many trips abroad, and she clearly goes on other trips and most likely wrote other letters, but these letters are missing. I have cut out repetitious passages and corrected some—but not all—of Pauline's spellings and have given background details to complement her writing—adding information about the well-known people she refers to. Others will either be recognized or will have to remain mysterious.

Bertha Honoré Palmer.

INTRODUCTION

The Palmer Letters, a correspondence between Pauline Kohlsaat Palmer (1882–1956) and her mother, Mabel Blake Kohlsaat (1861–1959), give a glimpse inside the lives of an influential early twentieth-century Chicago family. They tell of family life, European travels, art collecting, and Chicago history. The first letters are those Pauline writes on the honeymoon trip to Europe with her new husband, Potter Palmer II, in 1908. She continues to write during the intervening years until her children, as teenagers, go off to boarding school in the mid-1920s.

The Palmers were socially prominent— viewed by many as Chicago's "first family." When Pauline Kohlsaat married Potter Palmer II, newspaper reports went into great detail about their wedding and other events in the young couple's lives. After all, Pauline's mother-in-law-to-be was the famous Bertha Honoré Palmer, a very visible personality in the city, known for her accomplishments, her lavish entertainments, and her reputation as a figure in international society. Although one would have thought that young Potter Palmer would be married with great fanfare, the wedding on July 26, 1908 in the

Kohlsaat's house was an intimate gathering "open only to relatives of the bridal couple." A wedding breakfast was served after the ceremony. No formal announcement was made about bridal gifts, "though it was reported that Mrs. Bertha Palmer returned from Europe with a $5,000 tiara as well as a silver service set for the bride."

Pauline begins writing her mother in the days after her marriage, and her letters of the next two decades tell of the social rituals and family events of a well-off young matron at the top levels of society in America's fast-emerging Second City. These are the years before, during and after the First World War, a time seen in American history as the end of the Gilded Age and the beginning of the modern age of the twentieth century. They record, therefore, a particular cultural and social history while America was gaining sophistication and emerging as a power on the world stage. Potter Palmer II and Pauline Kohlsaat Palmer are interesting to observe as they live the lives of a privileged American family in these decades, enjoying the prosperity enabled by business success and one of America's newly made fortunes. They were members of the enthusiastic group of Americans who

Pauline Kohlsaat

were eager trans-Atlantic travelers, often touring abroad and hunting for artistic treasures. Their lives touched upon some of the celebrities of the day—Pauline talks of meeting the famous novelist Henry James and watching the funeral of Edward VII, her mother-in-law's friend.

The letters also illustrate a particular time in Chicago's own history when the former frontier town was establishing itself as the preeminent city of America's heartland. The Palmers were cultural leaders in the city. The first Mrs. Potter Palmer had reigned over the World's Columbian Exposition in 1893 as head of the Board of Lady Managers. Because of her husband's wealth and her lively personal style, she also ruled Chicago society, entertaining lavishly at either the Palmer House, their enormous luxury hotel, or at "the Castle," a gigantic medieval-style building with towers and crenellations and a huge gallery that housed her impressive art collection. Both generations of Potter Palmers were active promoters of the Art Institute of Chicago, which began in a rented space in 1879, moved to a new home at Michigan Avenue and Van Buren Street in the 1880s, and to its current handsome Beaux Arts building in 1893. As the city worked hard to

catch up to the more seasoned East Coast cities—New York, Philadelphia, and Boston—the Palmers, with their large bank accounts and energetic personalities, played leading roles.

While the society columns covered the young Palmers' wedding and their public appearances, the letters of Pauline give us an insider's look into the young couple's life. They are written from Europe; from Sarasota, Florida, the family's winter haven; and during summers from Maine, first Biddeford Pool and later Bar Harbor. Pauline talks frankly—although still a bit reticently for our day—about their children, their family life, their friends, and the personal things that concern her. Her comments about her husband, known as Min since childhood, when a nurse saw him as small, are relatively slight, leaving his portrayal somewhat mysterious. Pauline only occasionally gives her mother comments on his behavior and she tells us little of his personality. Her mother does not get the details of Min's business trips. He supports Pauline in her dealings with the servants, helping to keep the household running smoothly, and he works hard at setting up the new houses and buildings and clearing the property in Florida. He dislikes meeting strangers, and later on was seen by grandchildren and nieces and nephews as very quiet and shy. There was always a card table in the Palmer living room, and Min often played solitaire.

Lengthy letters are an anachronism in our age of hastily typed e-mail messages. Yet they continue to fascinate. Intimate personal letters served many purposes. They were meant to pass along information in an era when long-distance communication was expensive and infrequent. They were a way to keep family members close and informed about goings on when separated or traveling. Pauline gives her mother every detail about her children's behavior, whether it is an amusing incident—"Bertha tells me she is studying 'art distrophy!'"—or a new stage: a toddler's walking, or a young child's growing awareness of the ways of the world, or a puzzling symptom of bad health.

Pauline's mother-in-law, Bertha Honoré Palmer.

Writing letters to her mother also gave Pauline a time to collect her thoughts, to rethink her own life and restate her values as she comments on and critiques what she sees around her. The subjects she describes range from the beauty of Venice to shocking behavior at a Chicago costume party: "restraint [was] thrown off with conventional dress." The letters also served to maintain the affectionate emotional connection between the two, as both mother and daughter need encouragement and understanding. Pauline urges her mother not to feel "blue" and thanks her mother for frequent compliments.

As a daughter is writing to her mother, the letters also give us portraits of ladies and tell of women's concerns at that time: keeping a husband happy and healthy, looking "well-turned out," shopping for the latest fashions (in Paris), managing a large household, enjoying life, traveling, and contributing time and money to civic and cultural institutions. Above all, they show the relations between members of different generations in the same family. Many stages of a woman's married life are chronicled: the honeymoon, the children's infancy, in-law rivalries and difficulties, building a house, dividing up the spoils when a member of the older generation dies, and separating from the children when they become teenagers and venture beyond the nest. We also see Pauline sharing her observations of human behavior within the social realm, commenting on the behavior of in-laws at an upcoming wedding, or the change in fashions and manners after the First World War. As Pauline matures we see her become more philosophical about life and ready to give her mother the benefit of her wisdom. In reading these letters written early in the twentieth century, we conclude that while certain lifestyle details—like our modes of communication and travel, have changed—other things, like human behavior, remain the same.

Pauline's father-in-law, Potter Palmer I, had first become a power in the second half of the nineteenth century. Born into a farming family in upstate New York, in the mid-1840s he went west to Chicago. There he started a dry goods store, first called P. Palmer & Co., then Field and Leiter, when Leiter and Field succeeded to the business. Eventually, under Field's management, it would become the hugely successful Marshall Field & Co. Palmer soon started a second career as a real

Potter Palmer I

estate developer and made himself into one of the richest men in Chicago. He bought up almost a mile of what would become State Street, then, as historian Donald Miller describes it, "a muddy alley, narrow, poorly paved and lined by a squalid collection of pawn shops, saloons, boarding houses, and blacksmith shops." He had the street widened, and built about thirty stores and office buildings, including the first Palmer House. All his buildings burned during the great fire of 1871. With loans secured quickly in New York based on his good business reputation, he soon rebuilt the Palmer House and continued his building along State Street and the near North Side. Although a Quaker and quiet by nature, he was a daring businessman and successful entrepreneur before and after the fire. When the second two-million-dollar Palmer House opened on November 8, 1873, it was said that the barber shop floor was studded in silver dollars. He challenged competitors to set his fireproof rooms on fire.

Potter Palmer was one of a number of adventurous entrepreneurs who had seen the opportunities in this challenging, well-situated city. When he arrived in the mid-1840s, Chicago was earning its reputation as a place of dynamic business possibilities. The city named Chicago (after the Indian name for wild onions) was no longer just a fur trading post on the edge of the frontier or merely the site of Fort Dearborn. It was a growing and energetic business center, and it attracted other ambitious men who made their mark at this time. Marshall Field, who started as Potter Palmer's

business assistant, built a retailing empire. Aldophus Swift would establish a successful and innovative meat business. Cyrus McCormick arrived from Virginia in the late 1840s to set up the McCormick Reaper Works and to market his new invention, a farm machine that would revolutionize harvesting and be bought by farmers around the world. These industries employed workers by the thousands and their labor problems were well known. The Haymarket Riot of 1886 brought attention to the Anarchist movement that demanded better working conditions for the thousands who had immigrated from Ireland, Scandinavia, and Eastern Europe. Upton Sinclair's *The Jungle*, an exposé on the stockyards published in 1906, called attention to the tensions between labor and capital and the growing gap between rich and poor.

After Potter Palmer married Bertha Honoré in 1870, he retreated somewhat from public view. His brilliant wife, twenty-three years younger, had herself become one of the leaders of the Second City. She led its cultural life beginning in the 1880s and culminating in the World's Colombian Exposition of 1893. This World's Fair

marked the 400th anniversary of Columbus's discovery of America and also celebrated Chicago's prosperity, its recovery from the devastating fire, and its emerging role as one of America's preeminent cultural centers. Bertha was welcomed at the White House during the Ulysses Grant administration (her sister, Ida, was married to Grant's son), and led a cosmopolitan life with houses in London and Paris, in addition to the Chicago "Castle." The situation of the Palmers' enormous castle, built in the early 1880s, encouraged other socially aspiring families to move up north from the South Side and join the newly chic residential area looking out over Lake Michigan. Bertha's large art collection—she was an early collector of canvases of French modern painters of the Impressionist and Barbizon schools, including a large number by Monet—became an important element in the lives of Pauline and Min. After she died they took over her role as patron of the arts.

Bertha Palmer's personality and position in Chicago were both similar to and different from that of her new daughter-in-law, Pauline. Bertha had come from a cultivated Kentucky family of

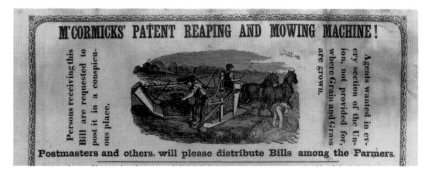

Left, clockwise from top: The Palmers' Chicago: The Palmer House, Grand Hall; Advertisement - "Thoroughly Fireproof Hotel," "Potter Palmer Owner and Proprietor;" Cityscapes, 1904–1913: Michigan Avenue with Art Institute (background, right); Marshall Fields; State Street with Carson Pirie Scott (corner, right). Above: McCormick Reaper broadside.

French background and had been educated at a Washington finishing school. Her father, Henry Honoré, had worked with Potter Palmer I in the real estate business. With her southern charm, regal presence, and keen mind and ambition, Bertha became well known in Chicago and later in London and Paris. In the planning of the World's Columbian Exposition she managed to edge out rival women for the position of greatest power, allowing her to fulfill her goal of creating a women's building, to showcase women's accomplishments separately instead of alongside men's. As the head of the Board of Lady Managers, she led a committee of strong-minded women from all over the country. When the Fair opened on May 1, 1893, Bertha, decked out in her famous diamonds, graced the impressive procession by riding in the carriage with the Duchess of Veragua, whose husband was a direct descendant of Columbus. Passionate about feminist issues, she also campaigned and spoke out for women's equality. In these decades before women got the vote, she preached that they should not be dolls, drudges, or angels for men, but true equals.

In the post-Fair years Bertha spent more time in Europe, entertaining in her London and Paris houses and enjoying the ambience and culture of the cities abroad and the society of other well-off Americans on the Continent. As a friend of Edward VII, who was a great admirer of American women, she took part in the lively social life around the King. After her husband's death in 1902, she turned her mind to business in Florida. She purchased and developed some 140,000 acres of land on the west coast near Sarasota, doubling her husband's fortune before her own death in 1918.

While Bertha was known as the Queen of Chicago for her entertaining, her leadership, and her larger-than-life personality, Pauline, her daughter-in-law, was quiet and soft spoken by comparison. She had elegance and charm, however, and the word that later generations used to describe her was "serene." When she married at the age of twenty-six she proved herself immediately adept at stepping into the role of Mrs. Potter Palmer II: running a household of numerous servants, being a good wife and intelligent companion, and with her great caretaking instincts, bringing up a family of four children. As her letters show, she was an astute observer of the social customs around her. She does not comment on her mother-in-law's personality except to be grateful for Bertha's interest in the new generation of Palmers that start arriving in 1909. The curious reader senses, however, that with her wise approach to life, she managed to coexist comfortably with the powerful Bertha.

While Potter II's parents were legendary, Pauline Kohlsaat's parents were not such celebrities, but were still important figures in the growing, vibrant city. Pauline's mother was Mabel Blake, from a Boston family who came to Chicago in 1868. The daughter of a successful businessman who became the first president of the University of Chicago's Board of Trustees, she was a determined, competent, and adventurous woman. In 1901, when her daughter Pauline made her debut, Mabel was described as "the handsome Miss Blake of Ashland Boulevard before her marriage. Mrs. Kohlsaat has not lost one whit of her youth or beauty. In fact, her face is almost as young as her daughter's. But she has the serious, pensive, severe look in her eyes of a woman hampered with many cares. It is known that H. H. Kohlsaat depends upon her judgment in many financial and journalistic matters of the greatest moment. That explains, perhaps, the absent, distrait gaze and the all too infrequent smile."

Mabel spent her time in Chicago, seeing Pauline and her family, and in Madison, Wisconsin, visiting her younger daughter, Katherine Kohlsaat Shepard. She also went abroad often, particularly to Italy, and had taken her two daughters with her before their marriages. Her keen visual descriptions of travel were clearly an influence on Pauline, who knows her mother will appreciate similar descriptions of her own touring. On a trip from Paris to Limoges Mabel writes: "Beautiful little towns—fertile fields all cultivated—wheat and sweet potatoes. Lovely trees. We crossed the Loire, Cher and the Creuse on beautiful bridges." At the home of Francis I "all the windows were filled with pink geraniums and the gate to the courtyard [was] magnificent. We drove for a long time through tall pine trees." The ground was "carpeted with heather—deep magenta, most lovely and unusual." Mabel Kohlsaat also has strong ideas on current events—both American and European. In a post-war diary entry she writes: "The politics of France should be to make close friends with Italy…instead of enemies….Germany [is] assiduously courting Italy. England is well nigh Bolshevist and never friendly to France excepting when France is pulling her chestnuts out of the fire."

Pauline's father, Herman Henry Kohlsaat ("H. H." outside his family), was respected and enjoyed by all—"a lovely, lively man," his granddaughter remembered. His life was an example of the American dream, and not just because he

married off his eldest daughter to the son of arguably the richest among many rich men in Chicago. H.H. was raised on an Illinois farm. His parents were immigrants: his father, Reiner, once an officer in the Danish army, came from Schleswig-Holstein; his mother, Sarah Hull, was born in Surrey, England, and brought to Illinois by her parents. Yet another self-made businessman in the age of enterprise after the Civil War, he was fourteen years old when he started to work for the Chicago Tribune as a "carrier boy." Soon he switched jobs, becoming a salesman for a wholesale bakery, and rising up there to make an early fortune by building a chain of bakeries and restaurants. But for the rest of his life he was a newspaper publisher, buying and selling interests in a series of unprofitable Chicago papers— the Inter-Ocean, the Times-Herald, the Post, and the Record-Herald—the wreckage of which was eventually acquired by William Randolph Hearst. According to his grandchild Constance Shepard Otis, he "made and lost fortunes," and after his death, Mabel Kohlsaat had very little money to live on. Letters from the daughter to the mother express Pauline's concern about her father's business dealings. It was said of him: "He loved newspapers, but his interest centered wholly on the influence and power his paper might assert, rather than in its commercial success."

That power and influence was used to support the Republican Party. H. H. was a loyal and diligent Republican during an age when the Republican Party dominated—electing all the presidents from the Civil War until 1912, when the Democrat Wilson was elected only because two irreconcilable Republicans, Taft and Roosevelt, split what had been the Republican

MRS. POTTER PALMER.
PRESIDENT WOMANS DEPARTMENT WORLD'S FAIR.

The great buildings of the World's Columbian Exposition, 1893. Bottom right: the Woman's Building.

Top left: The Palmer family: Honoré Palmer and Potter Palmer II as boys. Top right: Honoré Palmer, Potter Palmer II, and Honoré as boys, and Potter ("Min") at the time of his marriage. Bottom: The Palmer family out for a ride.

Top left: Herman H. Kohlsaat.
Above: Pauline Kohlsaat as a girl.
Below: Mabel Blake Kohlsaat, and
bottom left, Pauline Kohlsaat as a teenager.

vote. He was an intimate adviser to numerous politicians—McKinley, Theodore Roosevelt, Taft, Harding, Coolidge, and even Wilson, a Democrat—and had advised T. R. not to run. When H. H. bought the Times-Herald he told the editor: "The paper under my ownership will be independent in politics, but for William McKinley and anything William McKinley wants!" When the editor pointed out that this would ruin the business, saying "I don't believe [the paper] has a reader who isn't a life-long Democrat," H. H. replied, "I'll still have the bakeries." Sure enough, readers dropped away along with H. H.'s investment, and he learned what it was to rush to the bank for a loan to meet the paper's payroll. His enthusiasm for McKinley, however, remained unabated.

When Pauline Kohlsaat and Min Palmer were married in 1908, Chicago had long since recovered from the fire. Sitting as it did in an enviable geographical position—reachable through the Great Lakes and at the center of the country's railroad web—the city continued to be a growing, vibrant business center. Pauline's life took place far from the stockyards, and there is little mention in her letters of Chicago's poor or the vice and violence for which the city was also known. We imagine her bundled in furs or the latest warm coat from a Parisian shopping trip, riding in a chauffeur-driven automobile through the streets of the Windy City on a frosty winter day.

The descendants of Chicago's early business successes—the Fields; the McCormicks of the harvest machine fortune; the Swifts and the Armours, who made money in the meat packing business; and the Ryersons, who managed their family's lumber and steel empires—made up the privileged society that Min and Pauline knew. They lived in mansions on the North Side; they sent their children to boarding schools in the East; they traveled to Europe frequently, filling their homes with the furniture and decorative arts collected while abroad; they entertained lavishly. They also worked hard to beef up cultural institutions like the Art Institute, to which they donated their collections of paintings.

At the end of the nineteenth century and the beginning of the twentieth, well-off and cultivated Americans looked to Europe as an irresistible destination for travel—for beautiful scenery, to view art and architecture, to understand a longer history that Americans lacked but felt a part of, and for adventure. Pauline, Min, and their parents before them were constantly in England or on the Continent. An expatriate excitement runs through the letters. Even when Pauline is in Europe she is planning her next trip, imagining the hotels she will visit, the Italian towns or German spas she will enjoy. In their art collecting the two generations favored subjects that would remind them of their travels: Pauline collected some one hundred Whistler prints including scenes of Venice, London, France, and Holland, while her mother-in-law's famous gallery showed off canvases evoking Paris and the French countryside. The younger Palmers were not particularly erudite travelers, but they enjoyed the fun of being away from home—the nightclubs, the shopping, and seeing their American friends abroad.

For society watchers in Chicago the marriage of the young Palmers was an event to make the Second City proud. Although Pauline and her family had chosen to have a small wedding, weddings at the time were an important social ritual, and many wealthy Americans turned them into colossal events. During the 1890s, several of the young Vanderbilt women were married in the East at enormous affairs. For example, when Florence Adele Sloane married James Abercrombie Burden in 1895, the bride's trousseau cost $40,000, and the wedding guests were transported in 180 broughams brought from New Haven at the cost of $40 each and put up at one of the largest hotels in Lenox, Massachusetts.

When Pauline and Potter became engaged, the breathless tone with which the society writers sketched in the details of the young couple's history encouraged the fascination readers had with events in the lives of prominent families. Readers learned that their mothers—Bertha Honoré Palmer and Mabel Kohlsaat—had been friends for years and that Potter and Pauline had "met often abroad when traveling with their parents." Pauline had spent her young life in Chicago with the exception of one term at Miss Masters School in Dobbs Ferry, New York. She was described as artistic and social, and one of her interests was "modeling." When Pauline made her debut in 1901, a society columnist commented that it seemed only yesterday "that Pauline was a rakish little auburn-haired miss in short skirts, with the brightest little mischievous eyes. Suddenly she has grown into a stately young woman very much like her mother."

Potter, nine years older than his bride, "had been ranked as the most brilliant match among Chicago's contemporary bachelors" because of his "fortune and social prominence." "An indefatigable traveler," he had just arrived back in town after crossing the ocean on the Lusitania with his mother. A Harvard graduate, "widely popular," with a "winning personality," he was much in demand "as a leader of cotillions." He was credited with having " no fixed business or profession," but acted as an overseer of his family's large real estate holdings. Although his personality was a quiet one, he had a dry and appealing sense of humor. After his marriage he worked at his mother's real estate company in Florida and the family's bank there, and after her death in 1918 he would focus on renovating the Palmer House hotel and serving as president of the Art Institute.

The wedding ceremony, held on July 27, 1908, was "all green and white." The bride's robe was trimmed with silver and satin embroideries, and her long tulle veil caught with "a tiny coronet of orange blossoms, and atop of these the $5000 diamond tiara." The service was "solemnized in the parlor" with Johnny Hand and his orchestra hidden behind ferns. Hand would play his "sweetest" because "didn't he perform a like service thirty-seven years ago" when the bridegroom's parents were married, and the same ten years later when the father and mother of the bride were wed?

Even though the guest list was small, the presents poured in; newspapers reported that they "outrival[ed] any similar array of presents ever seen in Chicago. Cut glass, silver, house furnishings of all descriptions and souvenirs of priceless value." Civic pride was apparent in the closing remarks of one writer: "The marriage will climax a romance that society has smiled upon approvingly, for six years past. It is delightful too, that Chicago boy and girl as they are, Mr. Palmer and his bride will continue to live in their home city."

"Min calls me Mrs. pretty well,
but I can't say it yet! Seems a little strange still."

EUROPEAN SUMMER, 1908

In the first letter after her marriage, Pauline Palmer writes her mother, Mabel Kohlsaat, from New York on a hot summer's day, commenting happily on the wedding and its coverage in the papers. The next day she and her new husband will sail to Europe for their honeymoon. After their wedding they had gone to Mattapoisett, Massachusetts, where Potter and Pauline visited with Potter's brother and sister-in-law, who had a cottage there. They then sail from New York on July 30th and on August 6th arrive in Plymouth, England.

Pauline and Potter set off on their European tour in the great age of Atlantic voyaging. Ocean travel by steamship had improved vastly from its beginnings in the 1830s. As writer John Maxtone-Graham describes it, by 1900 "the world's greatest merchant ships sailed the Atlantic, flying the colors of half a dozen energetic companies." No longer did passengers have to endure damp and unappealing food, cramped quarters, or more than six or seven days at sea. Charles Dickens had described his fifteen-day voyage from east to west in 1842 on Cunard's Britania in a cabin that was "utterly impractical," a "profoundly preposterous box." Meals were served in a "hearse with windows," and featured "rather mouldy" desserts following spreads of "pig's face, cold ham, salt beef" or a "smoking mess of hot collops."

At the beginning of the new century, Cunard, a leading ship-maker of Britain, which led the world in building steamships, had launched two liners that would revolutionize ocean travel. They were driven by a new type of engine, the steam turbine, and would have very different destinies.

While the Mauretania, who made her maiden voyage in 1907, became Cunard's "golden ship," holding the Blue Riband for the fastest transatlantic crossing for twenty-two years, her sister ship, the Lusitania, launched several months earlier, was sunk by a German submarine in 1915.

On the Mauretania, the grand salon was decorated in panels of mahogany trimmed with mouldings of gold and a skylight capped with a "ground-glass, bronze-filigreed ellipse." This gave the room a "quiet grandeur." In first class no expense was spared. There was paneling and meticulous woodcarvings in all the rooms: "mahogany in the lounge, stairs and passages, maple in the drawing room, walnut in the smoking room and weathered oak in the triple-decked dining room." And although the Mauretania was spectacular in these respects, she was designed for speed rather than comfort.

The ships of the White Star Line (including the ill-fated Titanic) were even more luxurious, as they sacrificed a few hours of speed to comfort and grandeur. There was a "high servant ratio" and "sumptuous decoration." For first-class passengers on the Olympic there seemed to be limitless space and "a profusion of time-killing diversions," important for travelers on these crossings where the hours grudgingly crawled by. These included a small swimming pool, Turkish and electric baths, and a gymnasium.

The Palmers started their honeymoon voyage on July 30,1908 and arrived in Plymouth on the 6th of August. Although the departure on such a voyage might bring forth feelings of anxiety as the ship made its way down the Hudson River past

Sandy Hook and into the dark and often threatening ocean, Pauline only voices feelings of happy anticipation. On arrival in Plymouth she described how " I have done nothing but sway and clutch things all day to keep my balance." They had to wait "for hours" while a friend's "machine" (car) was hoisted off the ship. In these early days of automobiles some adventurous travelers brought their own with them for touring.

Because of the Palmers' celebrity status in Chicago, the newly married couple is well known on the boat: "Everyone on board rubbered every time they passed us. The man who sat next to us at table was a Mr. Waugh of the N.Y. World, and he knew our separate histories from a to z." After landing in Plymouth and journeying up to London, they spend a few days there staying at Claridges and two weeks in Paris where Pauline shops for clothes. "There are millions of dressmakers in town, and everything is at half price, and I can't possibly keep my head." They take a night train through France and Switzerland to Italy: "The wonderful mountains came into view about 4:30, so we missed them, but managed to see the beginning of the Simplon."

In Stresa, on beautiful Lake Maggiore, which is surrounded by the Alps, they board a boat to Luino, and then a train to Lake Lugano. At Porlezza they take a train to Menaggio and another boat to Bellagio, towns on romantic Lake Como that were popular tourist stops. "There is a moon…and men singing and playing mandolins and guitars. Everything is gay and happy, and we are having such a good time." After Bellagio they spend a week in Venice, and then go on to Florence. From there they motor to Gubbio, Urbino, Rimini, Ravenna, and Forli before taking a train back to Paris on September 29th.

In Italy Pauline's enthusiasm for beautiful places emerges. It is clear she has traveled in Europe before. She is happy to see familiar sights, and is struck by spectacles and the beauty of the landscape and architecture. Arriving in Venice, she writes about "the usual excitement at the station and a great deal of bustle about getting the trunks and starting off… The sun was setting and everything was pink and we started up the canal with the moon just beginning to make the palaces white." On a later day, as they come into the Grand Canal, "a mass was just finished in the Salute, and all the people were streaming out. Men in red gowns carrying huge lighted candles and priests in white with different coloured banners. In the twilight it was a marvelous sight."

Pauline watches the other travelers with great interest, amused by the Americans in Paris "who got drunk and began kissing and hugging each other." While Pauline loves to visit the museums, "Min can't be lugged to see a sight so I have to get him there unsuspectingly." She is gradually easing him into doing things the way she likes to do them. The letter of October 11th is from Min, and shows his dry sense of humor in his comments on shopping, as well as his and Pauline's reactions to the Christian Scientist healer.

Toward the end of their trip, Pauline advises her sister (Kay is in Paris while the newlyweds are in Italy) to tell Callots Soeurs to have her dress finished by the beginning of the next month. She reports on October 15th that she has ordered a "'maternity' corset, which seems composed entirely of laces and elastic, and might be very comfortable." And "Min says I shop with my head in the clouds and forget what I've said as soon as I've said it! But he still goes with me." They visit every antiquity store they come upon. Pauline anticipates that their house at "183 [Lincoln Park Boulevard] is going to be a wonderful place."

The Mauretania, Cunard's "Golden Ship," 1910.

Bertha Honoré Palmer with General Frederick Dent Grant leaving Pauline and Potter Palmer's wedding, 1908. Grace Palmer is in the background.

New York, NY
July 29, 1908

Mrs. Herman Kohlsaat
186 Lincoln Park Boulevard
Chicago, Illinois

Dear Mother:

Well, how are you? I am fine, and having a perfect time. We have a northeast corner on the eleventh floor, and ever since we arrived the wind has been n.e. and east, so it's as cool as can be up here. Down on the street it's pretty bad. Coming on there was an electric fan in the stateroom which helped matters a good deal and managed to save our lives.

All the clippings, telegrams, and letters came this morning and I've never read anything funnier than some of those clippings. Tell Kay that we think the joke's on her about having her picture taken, and another one is on you, where your picture is printed. Tell father I hope he appreciates my smile on the way to the machine! It certainly is a won-

der. The more I think about the
wedding the nicer I think it was.
We don't think it could have been
better possibly, everything was
lovely. The room was perfect. So
was the food, and everybody
seemed to enjoy it a good deal.
Didn't you think so? I think we all
looked proud, especially myself! So
everybody's happy.

In all the excitement I forgot to get
those things out of the library, and
so Min telephoned for them. It's a
good thing we did too, as that van-
ity box stands for 315.00 and it's to
my credit at Tiffany's now. We
looked at tiaras there, but there
weren't any that could begin to
compare with mine. It's so lovely.
Every time I go out I can't help
thinking of the Squill and what a
delirious time she'd be having here
in the shops. Everything is about
1/4 price and perfectly fresh and
new! I nearly lost my head today

Katherine Kohlsaat leaving Pauline and Potter's wedding.

over some things and only my great force of will, and the vision of packing them, kept me
from falling in completely. I'm sending the pink slippers back as they were made too
small and of a kind of silk that has already begun to fray and wouldn't stand wearing
more than twice. Too bad, but we'll go to that place on the corner of the Place Vendome
and get another pair, which will be just as good.

Min calls me Mrs. pretty well, but I can't say it yet! Seems a little strange still. Sailing
tomorrow, and I think it will be cool. Goodbye, and be sure you write me often and tell
me everything! Kay was a sweetie to write me, and I'll answer it as soon as I get on board
ship—all those 295000000 letters, telegrams and presents, too. It's nearly driving me to
drink. But I guess I'll finish them some day. Min says to have everything boxed and the
bill sent to him. Best love to Father and K. Loads to you, from us both.

Pauline

Tell Hannah my trunk is fine.

Stapleton, NY
July 30, 1908

Mrs. Herman Kolsaat
186 Lincoln Park Boulevard
Chicago, Illinois

Dear Mother:

Just a line to say I'm feeling fine, and we are as happy as two clams without an idea in the head. We had a beautiful time in N.Y. Last night we dined at Martins with the Clarks and had friends over. This morning we started off bright and early without the least hurry or trouble and got down here in plenty of time.

It makes us laugh to look out of the porthole and see the ships. Sara and Stanley are on, sailing down the harbour about half a mile ahead of us!

My trunk is all unpacked and everything out in its place, so every last thing is done. Min only knows one man on board, and I only know one, that Mr. Bacon of Washington. Miss me a lot, and write me a lot. We both send love, and loads of it.

Pauline

Claridge's Hotel
Brook Street. W.
August 7, 1908

Dear Mother:

We got here early this morning, 3:30 in fact, and it does seem queer to be here, and on land, again. I have done nothing but sway and clutch things all day to keep my balance. Min is just as bad. The boat got to Plymouth at 9:15 P.M. We got off into a founding tender and then sat hours waiting for Janet MacDonald Grace's automobile to be hoisted on. It seemed so funny to think of it being their machine. I don't know why, but it did. We kept thinking of Janet on the boat with the Elys and Farquhars, trying to keep away from them all the time, and their motor on our boat, where it was quiet and nobody spoke to you! Nevertheless, it's still "hell to be famous," for everyone on board rubbered every time they passed us, and the man who sat next to us at table was a Mr. Waugh of the N.Y. World, and he knew our separate histories from a to z. Started conversation on the subject, in fact, but as usual, met little or no success. We were actually sorry for him, but he didn't realize that. It was a perfectly smooth trip the entire way, and very pleasant, not at all warm. I ate so much that I had an attack of indigestion. Aren't you glad you weren't there to hear me complain?

We have wonderful rooms here, quite katosh, with an entrance hall and dressing room! We don't think we'll do it often, though. I'd rather get furniture. We have been shopping all the afternoon, and for some cretonne, which is most unusual and lovely, and a chair! Oh, I must tell you what happened on the boat. I lost my toothpowder box down the W.C. The one to my new bag! I dropped it, and in trying to catch it before it touched the floor, gave it a hit just as neatly as could be into the thing across the room, and it went down! We went and got another today at Aspreys, not quite like the old one, but very nice. I've nearly lost my head over the shops. They are so wonderful. Everything is a "sale," but I'm going to wait until Paris for a voile dress, for they will have them there, and much better. My clothes came out pretty well, only a few wrinkles, which I think is pretty wonderful. I'm going to wear the tea gown tonight. There isn't a wrinkle in it!

I'm going to take Min to a couple galleries before we leave. He isn't very anxious to go, but I think it will do him good to see one or two. Will you send announcements to the Misses Masters, Dobbs Ferry, and Nathaniel Pride, Southboro, and Lesla? Love to Father and the Squill and your honey self.

Pauline

Hotel Meurice
Rue de Rivoli
Paris, France
August 16, 1908

Mrs. Herman Kohlsaat
S.S. "Rotterdam"
Holland-American Line
Arriving August 18th
Boulogne-sur-mer, France

Dear Mother:

We nearly fainted when the cable came saying you had sailed on the "Rotterdam." It is splendid, and the very best thing you could have done. I hope you had a good trip over. We are crazy to see you both, and Min is plotting to insult Katherine several times! We came over from London last Thursday and expect to stay here two weeks longer. Then we are going back to Italy to Turin, I think, and get a machine, and tour all about for a month. Then back here the first of October and stay until we sail sometime about the 20th. Now you know all I know. You see, I got your letter congratulating me on the lack of news I sent in my letter from N.Y.

London was horrible. I got so blue and hated to go outside of the hotel. We stayed at Claridge's and were quite grand. Marion Farquhar was there, too, for a day, and lunched with us, and was awfully nice. She gave us a most attractive travelling clock for a wedding present. We had the dinner with Mrs. Ely and I put on all my good clothes and dined in the broad daylight, as it didn't get dark until 8 and felt about as uncomfortable as could be. We went to the theatre with Mrs. Ely to see the "Girls of Gottenberg," which was very good. Min and I went the night to see a comic opera called "Havana," and there was one joke in it, which would have pleased you both, as it was a good one on me. We saw Maud Allen, a wonderful saucer, who dresses either in chiffon or beads—nothing else. Everything very visible, and she did "Salomé," which was so disgusting that I couldn't watch it. We found the most lovely old tea set there in an antiquity store, and Min gave it to me on the 13th. Isn't he a sweetie? Then we got some cretonne and a chair! and the china and glass that we meant to get. I guess that finished London.

There are millions of dressmakers in town, and everything is at half price, and I can't possibly keep my head. We have had a lot of fun lunching and dining around. We went to the Ambassadeurs the other night, and the only amusing thing there was a woman who smoked a cigar. And last night we went to Armanoville with a friend of Min's, and I wore my yellow dress and no hat, and Min paid me a compliment on my looks! There were about 20 people in the place, all dull except some real "Americans," who sat at the next table and got drunk and began kissing and hugging each other.

It will be great fun having you and Kay here, and we are planning to do lots of things with you. Why don't you come to this hotel? It's very nice, and hardly any more than the Normandie, and ever so much nicer, newer, and cleaner. We have a sitting room, bedroom, and bath, and it's all paneled with grey and papered in the bedroom with blue. The furniture is white and grey and is most attractive. So come. It will be so much nicer all being together. I can't get used to being called Mrs. yet and think everybody who does call me it is laughing at me! Min has an awful time doing it and last night messed it up beautifully introducing me. So I am making him call me "my wife" to get used to it! He's wonderful.

Well, good night, Honies. You are about 35 longitude 45 latitude tonight, but when you get this you'll be on the same side of the Atlantic as we are, and we certainly will be glad to see you two again. Ever so much love from us both. Isn't this a chatty letter?

Pauline

Venezia. — Ponte dei Sospiri.

Grand Hotel et de Bellagio
et
Hotel Villa Serbelloni
Bellagio (Lac de Come)
September 2, 1908

Mrs. Herman Kohlsaat
Hotel de Normandie
rue de l'Echelle
Paris, France

Dear Mother:

I know you are surprised to get a letter and are sure that one of us must be ill or something. But really I haven't had more than six minutes to sit down and write in. Did you get all the postals? We picked out the prettiest ones we could find. The trip down was quite nice. I didn't enjoy it much because I began thinking about all the stories I had ever heard about the beds on the "wagons lits" and was on the lookout for trouble all night. But nary a one, and it was very clean and fresh. The bed, I mean. All the wonderful mountains came into view about 4:30 so we missed them, but managed to see the beginning of the Simplon.

Stresa is so different from what I thought it would be. There was scarcely an American at the Iles Borromées Hotel, but loads of French, who were most amusing, and we spent most of our time watching them. We had a room on the front with a balcony facing Pallanza and the Isola Bella and the other two. Min was really thrilled and most enthusiastic. We had a bath, too, which was very nice. It was cloudy most of the time, and on Tuesday night there was the most awful thunder and lightening storm with torrents of rain, just at dinner time. The café was enclosed with glass, and the rain paid no attention to the fact, but poured in. The floor was covered with streams of water, and people had to change the tables, and there was great excitement, and in the midst of it all, every light in the house went out! They brought out candles and stuck them into anything that was handy, from a wine bottle to a washstand carafe. In the hall it was most amusing, for everyone was sitting out there after dinner with a candle on the table before them, and one set of gay old French ladies was playing bridge by the light of the candles stuck in water carafes. They certainly did look sporty. About ten the lights came on again, and all the candles were removed, and the band began to play, everybody gay, and then the lights went out again!

We couldn't do any packing that night, so had to get up early Monday A.M. and do it, and just managed to start on time for the boat at 8:45. It was an absolutely cloudless day, and we had a wonderful trip over mountains and across lakes, arriving at the Bellagio at 6:30.

We took a boat from Stresa that stopped at every backyard, but in doing so gave us every possible view. It took us to Luino, where we took a funny little train up the mountain to the Lake of Lugano, which is much higher than either Maggiore or Como, as I suppose you know. Then we went all around Lugano until we reached the town of Lugano, where we had to wait 45 minutes and change boats. Then we went over the rest of the lake to Porlezza, where we boarded another little train—the same one we took when we left Bellagio before—do you remember?—and got out at Menaggio, where we got a steam boat and came over here. It was a glorious trip, and we enjoyed every minute of it. We sent our trunks over a shorter route, which saved us the trouble of having them examined by the Swiss and Italian customs. Bellagio is the same—cool, clear, and lovely. There is a moon (which will be full while we are in Venice) and men singing and playing mandolins and guitars. Everything is gay and happy, and we are having such a good time.

Tomorrow we start for Venice to stay a week, and then to Florence, and then the motor trip. Min is having a most surprising time, for I think that he is finding out he likes scenery! The Orson Smiths are here and fell on our necks last night. They are awfully nice. Haven't any more time to write now, but will try it again as soon as I can. Am looking forward to letters in Venice. Love to you both from us two.

Pauline

Hotel de L'Europe
Venice, Italy
September 8, 1908

Mrs. Herman Kohlsaat
Hotel Normandie
rue de l'Echelle
Paris, France

Dear Mother:

When I left Paris I had an idea of writing to you every day while I was away. But somehow I don't find that there is any time to sit down and write, and if I send you a letter once a week, I think I'm pretty smart.

It sounded in your letter as if you were enjoying Paris almost as much as the Squill! Glad to hear it. We had a splendid trip down here from Bellagio, by way of Lecco to Milan where we stopped off long enough for lunch at the Palace Hotel. And such a good lunch!

The trip here was cool and comfortable, but dusty as usual. It was an unusually clear day. So we could see mountains to the north every inch of the way—and it was beautiful.

There was always the usual excitement at the station and a great deal of bustle about getting the trunks and starting off. We arrived at the station just as the sun was setting and everything was pink and we started up the canal with the moon just beginning to make the palaces white. Min was thrilled and has had as good a time as he looked forward to having. He expected to have a wonderful time, and said today that he was not disappointed. I'm glad we haven't done very much sightseeing but we've had lots of lovely rides, and plenty of looking around in antiquity shops and have succeeded in getting some more chairs! Mrs. Ely left this morning for Paris. We have seen her more or less— she nearly fainted over the necklace. I thought she would.

We are at the Europe and like it much. The food and service are excellent, and so are the rooms. There are some of those water bugs loose in the bathroom which makes me rather nervous, but I'm getting used to them. Mostly everybody is a foreigner, and what Americans there are are nice and quiet. One very handsome man has his lady friend here, and she has the most lovely clothes. I have great fun watching her. Friday we took a long ride in the "piccoli calli" and out in the Lagune towards Murano, then down the Ghetto Nuovo, and to the Ghetto Vecchio. Then on the south side of the canal, in the "p.c.'s" until sunset, and which we saw from the Guidecca, red, red seen disappearing behind the Padova Mountains and the full moon coming up over San Giorgio Maggiore! Friday is a festa, and as we came into the Grand Canal from the Guidecca a mass was just finished in the Salute, and all the people were streaming out. Men in red gowns carrying huge lighted candles and priests in white with different coloured banners. In the twilight it was a marvelous sight.

Thursday we go to Florence, and I think we'll stay at the Hotel de La Ville. The next address after that will probably be Perugia! Can you bear it? I scarcely can.

I'm hoping for a letter from you both in the A.M. So have a good time and don't forget Min and me.

Lots of love to you and the Squill from Min and me.

Hotel Royal Grande Bretagne
Florence, Italy
September 14, 1908

Miss Katherine Kohlsaat
Hotel de Normandie
rue de l'Echelle
Paris, France

Dear Squill:

I am much impressed with the two letters from you and think you are a sweetie to have written them when you had so much else to do. Mother said you looked lovely the night you went to the Ritz for dinner. It must have been very gay there. Weren't you thrilled?

We went to get your coat on Saturday and found the darkest blue, a very bright blue, which wouldn't be becoming to you, so we ordered a blue grey, quite light. It came tonight, but we sent it back because the collar was too big. It is very good looking, and I hope you like it. $30.

The antiquity shops are fascinating, but we haven't gotten anything. This hotel is as nice as ever, and everybody is so polite. Two fioris here, who make it more or less amusing. One picked up a man in the hotel last evening, and they haven't been separated since. Nobody gets served in the dining room, as the waiters are so horrified that they can't take their eyes off of the couple. The Duke and Duchessa of Riario Sforza are here with two children and four servants, and a banker's family of seven from Brussels has just left— who had six servants—so we feel that we are most unimportant doing our work ourselves. I have never seen such a dirty people as the Belgians here. I'm glad they've gone.

We are going to Siena sometime this week, in a machine, and then down to Perugia, and expect to get to Paris the morning of the first. I wish you weren't sailing so soon, for it will be horrid just seeing you for a couple of days only. I am having an awful time trying to finish up my summer clothes because I've just realized that they can only be worn two weeks longer. All my pretty things have to wait until next year. Some of them are going to die this, though. If you go to Callots, you might suggest that I'll be there around the 2nd and expect my dress to be finished.

There is a singer singing outside. They come every evening, as they used to. The old man who sang where he sold papers isn't around anymore, and I miss him. Min can't be dragged to see a sight so I have to get him there unsuspectingly. We went to the Pitti today for a half-hour and saw the Uffizzi in 20 minutes the other day! He has no shame about using the Italian language on all occasions, either. You ought to hear him—worth the price of admission. The singer is singing "Santa Lucia" now, in high g.

Goodnight little Squilly. Hope you like your cape. If you don't, I'll take it. Will telegraph where to write next. Probably to Perugia. Don't you wish you were coming, too? Treat your mother well and politely, and write your sister another letter. Much love to you and to Mother from Min and me.

Pauline

Grand Hotel (Brufani)
Perugia
September 22, 1908

Mrs. Herman Kohlsaat
Hotel Normandie
rue de L'Echelle
Paris, France

Dear Mother:

Everything is about the same—except Lucia is resting, the headwaiter is new, and the dining room is all little tables and more formal. It's so nice to be back and to wander around the funny old streets, looking at the same old things. We have the room on the 2nd floor above the old sitting room, at 10 francs, and a fine bath for five more. We are very comfy and Min loves it. He is having an awfully good time, I think, because he said this was no way to do it—we should come back and spend a day at least in each place to see it thoroughly. So you see he wants to come back, and that means that he is having a very good time. We have taken loads of photographs, so you will have a lot to look at when we reach Paris. We arrive at 2:40 the 30th of Sept., but I suppose the train will be late as usual. Come to the Meurice about 3:30, will you, and stay for tea. I got K. a birthday present, nothing much because I couldn't remember everything she wanted except a diamond bracelet and a gold bag. But I haven't forgotten her.

We leave here this morning for Gubbio and Urbino, Rimini, Ravenna and Forli with perhaps Bologna, arriving Florence the 28th, and leaving again, for Paris at two, the 29th.

Now I must fly—

So goodbye, much love to you two from us.

Pauline

Hotel Meurice
Rue de Rivoli
Paris, France
October 11, 1908

Mrs. Herman Kohlsaat
186 Lincoln Park Boulevard
Chicago, Illinois
Dear Mother and Family,

Just at this moment we are in a temporary collapse after the strain of calling on the Harold McC.'s and the Howards, so I am requested to dash off a few burning words on topics of the day.

Since you left we have been feeling gradually better (this is not intended as an insult). There are still moments when life is not entirely rosy, but the hunt for clothes and furniture is on again in a mild but interesting way.

We have also discovered a beautiful renaissance dining table. Only it will fit neither our dining room or our tablecloths. We have figured out that by taking the longest one we got and folding it three times something might be done. (By "it" I mean tablecloth, not dining room).

We have also received two wedding presents. From Mrs. Chauncey Blair an Empire chocolate breakfast set and from Hazel Trudeau a small dark brown pillbox with appropriate scriptural quotation on the cover.

We are now being treated by a very dressy but casual scientist, a most amusing, impersonal being who blew in one night in a purple velvet opera cloak and "chick" theatre gown with here and there a dash of blue velvet.

I was nearly bowled over when I answered the door, and Pauline's feelings on receiving her in a wrapper may be left to the imagination. The interview was quite amusing according to Pauline's account.

She amuses Pauline a great deal by her impersonal scientific point of view, apparently devoid of sympathy, and by always calling us Mr. and Mrs. Lawrence. But apart from her amusing sides Pauline thinks she is very good and helps her, which is the important thing.

Now, having given you the views of the head of the family, I will descend to the other member, me. Please thank Mr. Kohlsaat for a most kind cable he sent me on my birthday. I enjoyed it all the more because it was unexpected.

Most sincerely, Min

Hotel Meurice
Rue de Rivoli
Paris, France
October 15, 1908

Mrs. Herman Kohlsaat
186 Lincoln Park Boulevard
Chicago, Illinois

Dear Mother:

It was awfully nice to get your cable, and we are so glad that you had a smooth crossing. You will get this about a week or less before you have the pleasure of beholding us again. For we said Wednesday next I expect to get a good quiet rest all the way over and feel like a new person when I reach New York. We have been doing a good deal lately, and I think a rest will help. My clothes are nearly all finished, and are very pretty. I have ordered a "maternity" corset, which seems composed entirely of laces and elastic, which ought to be very comfortable. [Mrs. Ely] paid sister a most lovely and spontaneous compliment the other day about how lovely her pearls were against her skin that night at the Ritz and what a wonderful skin she had anyway. It seems she was much impressed with the Squill, as who isn't?

Helen Goody asked us to tea at the Ritz the other day, but we declined, which means a call, I suppose. Tuesday we go to call on the Greens, Goodys, and C. Blairs. Pleasant day. Ordered a lovely red tweed coat lined with grey fur from your fur place. I guess people will see me when I'm coming! And I have another coat from Jeanne Hallie, and a couple of blouses and some underclothes, wreathed in Jewish lace! Simply divine. Min says I shop with my head in the clouds and forget what I've said as soon as I've said it! But he still goes with me. He has developed a passion for antiques, and never comes in without a handful. He can't pass an antiquity store! 183 is going to be a wonderful place. Love to Pa and Kay from us both, and a lot to you too.

Pauline

Notes

July 29, 1908: When Chicagoans went east by train, they called it "coming on," and an automobile was then called a "machine."

Pauline's sister, Katherine, is called both Kay and "the Squill." Bertha Palmer, Pauline's mother-in-law, had given her a tiara valued at $5,000.

July 30, 1908: Sara and Stanley Field are friends of the Palmers. Stanley was the nephew of

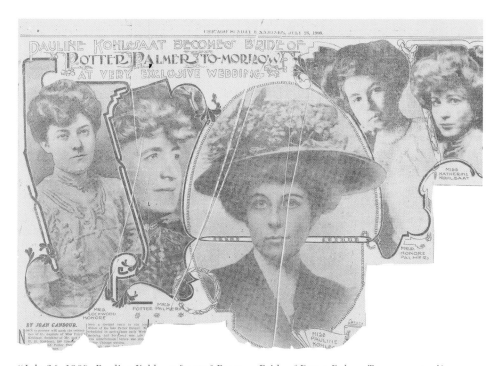

"July 26, 1908. Pauline Kohlsaat [center] Becomes Bride of Potter Palmer Tomorrow at a Very Exclusive Wedding." Attending will be [left to right] Mrs. Lockwood Honoré, Mrs. Potter Palmer, Mrs. Honoré Palmer, and Miss Katherine Kohlsaat.

Marshall Field, at one point Min's father's business partner. Other Americans whom Pauline tells her mother she sees are the Clarks, Janet MacDonald Grace, the Elys, the Farquhars, the Harold McCormicks, the Howards, the Chauncey Blairs, the Greens, and the Goodys. There are many Americans in London and Paris and they get together for lunches, teas, and evening parties. The significant friends will be identified in the notes.

Pauline wanted wedding announcements sent to their schools—the Masters School in Dobbs Ferry, New York, and St. Marks School in Southboro, Massachussetts.

August 7, 1908: A founding tender is a smaller boat which ferries passengers from a larger boat to the shore.

September 14, 1908: Pauline writes this letter to her sister, Kay, or "Squill," who is in Paris with their mother. Callots is Callots Soeurs, a couturier.

October 11, 1908: This letter is written by Min. The Harold McCormicks are Chicago friends, son and daughter-in-law of Cyrus McCormick, inventor of the reaper and founder of the McCormick Reaper Works. Mrs. Harold McCormick was the former Edith Rockefeller, daughter of John D. Rockefeller, Sr.

The scientist mentioned would be a Christian Scientist practitioner of health. The Kohlsaats were Christian Scientists, while the Palmers, originally Quakers, had become Episcopalians. Pauline and Min agreed to raise their children in the latter tradition.

GRAND HÔTEL DE RUSSIE

★ ROME

Mrs Herman Kotelaet.
844. Lincoln Park Blvd
Chicago: Illinois
U.S.A.

"The [King's] funeral was most impressive. It went down
the Mall, so we saw it beautifully from the terrace.
It began early, so people began to assemble under the window
all night to get their places."

2

Italy, Paris, and London, 1910

In the early spring of 1910, almost two years after their wedding, Pauline and Min again cross the ocean to spend three months in Europe. This time they sail on the Berlin, of the Nordeutscher Lloyd shipping line. Potter number three, born in April 1909, is with them, as well as Elise, Pauline's maid, and Julia, a nurse for the baby. The baby is almost one, and the letters are full of affectionate descriptions, as Pauline wants to inform her mother about every new stage: "He has learned to smell flowers and watches children and dogs with the greatest interest. If anything gets in his way he simply brushes it aside! He nearly drives Julia wild, for he is always smiling and always bad."

This is the period of "democratic" seating, when one is placed at table with unknown companions. Min does not take easily to making friends with strangers. "Two very nice well-meaning common people sit at our table, and they are very funny.... We nearly die trying not to laugh sometimes. Several men have begun to talk to Min but haven't found his welcome cordial and have given up." Today Pauline's remarks may sound snobbish and condescending, but in her time, class distinctions were rigidly observed.

After an ambitious trip to Italy, they go up to Paris, and it is here that Mrs. Potter Palmer I (Bertha Honoré Palmer) makes her first appearance in the letters. Pauline comments on her mother-in-law's Parisian apartment: "There are such wonderful things in it that you find something new every time you look." Located at 6 Rue Fabert, in a grand old hôtel particulier with a walled-in garden running parallel to the Esplanade

des Invalides near the Seine, it later became the Austrian ambassador's residence.

Pauline and Min go shopping with Bertha to Worth, the number-one stop on a well-dressed woman's itinerary. Charles Worth, a young Englishman, had arrived in Paris in 1845, bringing the talents of English tailoring to a city where flair in fashion reigned supreme. His couture house became a "must" for ladies who wanted to make an impression, including the wives of rich Americans. Worth set the style, reshaping the enormous crinoline, flattening the bell-shaped skirt in front and cutting it full in the back so a woman's silhouette became more feminine. His Paris salon had blacked-out windows and gas-lit sconces so a woman fitting for a ball gown could see how she would look at night, on the dance floor. When Bertha, Pauline, and Min go to shop there in 1910, the business is being run by Charles Worth's sons, who maintain their father's standards of "preparing a client for her social responsibilities." For a ball gown, the bodice is tight-fitting, with a becoming decolletage and a well-draped skirt, all expertly made in exquisite fabrics. Bertha Palmer is a well-known Worth customer.

Several days later they all go to London to attend Edward VII's funeral, staying at a house Bertha rented. Bertha was a good friend of the King's. Pauline describes the King's funeral, and how "dismal looking" London is with everyone wearing black—even Americans. The younger Palmers are thrilled by the beauty of Hampden House, Bertha's London residence, particularly the room with "Chinese things."

The Edwardian age was unrivalled as a time

of unusual gaiety, the example being set by the monarch, a bon vivant who loved a good time. The papers in America imagined Bertha in the thick of this social exuberance. Her entertaining in England at that time—Bertha would rent several houses outside London as the social season moved along—was well known from pieces in Chicago newspapers. The Chicago Sunday Tribune reported an exaggerated account in September 1907: "Everywhere [Mrs. Palmer] goes she is the widow with $500,000 a year, the royal entertainer—'the only American who knows how to spend her money!' When she is in London, invitations to her London residence—the historic home of the Hamiltons—are as anxiously sought as are the invitations to the castellated mansion at 100 Lake Shore Drive when Mrs. Palmer is in Chicago. All London society waits as breathlessly for cards from Mrs. Palmer as they await the invitations to the houses of royalty bearing the arms of the king or of Wales." "Phyllis," the Tribune reporter, notes that "celebrated Parisian bands and world famous divas are brought from Paris and from Berlin to entertain the guests," while a cross-the-page headline asks rhetorically: "Is Mrs. Potter Palmer the only American woman who knows how to spend a fortune?" Indeed, at one event British royalty were invited to attend (they didn't) and Bertha had Olive Fremstad, a prima donna, come over from Paris, fee undisclosed, to entertain her guests by singing from the scandalous Strauss opera "Salomé" based on Oscar Wilde's banned play.

On another occasion the entertainment included an evening of songs by Boris Chaliapin, his first visit to England, lured by an astonishing fee. The story is that before his debut, he heard a nightingale sing, and thought, "Ah, England and the nightingale!" However, he was puzzled that the bird could sing over the loud chatter of the audience. "When he expressed surprise, the butler informed him that the bird was an artist with a whistle who sat in a tree in Mrs. Palmer's garden and trilled for ten pounds an evening."

While the Chicago press made Mrs. Palmer into a larger-than-life spender in London society, Pauline describes a thoughtful human being. When they are all together, Bertha is very affectionate with little Potter, as she will be later with the younger grandchildren. Although the exact nature of the relationship between the high-powered mother-in-law and the serene and capable Pauline is not altogether clear, they seem to get on well. Bertha must admire Pauline's panache in managing her family. Bertha had written and preached extensively on women's self-development, and had proclaimed: "Our highest aim now is to train each to find happiness in the full and healthy exercise of the gifts bestowed by a generous nature....We advocate therefore, the thorough education and training of woman...not only to prepare her for the factory and workshop, for the professions and arts, but more important than all else, to prepare her for presiding over the home." Pauline was certainly superb at home and, later, in her work for the Art Institute.

After a return to Paris and then again to London, Pauline and Min visit Scotland and their friends the Pecks. There is much talk about servants in this collection of letters, which shows Pauline's keen observations and her expertise in arranging a household. "Allen isn't coming back after all. He has acted in a very silly way—like a big baby—and has decided not to come back. If Mrs. Blair's man is still free, would you mind getting him?...I want a laundress, too....I don't want the house opened any more than necessary—just the dining room and enough plates to use."

The Kohlsaats' concerns mentioned in these letters are Katherine Kohlsaat's wedding in mid-July, and news of the sale of the Chicago Tribune, of great interest to Herman Kohlsaat, who is active in that business. Kay's fiancé is Roger Shepard, a bright young man from a prominent St. Paul family.

The funeral procession of Edward VII. May 1910.

The Chicago Sunday Tribune.

PART SEVEN   SEPTEMBER 22, 1907.   SPECIAL FEATURES

Is Mrs. POTTER PALMER the ONLY American Woman Who Knows HOW to SPEND A FORTUNE?

By PHYLLIS

THE only American woman who knows how to spend her money"—that is the way London describes Mrs. Potter Palmer. It's the way Paris speaks of her, and Berlin, and St. Petersburg, and even Carlsbad, and Spa, and Nice. In the courts and on the Riviera—everywhere—Mrs. Palmer is "the American woman who knows how to spend her money." And for ten months in the year she spends it—spends it entertaining dukes and counts and all sorts of titled folk from kings and queens down to ordinary knights and pawns, spends it traveling from London to Paris, from Paris to Berlin, from Berlin to St. Petersburg, and stopping long enough in each capital to reclaim the social sceptre. Everywhere she goes she is the winter with $350,000 a year, the royal entertainer—"the only American woman who knows how to spend her money?"

When she is in London invitations to her London residence—the historic home of the Hamiltons—are as anxiously sought as are the invitations to the castellated mansion at 100 Lake Shore drive when Mrs. Palmer is in Chicago. All London society waits as breathlessly for cards from Mrs. Palmer as they await the invitations to the houses of royalty bearing the arms of the king of Wales.

Nomad Queen Rules Many Capitals.

When Mrs. Palmer crosses the channel and opens her Paris residence the royalty of the old empire gathers around her, and her invitations are as eagerly sought as the invitations to the mansion of the president. So it is wherever she goes, whether it be in Paris, Berlin, or St. Petersburg. Mrs. Palmer is the wandering society queen. In Chicago, in London, in Paris she is a leader.

For ten months she occupies herself with the task of spending the Palmer fortune in Europe; for the remaining two months she takes up the same occupation in Chicago. It is the same story wherever she goes. Money is spent with a free hand; one entertainment after another is given. Expense is not considered. Celebrated Parisian bands and world famous divas are brought from Paris and from Berlin to entertain the guests of Mrs. Palmer in London. Entire interiors are reconstructed to give fitting environment for her gorgeous receptions. Perhaps gowns makers are paid fabulous prices for the next creations of their brains. Houses are rented in London at $4,000 for the season and $150,000 is spent in entertaining; a house is maintained at Cowes, a residence at Goodwood. Then there is the imposing castle on the Lake Shore drive, to say nothing of the summer home which Mrs. Palmer rents at enormous cost wherever with and fancy take her for the summer season.

Center of Social Life Everywhere.

Mrs. Palmer has had villas at Newport, where she was so greatly sought after as abroad; she has spent June at Monte Carlo, gone over to Nice for July, and to Carlsbad for August, entertaining lavishly wherever she went. Everywhere she has ruled over society and everywhere her invitations are as much sought for as the invitations of royalty. The winters are reserved for Mrs. Palmer's return to Chicago. And, although she never has spent a summer at Lake Forest, her place never seems to be filled during her absence. When she comes back to Chicago in October or November, or December, according to her fancy, she steps into her old place as society's leader and society does her bidding. Last year she returned in time to arrange for the big New Year's eve charity ball, and after Mrs. Palmer had given the last directions for the decoration of the First Regiment armory and the decorators had put on the last touches, not a vestige of the commonplace interior was left—the whole place had been transformed into a fairyland of color and lights. Mrs. Palmer has been the moving spirit in the Chicago charity balls every winter since the world's fair, with the single exception of the winter she wore mourning for her husband. Perhaps it was the world's fair that gave Mrs. Palmer the highest social place abroad that any American without a title to help her ever attained. Perhaps it is only her personality, her beauty, her talent for entertaining. Perhaps it really is because she is the only American woman who knows how to spend her money. Whatever the reason, it is true that whether she is at Hamilton house or at Cowes, at Paris, Berlin, or Newport, or at any of the other places where she has residences, she is the center of the social life.

Standing Army of Servants Retained.

At all these palatial residences a retinue of servants is kept, whether they are occupied or not. They are always in readiness to receive the only American woman who "knows how to spend her money." And always there are dukes, and counts, and princes, and duchesses, and countesses, and princesses waiting for an invitation to share her roof with Mrs. Palmer.

The famous question once asked of King Edward was propounded the other day to a London woman whose birth and beauty are as high as her monetary resources are low—"If not yourself, who would you be?"

Without a moment's hesitation the woman of title replied, "Why, Mrs. Palmer, of course!" And nearly every other woman in the throng gathered about the dinner table nodded assent.

Asked the same question, nearly every woman in London of noble birth would make the same reply; so would nearly every social leader in the other capitals of Europe.

In London today only two things are necessary to insure universal right of entry and entire social success when entered. They are money and the ability of knowing how to spend it. Mrs. Palmer has both. The leader of Chicago society for fourteen years has the art of entertaining at her fingers' ends. Perfect dinners, superb concerts—these are her specialties. A month ago Mrs. Palmer gave a great dinner in Hamilton house which royalty was asked to attend.

Excels All Others as Hostess.

When the guests were assembled around the tables Olive Fremstad suddenly appeared from behind a mass of palms and began to sing. Mrs. Palmer had wired to the great prima donna to come over from Paris to sing for her guests, and how much she paid to Fremstad never will be known. The song that Fremstad sang for Mrs. Palmer's guests was the censor tabooed "Salome" of Oscar Wilde and Strauss. The next morning, her fame having spread, she repeated the performance, this time for a more exalted audience. Unhappy people, other than Mrs. Palmer's friends, have to live without such treats. Wherefore Mrs. Palmer's invitations are sought as are a queen's. A few days later Mrs. Palmer again opened her historic London house to titled guests, and this time she had called from Paris one of the most celebrated bands. It is entertainments such as these, given at Hamilton house, at Cowes, at the handsome residence in Paris, and last season at Hampden house, the residence of the duke of Abercorn, that have given Mrs. Palmer the name of being the "only American woman who knows how to spend her money."

It is popularly suggested that Mrs. Palmer takes a proposal of marriage with her morning tea just as ordinary folk take their bread and butter. According to report that have drifted over from London from time to time princes and kings have asked for the hand of Mrs. Palmer, and a short time ago, according to these same reports, the king of Servia was the suppliant. But Mrs. Palmer seems to prefer to retain a social unique in London's Mayfair than a queen over twenty unenviable and unstable kingdoms elsewhere.

Anyhow the Londoners are of one opinion, that it would be definitely exciting to be Mrs. Potter Palmer. While queens and princesses are compelled to follow the customs of their lands and are not free to travel as they please, Mrs. Palmer has no idea; she may go and come at will—in London today, in Paris the day after, and in Berlin the next day—and wherever she goes she is sought by the great entertainers of the courts. She is a leader among them.

Lavishness Keeps London Guessing.

Everywhere Mrs. Palmer's residences are magnets to the nobility, to the great men and women of Europe, and what her lavish entertaining costs the Palmer estate can only be estimated. For her residences at Cowes and at Goodwood she pays enormous rents. Ask the Londoners, who ought to know, pretend to state positively that Mrs. Palmer paid $15,000 for the duke of Abercorn's historic town house last season and that the season's entertainment cost her $200,000. In return for her money she had the extreme satisfaction of possessing one of the most historic mansions in Mayfair—and one of the ugliest! But the house was particularly suited to extensive entertaining and Mrs. Palmer made the most of the opportunity. It was thought last year that she had nothing herself in the lavishness of her dinners, but this season London has been overawed and dumfounded by the entertainments that Mrs. Palmer has given. Londoners are asking one another, What has it cost her? And if the entertained more lavishly this year than last what are we to expect next year? With the present season almost over London is waiting breathlessly for the next, waiting breathlessly to see how the only American woman who knows how to spend her money will spend it next year—what new ways of entertaining her guests she will devise and what mistaken she will import to sing at her dinners.

And by all the titled women of Europe Mrs. Palmer is envied. Beauty, wit, freedom to go and come as you please, recognized social position, not a care or a worry, unlimited wealth, the historic house of the Hamiltons for her London residence, a palace in Chicago, a twenty house in Paris, at Goodwood, and Cowes, the best there is going, and a proposal per diem—what more could the heart of woman desire?

Hampden House

Egypt House, Isle of Wight

Mrs. Potter Palmer

843 Lincoln Park Boulevard
[from shipboard]
March 12, 1910

Dear Father, Mother, and Kay:

We received telegrams, letters, etc. and think you are dears to think of us. We are all settled, and the baby is asleep on the deck. Eleanor Robson and A. Belmont have the captain's cabin under the name of Smith. The boat has started. I can feel it jiggle a little. All the whistles are blowing. Keep your eye out for the sofa and glass we got from Vernay. We wish you were all on board. It's such fun to be going. Katherine and Mother must come this spring if they can and meet us in Florence. Goodbye, sweeties. Write us often c/o Monroe, Paris.

Much love from us all,

Pauline and Potter and Min

Nordeutscher Lloyd
Bremen
Damfer "Berlin"
March 18, 1910

Mrs. Herman Kohlsaat
844 Lincoln Park Boulevard
Chicago, Illinois

Dear Mother:

Well, the trip so far has been quite thrilling. The instant we got out of the harbour we began to pitch like sin and kept it up for two and a half days. Elise and Julia died naturally, and we took care of the infant, who never felt better in his life and was up to every kind of trick. Neither of us were seasick, so we got along famously. But I would never take up baby nursing as a job; it is too strenuous. The baby has gained and has the pinkest cheeks, and the damp air has made the 12 hairs into corkscrews. He eats everything he can get hold of: soup, crackers, zweibach, cookies, toast, anything. Everybody makes a fuss over him, which gets him excited, and Julia is so puffed up that I have to squelch her two and three times a day.

We have had a good time, Min and I. Min looks so well. He eats and sleeps all the time, and is getting stout. The people aren't very interesting. The Curtises have been nice and Mr. C. very amusing. He eats more than anybody on the ship excepting your grandson. Two very nice well-meaning common people sit at our table, and they are very funny.

51

They insist that Mr. Curtis has kidney trouble, as he takes all the exercises in the gym for that trouble and besides "has a special lot of crackers on the table, and that is a sure sign!" We nearly die trying not to laugh sometimes. Several men have begun to talk to Min but haven't found his welcome cordial and have given up.

We are expecting to meet you in Florence the last part of April. We get there about the 15th. Be sure you are there. Min isn't sure yet that he wants to see Louise married, but I have hopes, for she will probably be married at the Actons, and that will give us a chance to see some real antiques! Sunday we arrive at Gib [Gibraltar]. Can't you smell the place? Have you any new plans? Will you be sure and cable us about the Tribune? It's getting near the time now. You probably will know, by the time this reaches you. I hope it comes out right. I don't see, though, how it can do otherwise. So goodbye for a while. Much love to all from us, and be sure you write us once in a while.

Pauline

Bertolini's Palace
Naples, Italy
March 26, 1910

Mrs. Herman Kohlsaat
844 Lincoln Park Boulevard
Chicago, Illinois

Dear Mother:

Your letter from the Manhattan has just come. It took 14 days, which is quite a long time. You seem to have had a busy time after leaving us. Our trip over was a bounding one—two quiet days only. But after the first few days everybody was well. The baby gained weight, and I don't wonder. He ate everything he could get, and there wasn't a minute during his waking hours that he wasn't drinking or munching something. His cheeks were so red, and his hair curled and was red, and he made friends with everyone on board. I didn't get any too much sleep, but he was wonderfully good at night, only being restless when it was rolling very hard, and that made him mad, because turning over woke him up! He cried very little.

We have good rooms, and the baby spends most of the time either on the balcony or in the garden. He has learned to wave a very uncertain goodbye and to bite! He hurts, too. He has also discovered that matches are to be blown out, so whenever he sees a match lighted, he begins to blow as hard as he can. He climbs all over and gets onto his feet a good deal. He has taken the greatest liking for Elise. She is thrilled and does nine tenths of Julia's work!

Naples is much livelier than it used to be. There is a great deal of building going on—principally apartments. And the shops are much better. The things in the best ones are very pretty and smart! We start for Sorrento, etc. on Monday. Mrs. Bertolini has promised to look in at Potter every day to see if he is getting on as he should. We have been in every antique shop here but haven't found anything pretty as yet. So we have given up and are looking forward to Rome. Min has just said to tell you that there are cakes of ice floating in the bay, glistening in the moonlight! We drove to Posillipo this P.M., and it turned cold while we were out, and Min hasn't gotten warm yet. The "variously judged," otherwise Germans, are making life hideous. The hotel is filled with them and cheap Americans. All Naples is, too. We are going to Louise's wedding on the 2nd of May in Florence. Doesn't it sound lovely? We have had wonderful sunsets and have thought of you and how you would love it all. Expect to meet you in Florence. Don't forget. Give K. and Pa our very best love, and keep loads for yourself.

Pauline

Grand Hotel de Russie
Rome, Italy
April 2, 1910

Mrs. Herman Kohlsaat
844 Lincoln Park Boulevard
Chicago, Illinois

Dear Mother:

We have had a very thrilling life since I wrote to you last, and a very speedy one, too, as you will see. We are all well, and in great health (Min is talking to me so I may get a little mixed as in that last sentence). The baby has learned to make a very suspicious "day-day" and can play "peek-a-boo" to the queen's taste, and he talks all the time. It really sounds like a language as he lowers and raises his voice, and emphasizes the sounds every once in a while. I expect he will be walking soon, as we can't keep him off of his feet. He is never still and is thrilled to the bone over travelling. In the Naples station the other morning he was perfectly delighted and never lost a trick, and was so good and happy on the train. He is an ideal traveler.

We left the baby last Monday in Naples with Elise and Julia, and started out for Capri. Min wanted to see the blue grot [grotto], so we went in there. Min liked it, but was disappointed that it wasn't bluer. We had lunch at the Quisisana Hotel up in the town and spent the rest of our time there looking about. It is heavenly, and we want to take a villa there some time. At Sorrento they gave us an enormous room overlooking the sea. It was so cold that we didn't spend much time hanging over the balcony gazing! The next morning at eight we started for Amalfi. It was a wonderful day, and the drive what you can imagine it was. We arrived in time for lunch and directly after went up to Ravello. Such an attractive hotel, with a terrace and fascinating garden, with the most lovely view you can imagine. The next morning we went to Salerno and Paestum. When we arrived at Paestum the sky was quite blue and the clouds that greyish white and the hills grey with the olive trees on them and all about us. The largest temple is the most lovely—soft pinkish, yellow, and the one next to it a very brilliant greyish white. There were acanthus leaves growing about, and grey pieces of stone fragments scattered about in the grass, and a quantity of little English daisies growing everywhere. Lizards were sunning themselves and scuttling over the stones. We are going back the next time we come over.

It was good to get back to Naples that night and look at the infant. He didn't care in the least about seeing us the next morning when he woke up! He was feeling fine and on the look out for trouble. We took the early train for Rome that day, Thursday, and arrived at the station safely, but couldn't get a seat! So had to wait for the second section. It was much nicer, for we had a compartment to ourselves most of the time. A nice Italian got in, who was crazy about the baby and made friends with him.

At the Palace in Rome they couldn't give us quite the rooms we had expected, but they were comfortable and clean so we told them we'd keep them for three weeks. The next morning they said they'd like to move the baby into the room next to the one he was in. They said it was the same size and apparently wanted to give his room to the people who had the room next to him on the other side. I said very well, if the room was as big as the one he was in, and then we went out. When we came home we found the most disconsolate three humans huddled into a hole of a room with porters carrying in loads of things, which had to be put one on top of the other! I went downstairs and said I refused to be moved into such a hole, etc., etc., and went upstairs and had everything moved back. They, the management, looked very gloomy and said they didn't see what they could do. So I got into a towering rage and said we'd leave immediately. Min and I started out to look for rooms and found these at the Russie. The garden is heavenly, and the baby stays out in it most of the time. The funniest people in the world are stopping here. Very few Americans and thousands of foreigners, who keep Min and me and Julia and Elise in hysterics all the time. There is always something going on, which the baby loves. He can sleep through anything and eats all the time.

Please write us often. Tell Kay I am keeping my eyes open for things for her. Goodbye. Love to you all, from us all.

Min Potter and Pauline

Grand Hôtel de Russie
Rome, Italy
April 9, 1910

Mrs. Herman Kohlsaat
844 Lincoln Park Boulevard
Chicago, Illinois

Dear Mother:

This paper has been mussed and rumpled by your grandson, so I expect you to enjoy the letter just that much more. He has been playing in here for nearly an hour and has completely messed up the room. Now he is taking his 12 o'clock bottle and, I hope, is going to sleep. We measured him the other day and found him to be 29 inches long, which is eight inches longer than the average at one year. He is getting fatter, too. And his hair is growing. He has learned to smell flowers and watches children and dogs with the greatest interest. If anything gets in his way he simply brushes it aside! He is a scamp and up to every kind of mischief. He nearly drives Julia wild, for he is always smiling and always bad.

Today it is pouring rain, and we are staying in. I think Min is ready to go away. We have done up most of the antiquity shops, and he finds the rest of Rome dull. Yesterday we spent 3/4 an hour in the Vatican! It nearly did him up. But he's going again in spite of it. In that time we saw Raphael's stanze, tapestries, the Sistine Chapel, Raphael's Loggia, the Candellabri, and several other rooms. The town is overrun with the "variously judged," and they do get on ones nerves. We have the new rooms now, and they are lovely. All the windows look out on the garden, which is terraced half-way up the Pincio, and then the rest of the wall is thickly covered with vines. There are several cypresses at the wall, and you would love it. A fountain plays just outside our windows (each one has a small balcony), and there are several thrushes that sing all the time. We get the sun all morning until about 2:30 in the afternoon. The garden gets it all day, and the baby spends most of his time out in it. Julia takes him up in the Pincian and lets him see life. We called on the Roosevelts—that is, we left cards. They are dashing about as much as we are so have no time to waste seeing people. As I sit here writing I can see a rose-covered arbour, a magnolia tree, a hedge of spyrea all in the garden, then three cypress trees against the vine-covered wall, and a way above, between the cypress heads and coming out from some other—a corner of a marble balustrade belonging to the Villa Medici.

We are much interested in Bob Patterson's death—what effect will it have on the Tribune situation? I should think that they'd be stumped and have to sell it. We are waiting to hear.

The baby has no intention of sleeping as he ought to now. Min is playing solitaire, and it is still pouring. There is steam heat, and the rooms are comfortable and cheery. They are all white, with yellow hangings—makes it look homelike.

With our very best love to all.

Pauline

Grand Hôtel de Russie
Rome, Italy
April 15, 1910

Mrs. Herman Kohlsaat
844 Lincoln Park Boulevard
Chicago, Illinois

Dear Mother:

Two nice chatty letters came from you today, and I think that you had a good deal to say, considering you started out by announcing that you had "no news." We enjoyed reading them tremendously and hope you write often! We have been expecting to hear from you all about the Tribune. I hope that everything will go right. Father must have been very nearly beside himself with excitement from your account of Kay and her allowance—$300 in the bank and all bills paid—with you making over old dresses of mine. Min and I came to the conclusion that sister is getting near. What do you think? She probably won't let Roger ride downtown in the mornings—she'll keep his carfare. Your dress sounds lovely, and I know what fun you are having out of it. Isn't Madame Whitney a sweet creature—so refined. It sounds as if almost everyone had left Fields. They can't expect to ask huge prices and give nothing in return.

Our life is not without excitement. The infant eats a boiled egg and bacon every morn for breakfast. Also, he can take several steps holding your hand on a chair. He can raise himself up and down on his legs, holding your finger, and he has a great game of shoving a book ahead of him on the floor and then creeping after it. That certainly thrills him. Julia is so proud of him that she nearly expires over it. She saw the Pope Friday and took nearly the whole of Rome with her to be blessed! She has been no use to anybody since. So excited and talking at the top of her lungs. She was so grateful because we got her the permission that she nearly kissed us!

Delicate bits come floating through the rooms to us every once in a while, such as "I bet your gran'ma Kohlsaat would like to see you in that swell bonnet, you rat!" The "bonnet" is white-straw of Roman make. He looks like this [picture by Pauline]—oh no, he doesn't look a bit like that! It is banana-shaped and turns up in front, or down as one pleases. There is an elastic under the chin. If he had hair it would look ravishing on him, but as he hasn't, we had to laugh the first time he had it on and he cried. So now we jolly him. He is growing into the worst terror and is getting smarter every day. Julia put him in the crib today while she did some packing, and he threw the powder box at her and hit her in the head! Julia was so thrilled at his cleverness that she didn't pay any attention to the hurt. Sunday we go to Perugia for three days, and then to Florence. It's a good thing that the baby likes to travel. He's never happier than when he's on a train.

Oh, I must tell you more about our trip to Viterbo. Toscanella was perfect, and Min was wild over it. The church is on the top of its own little hill separate from the town. There are two ruined square towers beside it and a bishop's palace, which I think must have been built in the 10th century, too. It's so crumbly. The middle of the façade of the church is of curiously curved white marble and stone and simply too lovely for words. The ride over there isn't very interesting. After lunch at Viterbo we went on to Caprarola and discovered it was only open on certain days, and then one had to have special permission from the Farnese Palace in Rome! No one is allowed in the garden under any circumstance. We were quite annoyed, to say the least. It is wonderfully situated on the crest of a hill with the town of Caprarola below it crowded onto one perpendicular street. Like the one in Todi. The villa is at the head of the street and very imposing looking. The ride into Rome wasn't very interesting. It was windy, and the road bad. Viterbo was the same nice place. We walked all over and saw it all again, only we didn't go to Lante this time.

There was a woman at this hotel who came over on the boat with us, and she started yesterday to go to Perugia in a motor. She has a daughter of eighteen, who is a blossy dresser and knows Louise Bowen at Briar-Cliff and thinks she is "wonderful." Well! You can imagine how one would enjoy seeing the beauties of Italy with a companion like that. "If it's the least bit dirty and a chance of a bug I wouldn't consider spending the night." She wouldn't stay at Amalfi on that account, and her mother is helpless in her hands. They know about as much about traveling here and seeing things as the baby does. For instance, they were going from here to Perugia in one day by way of Viterbo and Orvieto! Min mildly suggested that there was something to see between here and there—and she said "Interesting, is it?" So he mapped out a trip for her, which I think will put a crimp or two in daughter's style. One night at Viterbo, another at Orvieto, and finally Perugia. They weren't stopping at Bracciano, even!

Well, goodnight, Mother dear, best love from us all to everybody. Pauline

50 Via della Scala
Florence, Italy
April 22, 1910

Mrs. Herman Kohlsaat
844 Lincoln Park Boulevard
Chicago, Illinois

Dear Mother and Family:

Here we are at the Lazzario, and most comfortably settled. Julia has the chambermaid under her thumb, for she can't get hold of the baby often enough and so does most of Julia's work as a bribe. And Elise is going home on her vacation in a few days. So we are all happy. Potter has learned so many new tricks that I can't keep up with him. His latest is to look very solemn and then suddenly clear the back of his nose as if he had catarrh! And then he beams and repeats the accomplishment. He takes a step or two holding onto one's hand and in fact is quite a wonderful child. We went from Rome to Perugia, and he was as good as gold. Stayed in P. two days and then came up here.

Perugia was lovely—wonderful weather and comfortable rooms with a bath and such a view! Julia saw nothing good in Perugia, as everything was so tumble down—and the hills "wore the legs off of her." Elise was enthusiastic. We walked all day and found some awfully pretty things. Your friend del Prato took quite a shine to us and insisted upon showing us the technical school of P., of which he is the President! It took 3/4 of an hour, and the best part of it was Min's expression! He nearly died. He asked us to his country place, too! But we didn't go. We went over to Assisi with the Count and spent the afternoon. I hated to leave Perugia, but we had to come up here on account of rooms. The town is filled to overflowing. Mrs. Collins asked for you and said you hadn't been there for 4 years and she couldn't understand it.

We have nice rooms here, good food, and splendid service. Min is satisfied and calls it an old people's home. We got some lace today—simply lovely—at that shop on the Ponte Vecchio. We expect to stay three weeks and then to Paris. Mrs. Palmer has asked us to stay with her, which will be very nice, and then we are going over to London for a short time before we sail. We expect to sail sometime between the 11th and the 20th of June, so you see our trip is almost over. The time goes like greased lightening. Louise and fiancé arrive in a few days, and we expect to see something of them once in a while, but I don't think we ought to interrupt much for we feel they should get acquainted. Give our best love to all, and write often.

All love,

Pauline

50 Via della Scala
Florence, Italy
May 13, 1910

Mrs. Herman Kohlsaat
844 Lincoln Park Boulevard
Chicago, Illinois

Dear Mother:

We have been so happy and well, and your grandson has gained five pounds (your daughter about 9) and is as strong as an ox, and your son-in-law is as happy as a king and hasn't done one thing he didn't want to do. Consequently I haven't seen the Ufizzi nor the Pitti and have only caught fleeting glimpses of the others. We know a tremendous lot about furniture and old brocade, etc., and have had great fun poking around. We have gotten some new things, which are very pretty—mostly chairs and tables. We have now 10 tables and 12 chairs! Mr. Ellsworth had just begun to get furniture two years ago, so we suppose that is why the stock was so low at that time. His villa is lovely—very grand—and such a garden! He has some lovely furniture, and some not so good. Neither he nor his wife enjoy it much, for none of their children will come over, and they have nothing to do but buy things and have guests. They look so discontented and hopeless. We have been up there twice, and I would like to go again on a lovely day to see the garden in sunshine, but the time is too short.

Yesterday was an ideal day, so we took one of Hutton's walks. We went to San Domenico in the train and got off to see the Badia. That was "molto sympathica." Then we took the train again, as they told us the walk from Badia to Fiesole was "rather stiffish." We had lunch at the little hotel in Fiesole, on the terrace looking over the valley of the Arno. The Hotel Aurora, it was, and then we started for our walk over the hills to Castel Poggio and Vincigliata. The most heavenly afternoon with great white clouds sitting just over the mountaintops and all the far mountains white with snow. The views were marvelous. We mentioned the other day that we were looking for an old tapestry, so someone said there was one for sale at Castel di Poggio and we might look at it, as the owners were away. So we got the keys and broke in. It was such fun. The tapestry was disappointing, but the Castel fascinating. Then we went on down to Vincigliata and that wasn't half as nice as it was when we saw it. Very disappointing. The day was so heavenly that we couldn't mind anything. We saw the Casa di Boccacio on the way to Ponte a Mensola. It looks most like the picture in Hutton's book. We drove back to Florence and arrived just in time to say goodnight to the infant. I thought of you on the walk, wishing you were there, too.

Today is another lovely day, and we are starting in a few minutes to see if we can get the Contessa a present before we go to Paris. She has been so lovely and has done so much for the baby. She gave him a cake and a candle on his birthday, and he came to the table.

Top: Pauline Palmer and little Potter, 1909. Bottom: Grace Palmer and her sons, Honoré (left) And Potter D'orsay (right). Opposite page: The Kohlsaat Family, left to right: Katherine Kohlsaat Shepard, young Roger Shepard, Roger Shepard, Potter Palmer III, Pauline Kohlsaat Palmer, Bertha Palmer, Potter Palmer II, Mabel Blake Kohlsaat, Herman H. Kohlsaat, 1911.

He cut his cake with a little help and then reached for a hunk of frosting, which he quickly ate! Everybody is wild over him, and he is as good as gold. Min is anxious to start, so goodbye, with all love.

Pauline

5 Carlton House Terrace
London, England
May 22, 1910

Mrs. Herman Kohlsaat
844 Lincoln Park Boulevard
Chicago, Illinois

Dear Mother:

Well, there is so much to tell that I can't stay on one subject for more than a line! When we arrived in Paris we were a sight to behold! The trip was hot and very dusty, and Julia got excited at the end and wasn't ready to get off when the train stopped! So we had to wait, and as we were finally starting off, the porter rushed down the platform with the seat of the baby's basket in his hand. Julia was covered with confusion, as the footman had come to meet us. Paris was nice, and everybody flying about so happy. We went to the opera and heard a rather poor cast sing Faust. Some Frenchies went with us, and they were charming. Mrs. Palmer took us to see an old hotel near the Invalides, which was too wonderful. Just think, there was a huge garden at the back stretching for over a block— and in the heart of Paris, too. It was all like one of Dumas' book and too beautiful. Tuesday I devoted to clothing myself, having arrived in rags. The things this year aren't very pretty, more queer than anything. The prices are frightful. I took a grey and pink theatre gown and a yellow and dark green evening gown among other things. Don't they sound ugly? And unbecoming? But I think they will turn out nicely. Min went with me to Worths and got so excited that he splurged dreadfully on a most wonderful evening gown of heavenly blue satin with a design in silver on it and made in the regular Worth fashion. Mrs. P. is going with me when we get back to Paris, I think. She was too busy to move when we were there. The apartment is lovely. There are such wonderful things in it that you find something new every time you look. We saw Aunt Del at Worths. She looks very well and says that Catherine nearly died when her baby was born—that she had received word that she couldn't live at one time, but the doctor managed to save her with salt.

Thursday we left to come over here, for the funeral Friday. And we left on short notice, too. Everyone had to wear black. London is the most dismal looking place—not a spot of colour anywhere. All the Americans even are wearing dark colours. One feels so conspicuous otherwise. The funeral was most impressive. It went down the Mall, so we saw it beautifully from the terrace. It began early, so people began to assemble under the window all night to get their places. Some of the guests arrived here at seven A.M.! Mrs. P. said for us to be ready at 9:30 and then came rushing into our room at 8:45 in a great hurry saying she wasn't half dressed and everybody was here and for us to come down as soon as we could! It was all over by 11 o'clock! Every shop was closed, and every museum, so we had a lot of time on our hands with nothing to do, but after all managed to go around in a taxi to see the crowds and decorations. The line of march was all draped in purple, white and black, and all very mournful looking. We had tea with Min's friend Mrs. Vanderbilt. She is so nice, and Min really is extremely fond of her. Yesterday morning we went to all the antiquity places with Mrs. Palmer and saw such lovely things. We are completely bowled over and don't know what we want. This house is wonderful— such a lovely collection of Chinese things that we sit in the room where they are every spare minute we can get. The house is tremendously imposing and dignified. There are lovely things everywhere.

Last night we went to see the Russian dancers, who are awfully good and most graceful. Today we go out into the country to tea with a friend of Mrs. Palmer's, who has a most attractive house and garden. Tonight Louise and husband arrive, and we hope to see them. Tomorrow we look at some more antiques in the A.M. and take the train for Paris at two P.M., arriving about nine. We stay in Paris until the 1st of June and then come over here to stay until we sail, which will be between the 18th and 25th of June. The Pecks are in Paris, and we are planning to do a lot of things together. They brought two Pekinese dogs and a chow puppy, two Pekinese birds and a Japanese nightingale over the Trans Siberian Railroad with them. Think of it! Worse than travelling with a baby. Annah almost got left at one place in Siberia, as her dog ran away from her while she was exercising it!

We are waiting to get the telegram about the paper. I know everything will come out right. Elise and I have parted. She isn't well enough to work, and we gave her a lot of money and told her to go home and rest. Julia is staying for a year longer. She has taken such wonderful care of the baby and adores him so that we think it best for her to stay.

Min joins me in best love to all. Take care of yourselves, and we'll see you in about a month from the time this reaches you.

All love,

Pauline

Cavendish Hotel
London, England
June 7, 1910

Mrs. Herman Kohlsaat
844 Lincoln Park Boulevard
Chicago, Illinois

Dear Mother:

We arrived safely from Paris and found the trip with the baby a very easy one. We sail on the Arabic June 18th, or a week from Saturday! Doesn't it seem soon? We go to Edinburgh Friday night and meet the Pecks there Sat. evening. Then Sunday we motor to Carlogie with them and stay until Monday night, arriving in London Tuesday A.M. Then early the next Saturday morning we start for Liverpool and sail from there. We have all kinds of luxuries on the boat—two large deck state rooms with a bath between and a huge sitting room! All for a great deal less than we paid going over on the Berlin and much less than they ask on the boats sailing from Cherbourg and South Hampton now! Just because nobody can take the time to go to Liverpool. We are delighted. We are going to 843 for a few days until we can get a house somewhere. This morning we are hunting for furniture with an expert! Time is too short to go out by ourselves and then have someone look at the things later to see if they are good. Sunday we went to the Victoria and Albert Museum and saw furniture and tapestry. We are going again to see the Salting Collection and to the British Museum too if we can get time. Tonight we go to see the Russian dancers with the Pecks, and perhaps we may go to the theatre again if we aren't too tired. It is difficult to go all day and then again at night, too! So we try to be a little careful. There is so much to see and do.

It is pouring today and dark—quite Londony, in fact. My shoes are all worn out. One hole goes straight through, so I expect I'll get my feet wet!

With best love from us all,

Pauline

Cavendish Hotel
London, England
June 17, 1910

Mrs. Herman Kohlsaat
844 Lincoln Park Boulevard
Chicago, Illinois

Dear Mother:

Isn't it nice about Kay? I am sure you are glad and sorry, too—and much too busy to think about yourself a second. We are wondering what has happened about the Tribune. Today is the 17th, and you have said that Billy Beale was sailing on the 16th, and everything would be arranged before he left. We are still hoping to hear.

Our life is not quiet either, as we decided yesterday to wait over for Cappy, and so put off our sailing until the 25th. We are coming on the "Baltic" and expect to get to Chicago the 5th or 6th of July. We are going to stay in town until after the wedding, and I think it will be such fun to all be together then. Is Whitney making Kay's things? I suppose so, unless Miss Dodd is back. Won't she be a lovely bride? Kay, I mean! Are you going to have a big wedding or a nice one like ours? We like it better every day.

We went to Scotland to visit the Pecks and had such a good time. Min behaved scandalously all the time and was so funny. We went to Edinburgh first and spent the morning looking at furniture and the afternoon looking at the town. It is so grey and dismal—anything but a cheerful town. We went out to Holyrood and saw Mary's rooms and the old chapel—that was all fascinating. It was a perfect day, and we had great fun. Our driver was a chatty Scot with a marvelous accent, and he insisted on telling us the history of everything. Once he stopped in the middle of the street where the train was and recited a Scotch poem to us several pages long. We couldn't understand a word of it. The Pecks arrived in their motor about eight, and we all had dinner together and then "exercised the dogs." It was so light that I saw a man in the park reading a paper at twenty minutes to ten! Father ought to go there and save gas bills!

The next morning we started for Carlogie in the motor. Six people, Mona and Peter, Joe's dog, a trunk suitcase, dressing bag, and my hat done up in a paper parcel on the floor! Can you imagine us? It got hotter and hotter as we went along and finally about lunch time Joe saw a lovely spot by a river where we could get out and eat lunch! Picnicking is their joy in life, and there had been some discussion beforehand about it, as they knew that Min didn't like it. But he agreed to suffer for once. Just as we were about to get out of the motor, a tire blew up, and then no one could find the lunch, and it was discovered that it had never been put in the motor. So we would have to lunch at the next inn! The Pecks nearly died of rage. Min was delighted. We finally lunched at a little inn where the food was good. We saw Stirling Castle, which was interesting. We got to Carlogie about six after a most wonderful ride. The country was lovely. Carlogie is too attractive and homelike, and we had great fun. Min fished, but the fishing was bad. We stayed two days and then came back. The baby looked at us when we came in and then went on playing!

Allen isn't coming back after all. He has acted in a very silly way—like a big baby—and has decided not to come back. If Mrs. Blair's man is still free, would you mind getting him? And would you mind trying to get me a temporary maid to wash the dishes and serve us (parlour maid)? I want a laundress, too. Miss Callahan will be alright, and if she hasn't anyone, try the Swedish National Association, 95 Dearborn St. Allen was going to do all this for me, so now I am up against it and so annoyed at him. I am sorry to cause you so much trouble when you are busy. I pay my laundress eight per week and nine if she will do the collars and evening shirts. I paid Allen 65. I don't want the house opened any more than necessary—just the dining room and enough plates to use. Eva knows about upstairs. Goodnight, nice Mother, and please be glad to see us when we get back. Give Father our best love, and Kay and Roger, too.

All love,

Pauline

Cavendish Hotel
London, England
June 24, 1910

Mrs. Herman Kohlsaat
844 Lincoln Park Boulevard
Chicago, Illinois

Dear Mother:

We are sailing in the morning on the Baltic, and I want to send you a line, hoping that it will go on a faster steamer and reach you before too! The Baltic takes eight or nine days, so we ought to get to Chicago Tuesday, July 5th A.M. Or perhaps it depends on the time we get off the pier on Sunday. We'll take the first train west. We have gotten a butler here. He is enormous and too ugly! But a "fine servant," they say. He glories in the name of Taylor.

We had great fun with Cappy and Grace. They went to Paris yesterday. I must send this off now and go see if the labels are on the trunks.

Much love from us all. Pauline

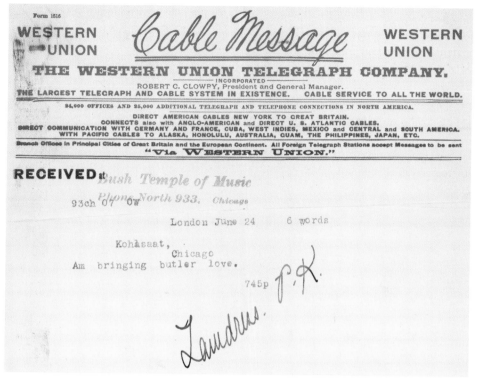

Cable from Pauline to her mother on the eve of sailing: "Am Bringing Butler, Love."

Notes

March 12, 1910: The first letter is on stationery from 843 Lincoln Park Boulevard.

March 18, 1910: They are sailing on the Berlin, a ship of the North German Lloyd line.

Pauline's question about the Tribune shows family concern over the sale of the newspaper. Herman Kohlsaat's own business prospects may have been somehow tied up in this sale. The paper's ownership continued to be in the McCormick family.

March 26, 1910: Elise and Julia are servants: Julia is the child's nurse, Elise is the lady's maid.

Pauline thinks her friend Louise may be married at the Actons' Villa la Pietra in Florence. Another Chicago friend, Hortense Mitchell, the daughter of William H. Mitchell, who had the controlling interest in the Illinois Trust and Savings Bank, was married to Arthur Acton, an English ex-patriate living at Villa la Pietra, so Chicago friends were likely to visit the magnificent villa.

May 25, 1910: She reports going on one of "Hutton's walks." Edward Hutton had written many guidebooks about Italy. Pauline probably has his Country Walks around Florence, published in 1908.

DE SOTO HOTEL,

W. L. PARKER,
MANAGER.

TAMPA, FLA.

OPPOSITE GOVERNMENT BUILDING.

U.S. POSTAGE
TWO CENTS

Mrs Herman Kotheoast
844. Lincoln Parkway
Chicago, Illinois.

"We went down to Osprey for lunch Friday.
Such glorious weather!
The water sparkled and seemed alive!"

SETTLING IN AT SARASOTA, 1910 AND 1911

In the fall of 1910 and the fall of 1911 Pauline writes her mother from Florida, where she and Min are visiting for the first time. During this period the Honoré family was becoming interested in Florida real estate. Min's great aunt Laura, married to Bertha's uncle Benjamin Lockwood Honoré, had just purchased twelve acres that became the nucleus of Bertha Palmer's 350-acre estate, Osprey Point.

It was the beginning of Bertha Palmer's Florida real estate empire as she directed her considerable talents to this new business venture. Bertha and her brother Adrian ("A. C.") Honoré, along with the real estate developer J. H. Lord, bought up nearly 90,000 acres of citrus groves, forest, and land on the coast, which when the land around Tampa was added, amounted to 140,000 acres. They organized the Sarasota-Venice Company: Lord was president, and Min and his brother, Honoré ("Cappy"), were treasurer and secretary. The company's holdings boasted sand beaches, exotic vegetation, and land good for farming. Bertha saw the importance of having rail access to her real estate holdings, and as a cutthroat business woman, she threatened to create a competing rail line if the existing railroad company did not comply. They did, building a railroad in 1911 from Tampa to Venice that crossed Palmer lands, adding to the value of the property.

At Osprey Bertha began creating her large, stately house "The Oaks" on land that was originally "a little settlement in the woods." A palm tree and an oak tree were intertwined near the original box-like house. The land belonged to Lawrence Jones of the John Paul Jones whiskey family of Kentucky. There was evidence, too, of an earlier era: mounds of seashells left by the Indians. It was a lovely site looking out over Little Sarasota Bay towards the keys—Casey Key directly west and Siesta Key to the north—which lay between the land and the ocean.

Bertha's house became a family refuge. She enjoyed gathering the large Honoré and Palmer clans around her to enjoy the mild climate. Pauline mentions Ida, Grandpa Henry Honoré, A. C., and Aunt Laura and Uncle Ben in these letters.

As Pauline describes Sarasota on first seeing it, "Sarasota itself is most wonderfully situated on the bay, with a chain of keys protecting it from the gulf. Such fish I have never seen—great big ones jumping several feet out of the water everywhere you look! They seem to be inviting you to catch them." In her letter of November 17th, Pauline jokes about her "Santa Claus figure," as she is several months pregnant with her second child.

In the 1910 letters little Potter, whom they call "Master Poppa," is being cared for by a nurse named Mary. Besides reporting on her child's activities, Pauline tells her mother that she and Min are looking at land on which to build a small house. In the second group of letters she writes of arriving in Sarasota again the following year in November, after a forty-eight-hour train ride. Little Bertha—named for her grandmother—has been born, and Pauline describes her as "very noisy as usual and manages to disturb everyone." It is balmy and pleasant compared to the harsh Chicago weather. After measuring out the space and having a well dug, they start building their new house, "Immokalee" in mid-December 1911.

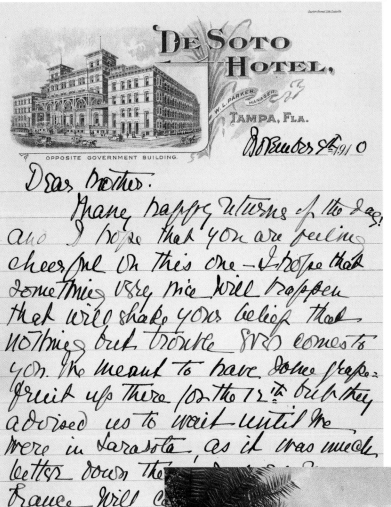

De Soto Hotel,
W. L. Parker, Manager
Tampa, Fla.

November 8 1910

Dear Mother,

Many happy returns of the day! and I hope that you are feeling cheerful on this one — I hope that something very nice will happen that will shake your belief that nothing but trouble ever comes to you. We meant to have some grapefruit up there for the 12th but they advised us to wait until we were in Sarasota, as it was much better down there

get down there and see what its like. It is a three hours trip, and they say that there is the greatest kind of difference between this part of the country and that. Yesterday we took a motor boat out onto the Bay for about 10 miles, then landed after much excitement, such as getting aground once or twice & finally for good! So that a small boat took us in shore. — Then we drove over a large piece of land — which wasn't very pretty nor interesting. Min & I drove in a buggy — with good horses. While the others were in a springless express wagon. They were pretty

Tampa, Fla. At the Fountain

Left: Pauline and Min stay in Tampa on the first trip to Florida.
Opposite: Pauline sends her mother "Kodaks" with views of their Sarasota land.
Top: "Docks."
Bottom: "Stable."

De Soto Hotel
Tampa, Florida
November 8, 1910

Mrs. Herman Kohlsaat
844 Lincoln Parkway
Chicago, Illinois

Dear Mother:

Well, here we are in Tampa, arrived last night after having come straight through from Chicago. It was a long trip, but not an unpleasant one. The baby did very well, getting tired late in the afternoons only. We arrived in Jacksonville in time for breakfast, which we took in the station, and strange to say it was delicious. Just as we were starting for the train, we met Mrs. Palmer and Mr. Honoré also on their way to the same train! They had just gotten in from a trip down the East Coast. So we all came down together. Mrs. P. was much surprised to find the baby so changed. He was very friendly with her and quite won her again. She liked Mary, too. She and Min have gone out for the day motoring, but as it was a bumpy ride, Min thought I had better stay at the hotel and rest up a little. In a few minutes my son and I are starting out on a leisurely ride to see the town.

Florida is lovely, and I am so glad to be down here. We may go to Sarasota tomorrow by boat. They say it is a lovely ride down, and Mr. H. is keen to go that way. It will be pleasanter for Potter, too. He is so full of spirits and minds Mary to beat the band. I am glad there is someone he pays attention to without a stern discussion! I don't see how she does it, for I have never heard her speak in anything but the gentlest of tones to him, and her only threat is that if he does what she wants him to do he will find something lovely, such as "such a lovely warm comfy bed for Potter to lie down and go to sleep on, if he will first try it once." Down goes Potter, and in two shakes of a lamb's tail he is sound asleep without a murmur! Min is eating everything he can grab hold of. Such an appetite! I think he's going to enjoy it down here, and he is crazy about it. It's amusing Min anyway, which is a good sign.

Must go now and put on a veil to go driving.

Move love to all. I will write soon again.

Pauline

De Soto Hotel
Tampa, Florida
November 9, 1910

Mrs. Herman Kohlsaat
844 Lincoln Parkway
Chicago, Illinois

Dear Mother:

Many happy returns of the day! And I hope that you are feeling cheerful on this one. I hope that something very nice will happen that will shake your belief that nothing but trouble ever comes to you. We meant to have some grapefruit up there for the 12th, but they advised us to wait until we were in Sarasota, as it was much better down there. So your remembrance will come a little late in the day. It is from all three of us with our very best love.

We leave for Sarasota at 7:30 in the morning, and I am wild to get down there and see what it's like. It is a three-hour trip, and they say that there is the greatest kind of difference between this part of the country and that. Yesterday we took a motorboat out onto the Bay for about 10 miles, then landed after much excitement—such as getting aground once or twice and finally for good!—so that a small boat took us in shore. Then we drove over a large piece of land, which wasn't very pretty or interesting. Min and I drove in a buggy—with good springs—while the others were in a springless express wagon. They were pretty well goggled up. We scarcely felt the bumps. We got back to Tampa about 6:30. I wasn't tired and really enjoyed it all very much. This afternoon we took an automobile ride over entirely different land that was lovely.

Potter and I went shopping this morning and found some lovely balls. He was so delighted with them that he will only give them up when food's in view! He seems to be enjoying the trip very much and Mary is a wonder—nothing bothers her, and she never gets flurried or seems in a hurry. Certainly Master Poppa is right under her thumb and eats and sleeps just as she wants him to. He slept two and a half hours at noon and then ate enough lunch for two or three babies. He is so cunning. Did you send Grandpa the pictures of him? Eva knows where they are. Send him one of the big heads and a smiling one, and put the date and his age on the back, "Sept. 1910—16 months." Mrs. P. is so crazy about them and thinks she never saw better nor more artistic pictures of a child. Tell Kay they are playing "Only one girl in this world for me" on a harp down in the lobby. It will make her think of Venice. How are all her plans turning out? Be sure and let me know just as soon as you hear. Tell Father that the Tribune is sold in Tampa. "Think of it!" How did you like the opera with Alice C. Howard?

I must get ready for supper now. Goodnight, with great love from us all,   Pauline

Belle Haven Inn
Sarasota, Florida
November 11, 1910

Mrs. Herman Kohlsaat
844 Lincoln Parkway
Chicago, Illinois

Dear Mother:

I am taking a rest today, so am writing in bed, which makes it a little difficult. So I hope you will forgive writing and ideas! We came down here yesterday, through lovely country, so rich and cultivated, in spots. They grow celery, lettuce, sweet potatoes, mainly, besides the oranges and grapefruit. Min likes it quite a good deal, which rather surprises me. I think he is somewhat surprised himself, to tell the truth! He hasn't any of his usual hopeless feeling about it. Sarasota itself is most wonderfully situated on the bay, with a chain of keys protecting it from the gulf. Such fish I have never seen—great big ones jumping several feet out of the water everywhere you look! They seem to be inviting you to catch them. We took a motorboat after lunch yesterday and went out for a five-hour ride inside the keys down the coast. It is a fascinating country, with wonderful vegetation. We got off at one place and walked a little way. Everything was very wild and dirty—so dirty that I nearly died. I don't see how people can bear to live surrounded by such filth, but they don't even seem to notice it. We saw a lovely blue heron flying near the shore and finally eight in the water. It is the first I remember seeing, and I was fascinated by its colour. The mosquitoes were very thick and vicious. Coming back to the hotel we stopped off on a key and walked over to the gulf side to see the afterglow. The beach was of very white sand and very firm and covered with thousands of different shells. The moon was getting bright, and the glow was fading off mild purple, so you can imagine what a wonderful sight it was. We have nice rooms here, and delicious fish, so I am very comfortable.

The baby is eating very well and I think is going to enjoy his stop here. He is so sweet and naughty. Min and his mother have gone off on some business this morning. I hope they get back in time to take me motoring this afternoon. I feel so well that it is hard to realize that it is a good plan to rest up once in a while. There weren't any letters for us from you all when we got here, and I was disappointed. I suppose I forgot to give you the address, as usual! I saw by the paper that you had our box Monday night. Did you enjoy it? The opera, I mean. Do write to me when you have time, for it would be nice to hear what you are doing, etc. We all send much love to you four.

Pauline

Belle Haven Inn
Sarasota, Florida
November 13, 1910

Mrs. Herman Kohlsaat
844 Lincoln Parkway
Chicago, Illinois

Dear Mother:

I lived, until last night, in the wild and crazy idea that today was the 12th, and so didn't get in a telegram to you that I intended to have greet you on your birthday. I'm sure the tale about the little behind hand was meant for me! We hope that you had a happy birthday. As far as any news from you goes, we might as well not know you. Nothing has come but the telegram in Tampa. We are all well and happy and rushing around like wild. I take a few hours off every once in a while to get my breath. This morning we went out on the bay, looked at some grapefruit groves, and then went over to a place called "Siesta" on the key and had a fish dinner. We had some wonderful things to eat. The fish here is so delicious and with the grapefruit is about all I eat. After lunch we looked at another grapefruit grove and nearly died of the mosquitoes and burrs. The latter are something awful to get rid of, and generally they leave little stickers in your fingers as a pleasant reminder. After that we came back here, and I came in to rest while the others went off in the motor. Potter is having a fine time and is up to everything. Min and I are having a good time, too. With much love from all,

Pauline

I ordered the grapefruit yesterday. Hope you like it.

Belle Haven Inn
Sarasota, Florida
November 17, 1910

Mrs. Herman Kohlsaat
844 Lincoln Parkway
Chicago, Illinois

Dear Mother:

We are having the most lovely summer weather down here that you can imagine. It is heavenly. Min and I are asking all over for a place to build a small house on, and we are having great fun over it. Min will have to be here a part of each winter, and it will be ever so much more comfortable to be in one's own house, however simple, than to stay in the hotel. And with this increasing family, it is quite necessary! The new member promises to give Potter a run for his money in the way of liveliness. I still look a little human, although am rapidly acquiring a Santa Claus figure. Min is inclined to take a most unsympathetic humorous view of the matter.

One day down here is very like another. We generally go off on a ride through the country to look at land. Sometimes it's timbered and sometimes slew or pasture. Here and there are tiny settlements or deserted cabins. The roads are all deep with sand so that we can't make very good time. The baby plays hard all the time and is a mass of mosquito bites. The other day when he was out with us Mary got a switch to brush the mosquitoes away, and he thought that she was trying to switch him and consequently got in a most awful passion at her. He really is becoming very fond of her, and doesn't fuss half as much when she takes him off.

I hope you are all well. You might be dead or dying for all I know.

Much love to all,

Pauline

[Pauline is now writing in 1911, the next year.]

Belle Haven Inn
Sarasota, Florida
November 12, 1911

Mrs. Herman Kohlsaat
844 Lincoln Parkway
Chicago, Illinois

Dear Mother:

After a very nice trip to Jacksonville and a very hot one from there down, we finally arrived at Sarasota a tired party, glad to get off the train. All things considered, it was a very good trip, and we all got along well. The baby was quite good, Potter, as usual, an excellent traveler. Forty-eight hours is a long time, after all. It is lovely here, and quite hot. Today it is cooler, and last night it was cool enough for a wrap outside. Everything looks in fine condition. Green and lovely. The bay is very blue, the sky cloudless. We are going down to take lunch with Mrs. Palmer today at her place. It's 12 miles down the bay.

Bertha Palmer (far right) with friends, probably at her inland property, Myakka.

We are going in motors, so it promises to be very bumpy. Aunt Laura, Uncle Ben, and Grandpa are at the Inn. They are all wild about Sarasota. Aunt Laura has been here since Sept. 1st and hopes to stay as much of the rest of her life as she can. We have gotten very good milk for the babies, and they are getting along finely. Bertha is very noisy, as usual, and manages to disturb everybody. They think she is a beauty and make a great fuss about her. Grandpa announced very impartially the other day, "This is going to be the favorite grandchild of all!" Kasper is most enthusiastic and tickled to death that he came. He spends all his spare minutes sitting at the water's edge gazing out at the boats. The idea of running a boat delights him. The furniture Min sent down has made the rooms very attractive and comfortable.

Will you get Eva to bring down Father's umbrella to him? Or perhaps it would be better to get it yourself to be sure about it. I left it standing in its box outside the sitting room door. This flower is off an acacia tree in Aunt Laura's yard. I hope it smells as good as it does now when it reaches you. Much love to all from us all. Many happy returns of the day.

Pauline

Belle Haven Inn
Sarasota, Florida
November 14, 1911

Mrs. Herman Kohlsaat
844 Lincoln Parkway
Chicago, Illinois

Dear Mother:

Min and I have been very busy these last few days, and I haven't had a chance to write you. For instance, yesterday morning Min said to me at breakfast, "Would you like to go over all the groves with me today? I am leaving within an hour and will be back by four or five." I went and got home about four very tired. We go to bed early and get up early. For everybody else gets up, and we are unable to sleep after seven anyway, at the latest. Today we went to our place to lay out the house, if you know what that means. That took several hours. While the men were getting their twine and pegs ready, we walked down the shoreline to see if there was any other place to put the house. That was quite a jaunt and took 1/2 an hour. It was very interesting.

There is a great variety of trees and shrubs on the place. Palms of every description nearly, live oaks, a few pine and cedar, a large clump of century plants, laurel and, oh, any number of other kinds. Several became trees, about a dozen. It is all lovely and wild. There are excellent grapefruit trees and oranges, guava, mulberry, and lemon! Quite a collection, isn't it? I can't describe it to you. You will have to come and see for yourself. We found another place for the house so meandered back along the shore among the fiddlers. Got home in time for lunch and then went out for a ride in the new boat for the first time. It's a fine Dandy and goes like a breeze. Kasper was so excited running it that we nearly exploded trying not to laugh at him. He did very well. We took Potter with us and finally landed on a lovely white-sand beach covered with shells. There Belle nearly fainted as she saw "shells that at home one had to pay money for, lying around!" For once in her life that I know of, she was speechless! Potter was thrilled and ran around to his heart's content. He'd pick up shells and show them to us—"Isn't dis pitty?"—and before we could see it, throw it into the water as far as he could. We are taking Bertha there next time.

Bertha is so cunning, everyone admires her. Min is getting fat and looks very well. And we are having a very good time. I see by the papers that it's cold in Chicago. I wonder if you went to St. Paul the night of the cyclone. But why wonder, of course you did! Give Kay and the Rogers my love. Am enclosing checks for stamps, envelopes, etc. Hope it's correct. Give Father my love, everybody's love! Loads to yourself!

Pauline

Belle Haven Inn
Sarasota, Florida
November 16, 1911

Mrs. Herman Kohlsaat
844 Lincoln Parkway
Chicago, Illinois

Dear Mother:

Yesterday we didn't do very much. I sat around most of the day and rested. Min went to the office for a while, and the children went out in the boat to the beach. They got some more shells that thrilled them a good deal. Kasper is so dippy about the boat. They all are, for that matter. It's lovely and cool today. The sun doesn't seem to be very strong. This p.m. we are going down to the place to look for a place to dig the well. I hope that things will get under way there before very long. I am getting thinner and Min fatter. The baby is in fine spirits and looks very well. She is as lively as a cricket. As for Potter, he still finds so much to do that the days aren't long enough. When it is too warm for him to run around he goes out in the boat, sits in Belle's lap, and gets nice and cool. Taylor always goes along. In fact, I don't think that we could have managed this year without him. He has done so much and has been a great help.

When are you coming down? Let me know, for I want to engage a room for you. Why don't you come about the first of December? It's very dull here. Nothing going on. Uncle Ben goes fishing all day. Aunt Laura sits on the porch or goes down to her place. Mrs. Palmer comes into town as seldom as she can. Grandpa Honoré is busy every minute, and Min and I take life easily and enjoy ourselves. You had better come down and help us! Don't plan to stay three days, for being in a hotel you can be very independent: have your meals when and where you want them, get up when you like, and go to bed when you are tired. Nobody dresses in anything but last year's clothes. All my summer things are coming in handy. You'd better bring Frances and come along. Or come without her. I am expecting a letter from you one of these days, but I am doubtful about getting it.

We all send much love to you and Father.

Lovingly,

Pauline

Belle Haven Inn
Sarasota, Florida
November 24, 1911

Mrs. Herman Kohlsaat
844 Lincoln Parkway
Chicago, Illinois

Dear Mother:

Min has the writing table in full sway, so you must put up with a pencil and my lap. I had a nice letter from you last night telling about your first opera going. It is too bad that Grace couldn't go with you. Aunt Mat was Aunt Laura's next older sister. Aunt Laura is terribly sad and broken up over it, although she is a little more cheerful now than she was at first. And now with Harry Honoré's death, everyone is feeling depressed and sad. Harry has been terribly ill with gallstones for several years and has suffered agonies. He has had pneumonia lately and died very suddenly. Don't say anything about his gallstones or suffering from them. Potter is down at Osprey with Mrs. P. He wasn't able to get decent food here and I thought looked thin and peaked. So when she suggested that she would like to have him visit her, Min and I were glad to have him go with Belle. We thought he might feel badly leaving us, but he waved good-bye very pleasantly and rushed off to play again! The baby is in fine form. Her cheeks are as red as apples, and her eyes are sparkling. Everybody in town knows her. I am so glad to hear that Kay's baby is doing well again. It's a great relief when they perk up, and then you wonder why you were worried so. Your descriptions of costumes and headdresses at the opera was very amusing. Rue must have been a sight. Ellen's I have seen and think that, as headdresses go, it is quite pretty. I am glad the box is so good. We had an idea from the number that it was very poor and off in a corner.

You won't notice having your teeth out nor know that you have been unconscious. Is Hyman going to put in false ones? Your news about your story is thrilling. I thought your decimal point was a zero and read it $20.50 or $2,050. I began to think I'd write. Still, as you say, washing sounds more lucrative. Well, good-bye. I have six letters to write, and if you know how I hate to write!

Much love,

Pauline

Belle Haven Inn
Sarasota, Florida
December 7, 1911

Mrs. Herman Kohlsaat
844 Lincoln Parkway
Chicago, Illinois

Dear Mother:

For one short moment I thought that there was no paper here except some that Min had beautifully illuminated with "hop-hops" for Potter! Luckily I found the rest of the pad. Min would have died of embarrassment—not that they aren't marvelous "hop-hops!"

We went over to Bradentown with Mrs. P., stopping at a nursery on the way. You can't think how interesting trees and plants and groves are when one is down here in the center of such things. Of course we aren't getting anything of the kind now, because it couldn't be planted on account of all the building, etc., that will be going on at the place during the next few months. Still, Min and I are keeping our eyes and ears open and expect to have a fine lot of information to fall back on when the time comes to plant. After lunch at Brandentown we went to see two grapefruit and orange groves. One has 80 rows of trees, each row a mile long! It is called the Atwood Grove—you probably know about it. Min is getting quite interested in grapefruit. He probably will change from his affection for city to affection for country life! Wouldn't it be a change? He is looking very well and fat and is enjoying his stay down here very much.

Aunt Laura is at Osprey until Mrs. P. gets back, so we are leaving Potter there. He is having the time of his life, and is too fresh for words. He is thrilled every second with the things to do. It's "watch me climb de tree" and "Oh, Mudder, see me pinkle" every second. He "pinkles" the lawn with an enormously long hose that lets out a couple of drops! He advised my not going in the direction of the spiget, as "it was wet there." So I see that Belle has him trained. We got back from there about five o'clock, and I was so sleepy that I couldn't keep my eyes open. This A.M. we went out to look at some land and took Bertha along with us. She is getting to like the boat more and more. Got in in time for lunch and then took the motor down to the place to see how the well-digger was progressing. He's digging a fine well. So you see we are seldom idle! Bertha is too adorable. She is very quick and notice[s] everything. We gave her the round mirror that Potter always liked so much, and she was perfectly fascinated by it and herself. She made such funny noises looking at her reflection! She would growl and snort and then lick it all over. Miss Hays is simply wobbly-eyed over her.

I suppose as usual I upset you a good deal about getting me clothes and things and telephoning Grace, etc., and all for nothing. Cappy wrote Min, and I had a letter from Grace this P.M. saying they were not going into mourning very heavily—merely not going out for a while and Cap wearing a black band on his sleeve. I'm glad it isn't different when I've first gotten all my nice new clothes. It seemed like another set to hang in the closet without wearing. Well, good night. Cheer up—we'll be home before long. And then you'll have all the trouble of coming up to lunch with me often.

Love to all from us all,

Pauline

Belle Haven Inn
Sarasota, Florida
December 10, 1911

Mrs. Herman Kohlsaat
844 Lincoln Parkway
Chicago, Illinois

Dear Mother:

We went down to Osprey for lunch Friday. Such glorious weather! The water sparkled and seemed alive. The air was warm, and there was a soft breeze blowing. We went out into the gulf and it was wonderful. Kasper says that the boat would "go much faster if all that water didn't follow it." So you see he is very observing. He runs the boat quite well but hasn't one particle of sea sense, if you know what I mean. We brought Potter back with us to spend the night. We will go back tomorrow. He didn't want to come. In fact, he cried. It is lovely down there for him, and he has a wonderful time of it. He is sending you the enclosed letter with his love. His hair is getting so long that I thought I'd cut off the longest end while it is curly. It gets so straight at home during the cold weather.

Now Min and I want you to attend to some Xmas shopping for us. We want to get Mrs. Palmer a clock for her living room at Osprey, either of wood or crystal or glass, not of anything that can tarnish or that needs to be polished, like silver. The face should be fairly large and readily seen from a distance. I suppose that a good clock would cost about $100. Min is particular that the works and face should be very good. About the rest he doesn't care, at least so long as it doesn't rust. I think it should be plain and good-looking. The living room has Jacobean furniture mostly, nothing French nor fancy. So the clock should be about one foot high or thereabouts and have straight lines. It is to be put on a high mantle. If you know what the clock on the mantle in Grace's sitting room is like, you can go by that for line and height, as that is about what we want.

Then could you go to Fields or Bests and get me six suits of winter underclothes for Potter and have them send them down here as soon as possible. He is quite big for his age and I think would probably wear four year size. He needs a very long seat, if you remember! I expect that you will get him terrible heavy ones! But don't get them too heavy. I can still remember how I itched. The baby is splendid. She gets better looking every day. Goodbye, much love to Father and you from us all.

Pauline

Mrs. P. is at home. You'd better call—at 1350 I think she is.

Belle Haven Inn
Sarasota, Florida
December 12, 1911

Mrs. Herman Kohlsaat
844 Lincoln Parkway
Chicago, Illinois

Dear Mother:

No letter from you for several days. What is the trouble? Have you gone to St. Paul? I don't care for such neglect! We are still progressing. Potter came in from Osprey yesterday, no, it was Sunday. Stayed until this P.M. I asked if he wanted to stay with us. "No," he said. "Would you like to go to Osprey?" "Yes!" very decidedly. So he went back today. He looks very well and has such an appetite! Egg, bacon, cereal, and five large pieces of toast and syrup for breakfast today. Sounds like enough to keep body and soul together, doesn't it? Bertha is as fine as a fiddle and keeps everyone jumping as usual. While she was out in her buggy today, a black cat came alongside, much to her delight. She leaned over the edge for some time, until the cat moved away. Then she flung herself back in the buggy and shrieked with rage! She knows just what she wants, and if she doesn't get it, she lets people know about it!

Tomorrow work starts on the building at our place. Doesn't it sound thrilling? We are going down there in the morning to see where the garage is to be put, as that will be the first building put up. Also, we are going out on the gulf to see about 14 whales that have gotten stranded on the sandbar outside the Pass and can't get off. One is 26 feet long. Mrs. P. got back today and said everything was ok with you and Father. I was glad to hear, as you haven't been letting me know how you are getting along with Hyman, etc. I

*Opposite: Min, Pauline, and their
two children in Florida.
Top left and bottom right: Potter III
and little Bertha.
Top right: "Bertha is too adorable.
We gave her the round mirror that
Potter always liked so much, and
she was perfectly fascinated by it
and herself".*

am hoping that a letter comes in this evening's mail. Did you get Father's umbrella from my house? I can't believe that Xmas is only 13 days off! It doesn't seem possible. Good-bye, much love from us all.

Pauline

Pauline Palmer and her sister, Katherine Shepard, relaxing in a boat near the Sarasota property.

Belle Haven Inn
Sarasota, Florida
December 15, 1911

Mrs. Herman Kohlsaat
844 Lincoln Parkway
Chicago, Illinois

Dear Mother:

I am writing to Eva either tonight or tomorrow about having the colonial furniture in the guest room moved downstairs into our room and the white furniture moved up to the guest room. Will you telephone to the Park Storage and have them send down two men to do it? The bed has to be taken to pieces. Their men took it down and put it up for us last summer. Then have them try to put the mattress that was on the white bed and has just been done over onto the mahogany bed. If it won't fit, never mind, but I hope it does. I want the chintz hangings put on the bed and the green velvet carpet put on the floor. You can get the work started any time after you get this letter. The bed can go where the present bed is. You can arrange the rest to suit yourself. I haven't ordered any curtains for the house yet! Isn't it shocking? But we can't find anything that suits our fussy selves. We are now considering madras very seriously. Anyway, I've ordered curtains for my front doors. Only took three years to do it! But the house will be charming when we get it into shape more. I expect to keep you busy after I get back helping me with curtains and rugs and a new suit.

I've lost at least five inches off my back, and nothing fits! Ain't it awful, Mabel? I hope I weigh under 140. But don't dare breathe it for fear I don't. There are still plump parts about me, as yet. But they won't be there long.

Bertha certainly is sitting up and taking notice! She has begun to creep and throw herself about. Her one tooth is still alone in its glory. It is growing so big that I am trembling for fear that the others will never catch up with it. She bites herself once in a while and gets as mad as a hornet. Her enthusiasm for Potter is pathetic, and his indifference and scorn are sublime. He absolutely ignores her most of the time! She squeals with delight every time she sees him. He is still at Osprey. We intend to bring him back here with us on Sunday. He won't want to come, as he adores it out there. Min and I have been very busy today at the place. We have placed the garage and cemetery and decided which trees will have to be removed. It doesn't sound like much but is a job when you get at it.

Much love to you both from us all,

Pauline

Belle Haven Inn
Sarasota, Florida
December 19, 1911

Mrs. Herman Kohlsaat
844 Lincoln Parkway
Chicago, Illinois

Dear Mother:

You see that the writing paper has finally come, also the Christmas toys for the children, and all the other things that were in the box that was sent by freight, and that instead of arriving five weeks ago, came last night. I was a little afraid that it wouldn't get here in time for Xmas, and then I would have been without toys, and that would have been a dreadful state of affairs. We are trying to work Potter up to some enthusiasm about Santa Claus. He is interested but not wildly so! He is getting to be such a big boy and has a great deal of character in his face. I am glad he belongs to me! Min is terribly proud of him, too. He and Bertha are quite a pair and well worth looking at. Aunt Ida arrived today looking very well, and seeming very happy. She is staying at Osprey for the holidays. She and Mrs. Palmer lunched here today. After, Aunt Laura took Aunt Ida and Min and me to look at her place. Tomorrow we show her ours. Next day I suppose she will see Osprey and the day after will take to her bed from exhaustion. If one isn't used to tramping around over rough ground and through thick underbrush, it is very tiring.

I sent you a telegram this A.M. about a cook. I wrote to Eva and told her to get Anna Johnson if she didn't have a place, and if she did to get Mrs. Jones or Miss Callahan to send someone. Then it occurred to me that I was rash, and it would be better for me to interview anyone before engaging them (clever thought, wasn't it?). So I telegraphed you to get a temporary cook if Anna was busy and have some others come to see me on Saturday so that I can engage one for the winter. I'll want the cook to prepare breakfast for us the morning we arrive and will send you word if we come another day. I suppose that we'll arrive about 7 A.M., but most likely we will be late. That train generally is. Grace's laundress is coming to me. I want a second man, but I doubt getting a good one very much. Taylor is attending to the matter, but if you should hear of a wonder that someone is letting go, on account of leaving town or anything, hang on to him and tell him to come Sat. A.M.!

Kay can use Potter's old buggy until we get home. I am sending Bertha's up from here on Monday or Tuesday by express and expect it will be at home by Sat., as Bertha is a good deal heavier and more difficult to carry than R[oger]. She will have to have the buggy until her own arrives. Then Kay can have the other as long as she likes. It needs new tires, so if you telephone Eva she can bring the wheels to you and you can have Field call for them and retire them for me.

Your letter about the ball was very amusing, and I am sorry you stopped for I was quite ready to keep on reading. I can't imagine what has come over Ellen Borden. She must be plain crazy. I think she imagines that she is smart and gay. I think it rather pathetic. You made no mention of Rue's get-up. Can it be that it was not noticeable? That, however, I can't believe. Mrs. Field sounded gorgeous. She must have been stunning in that ballroom. It has been such a long time since my last ball that I believe that I would not know what to do in a ballroom! Probably would get awfully bored and want to go home! As for Min, I'm sure he would yawn his head off. We are getting old and stuffy, and no mistake, I think that I get lazier every day.

Give our love to Father and keep a great deal for yourself.

Pauline

I am dying to know if you take out your teeth at night but have a feeling of delicacy about putting the question.

Notes

November 12, 1911: Pauline has read in the paper that her mother used her box at the opera.

    Kasper is the Palmers' chauffeur.

November 14, 1911: Belle is little Bertha's nurse.

November 16, 1911: Taylor is the Palmers' English butler.

November 24, 1911: Harry Honoré, who has recently died, may have been Henry Honoré Jr., who was in the family real estate business. In the next letter Pauline mentions that they weren't going into mourning "very heavily." She is happy about this, as now she can wear her "nice new clothes."

December 10, 1911: Pauline tells her mother to make a call on Bertha Palmer at 1350, or "the Castle."

December 19, 1911: Pauline refers to her mother's mention of Ellen Borden, a good friend Pauline often comments on who will become the mother-in-law of Adlai Stevenson.

"Today Mrs. Palmer took us all out
to Versailles in the motor....
It was the day the fountains played...
everything was so fresh and
green, after a rain, and smelt so woody."

4

Europe Again, 1912

In the summer of 1912 Pauline and Min are again travelling in Europe, this time for four months. They are with their two small children, Potter, three, and Bertha, one, who are being cared for by nurses Belle and Florence. While in London they are booked to stay at the Cavendish, famous hotel of Rosa Lewis, proprietor, caterer, and notable Edwardian personality. She remodeled her hotel in 1903—the first years of the Edwardian era—in the style of the country houses in which she was accustomed to cooking. Fashionable and attractive, it offered suites that had a club feeling and their own dining rooms—even one (probably seldom used) for Edward VII. As one historian put it, "Rosa's circle had always been decadent and now her hotel had become the flagship for the fashionable but racy." It was definitely a place where the well-off could enjoy their sexual adventures. Pauline is visiting later on in its history, and she is unhappy with the rooms. She gives Rosa Lewis a piece of her mind, showing her strong personality and how she has no doubts about what she wants.

While in London the Palmers see their friends the Jameses. William James, Jr., or Billy, married to Alice Runnells from Chicago, is the son of William James, the American philosopher and intellectual. They meet "Uncle Henry," or Henry James, the famous writer, but Pauline is not impressed, calling him "a puffy old soul and very pompous." At that time James had just published *The Golden Bowl* and was America's preeminent novelist.

One of James's important fiction subjects was the American in Europe; he himself was an American who felt a strong connection to Europe as a place with a history that was larger and more profound than that of his native country. James had spent a lifetime searching for the appropriate place to live, leaving America and settling first in Paris and later in London and then in Rye in Sussex. He had sent many of his American characters to Europe in search of an existence they couldn't find at home. Christopher Newman in *The American* and Chad Newsome and Lambert Strether in *The Ambassadors* all went to Paris, where they met with life-changing experiences. Daisy Miller, Roderick Hudson, and Isabel Archer met their fates in Italy. The American tycoon and art collector in *The Golden Bowl*, Adam Verver, who traveled abroad in search of artistic treasures, could have been modeled on one of the rich Chicago fortune-makers the Palmers knew. Pauline shows no sign that she knows the work of Henry James, but she senses that she hasn't reacted properly to meeting him. She cautions her mother: "Don't say that we found him queer. And don't be annoyed that I asked you not to!"

On June 11th, Pauline mentions that Min has given her "some beautiful etchings" for her birthday: "four Whistlers and a Schongauer, so I managed to do very nicely." Art collecting was an important interest in their lives. When Pauline died in 1956 her will bequeathed several hundred prints and drawings to the Art Institute. In Paris she and Min look at Chinese porcelain and tapestries.

They again spend time with Pauline's mother-in-law, and have a wonderful time visiting Versailles and shopping at Worth for clothes. Night-clubs are a prime amusement—at one they see "Moorish baths with nude ladies coming out of the tubs, chiffon scarf covering one spot, " and a "Harlequin in pink tights with black lace tights over it." It was "a very Parisian show, but not in the least coarse. The audience was just as good, and so the evening was most amusing and very exciting." At the Moulin Rouge there were "some very remarkable sights" that she will describe to her mother when she sees her, as "they can't be written." There is more talk of Paris fashions—at the clubs and in the shops after they get back from their trip to Switzerland and Germany—and purchases made at Drecoll, Chéruit, and C. Roget. While in Switzerland they stay at a resort hotel, which brings forth descriptions of prewar vacationing as they take walks in the breathtakingly beautiful scenery, watch tennis, and observe other tourists.

Again she confides to her mother about her servants, and we see Pauline's superb organiza-tional skills and how she is good at getting "the children, nurses and servants swung into line." With the two children and staff, they are a party of eight. Still, "everyone [and every trunk] has been on time, not one grumble have we heard, and everyone amiable with one another, and every face broad smiles." Potter, now three, is an awestruck observer. He has great fun in the park seeing the pelicans and baby ducks, and reports to his mother "in awestruck whispers with eyes as big as saucers."

Again Paris seems crowded with Americans. They see the Harry Howards, the Pecks—probably of the Ferdinand Peck family, Chicagoans who patronized the arts—and the Herricks (Myron Herrick was a friend of Herman Kohlsaat's). Bertha's sister, Ida Grant, is there with her granddaughter, also named Bertha, and Ida's son-in-law Michel Cantacuzène advises them on books to read, saying one should only believe fifty percent of what Chekhov writes.

Luzern. Die Hôtels Palace und Montana.

St. James's Palace Hotel
Bury Street, St. James's
London, S.W.
June 9, 1912

Mrs. Herman Kohlsaat
844 Lincoln Parkway
Chicago, Illinois

Dear Mother:

You see, we have changed hotels and are now very comfortably settled in this place, where the food is delicious, the service splendid, and everything is nice! The day we landed the boat kept getting later and later until finally we steamed into Plymouth about 8:15 and were on the dock about nine. Potter was so excited over the lights in the harbor and all the boats that his voice trembled. Min thought we had better go straight to London that night, as there were no good trains during the day if we decided to stay all night in Plymouth. We either had to start at eight in the morning and arrive when the children should be having lunch, or else leave at naptime and put in at three and so on. So we decided to have all the upsetting at once and finish the thing. We arrived in London at 2:30 and at the Cavendish at three.

As we had failed to arrive at 12, they had given up our rooms! There was a lovely suite of sitting rooms, two tiny single bedrooms, and two baths, and in the sitting room, a cot. Mrs. Lewis had gone to bed and left a cleft-palletted creature to meet us! We stirred things up a bit, and finally Min and I were given a room, dressing room, and bath belonging to a lord, who was not in town that night! His gloves, hair wash, and invitations were scattered around the room. The next day everyone slept, and nobody was any the worse for the trip. I interviewed Mrs. Lewis, and she told one lie after another until we got so disgusted that we said we would take rooms elsewhere. She didn't believe us at first, but finally the truth dawned on her. She was quite stunned. The Pecks had been staying here, so we came. It is very comfortable, they can't do enough for us, and it is half the price of the other place. The children get delicious things, the headwaiter coming up every day for their order.

We are near St. James's Park, and they have great fun going over there and seeing "pe'-cans" and "baby ducks," as Potter told me last night in an awed whisper with eyes as big as saucers. The first word means "pelicans." Florence is gone on her visit home, and Belle is managing the children beautifully. Min is sleeping ten hours a night, or rather morning, without waking, and is looking splendidly. We find we can't loaf; we're not made that way! We looked for etchings and found some nice ones, which reminds me that Min must write Roger that there is nothing rarer in England than the Venetian set, and to get all he can now at home. The Jameses we have seen, and they are lovely and happy. No news at all.

They lunched with us, and we are lunching with them tomorrow at a little restaurant called Queen's in Chelsea. They are so busy with Uncle Henry and social doings that we won't see much of them evenings. In the daytime we are going to hunt furniture. They have the fever badly. We are looking for their wedding present together. Min and I have seen some very pretty chintzes at one store and are out for more in the morning. I have ordered nurses coats and caps, aprons, collars, and cuffs for B. and T. and am expecting to arrive in Chicago looking neatly, even if I did leave looking like a mess. I went to Self-ridge's for them. That is the same nice store that Field's was when Uncle Harry had it. You are impressed the minute you go into it with the atmosphere of the place.

These are our plans: go to Paris the 16th of June, stay two weeks or more, then Munich for one week, visiting surrounding towns of interest, then Innsbruck for two weeks and settle infants there. We go down through the Dolomites to Venice, then to the Italian Lakes picking up the children on the way if it can be managed, then Paris August 16, and then sail on the 31st of August. We were taking the children to Venice at first but decided it too much of a jaunt for them. It won't be hot, for this is apparently a cool summer here. It is very chilly in London.

[scribbles drawn by Potter and a circle drawn by Pauline with the label "a kiss"]

He has just come in and has added this to my letter and kissed the spot indicated, so you must kiss it too. I don't know what his scribble means. I just asked him, and he said it means "Poor Banana." Why "poor," he won't tell. He looks very entrancing with his hair all curly and his cheeks pink from his nap. He is so amusing. Alice thinks him a beauty. Bertha is so good these days and happy. I am now writing under difficulties, as you see. When will you meet us, and where? We are counting on you coming over.

Yours with difficulty (as Potter is playing railway train on this paper, and I have to shove his car off to write a word) and with all love,

Pauline

St. James's Palace Hotel
Bury Street, St. James's
London, S.W.
June 11, 1912

Mrs. Herman Kohlsaat
844 Lincoln Parkway
Chicago, Illinois

Dear Mother:

I have never seen such a nice person as you to give me that lovely birthday gift. I am pleased and am planning to get a piece of Italian lace with it. It was a good deal of struggle not to open it beforehand, but I managed to save it until the 10th. Kay and Roger and "Little Uncle Roger" sent me a cable, and Min gave me some beautiful etchings—four Whistlers and a Schoengauer—so I managed to do very nicely, all told. Then your nice chatty letter came the next morning from Paris. I felt very old, much older than I do now! Min poked two or three very funny mean remarks at me, just to make me feel pleasant and at home. We lunched with Alice and Billy at a queer little restaurant called Queen's in Chelsea. There was a great deal of atmosphere about the place and Italian food. At one table a large man with bushy grey hair was talking French violently to a perfectly round woman in mauve, who answered him fluently in German. The Jameses are very swell together and seem quite fond of one another, to put it mildly. They gaze at each other and forget the world! After lunch we went to look at furniture, and we soon tired them out so that they left and we kept on alone.

We have been to the theatre twice to see a musical show called "The Sunshine Girl," which was very good but a little too long. Today we went out into the country to Hitchin to look at the furniture advertised in the Burlington Magazine as "The Manor House, Hitchin." We started at nine and weren't sure until we got to the spot and asked to be directed to the "Manor House" that we had gone to the right town. Min thought it was "Hitchon," and I thought "Hitchins," and the man at Cook's was a cockney and sure that Min meant "Itchins" and as our luck would have it, we couldn't find an advertisement in this month's magazines! We got there safely and found it to be a lovely Queen Anne House, old with such a pretty garden. The furniture was not as good as we expected, but it was pretty, and we got things. I had also the delicate pleasure of looking casually into a doorway while walking and saw a man skin a sheep. It always helps luncheon, a little scene like that. I ate asparagus, bread, rhubarb, and tea and thought on higher things. Florence is back again from her vacation. Bertha was so good while she was with Belle, and everything went very satisfactorily. Potter was of course very suspicious and followed Belle around like a lynx. He was good, though. I have written to Paris again about the rooms to be sure they are right and ready and have ordered the milk and told the hotel to put it on ice. That Bertha is growing out of her clothes! Her sleeves are too short on her dresses! It is discouraging. Such is life at 30 with a family!

Give Father our love and keep a great deal yourself.

Pauline

St. James's Palace Hotel
Bury Street, St. James's
London, S.W.
June 15, 1912

Mrs. Herman Kohlsaat
844 Lincoln Parkway
Chicago, Illinois

Dear Mother:

Well, part of our trip is over, and I can't even believe that it has begun. The time has gone so fast. We go to Paris in the morning. I shall be glad to be there again. The children are so well and look as finely as possible. Everyone now turns to look at Bertha because she is so lively. Florence said yesterday, "Bertha is now the centre of interest when we go out, not Potter!" Belle looked quite peevish, and Florence delighted to have gotten a rise out of her. Her face is clear and her cheeks pink. Still, Potter gets enough attention to make any other child impossible. They have taken such pains here to have things nice for us. It's such a nice place, where one can stay alone if it is necessary. One can go into dinner without dressing up and not feel queer. It is run by an Italian.

Today we went to see Alice and while there met Mrs. Joseph Stickney of N.Y. She was very amusing in more ways than she intended to be. Talking about Lady This and Lady That and how tired she was of going out every second. You can easily imagine how Alice felt! After she had gone, with a parting shot of "I am reduced to taxis, my dear, on account of a mix-up about my new motor," Alice said that she was only thankful that Billy hadn't been there to hear that last drop, as he would have died on the spot. Billy is terribly nice and not at all the superior person I imagined him to be. Just thoroughly nice in every way—very amusing and good fun, with the splendid brain that we heard he had. He and Alice are great pals and distinctly pleasant to be with. Really quite the nicest bride and groom you can think of. Min thinks Alice nicer than before and likes Billy, so things go smoothly when we are together. "Uncle Henry" James came in while we were there, and for a distinguished person, he is a puffy old soul and very pompous. I'd like to see him, Helen, and old Joe together. Perhaps three sentences would be finished in a day, but I doubt it. He has been too lovely to Alice and Billy, and they love him, so I shouldn't make fun of him. But he is funny. Don't say that we found him queer. And don't be annoyed that I asked you not to!

 Best love to you and Father from us all.

Pauline

[Hôtel Lotti
Paris, France]
June 24, 1912

Mrs. Herman Kohlsaat
844 Lincoln Parkway
Chicago, Illinois

Dear Mother:

I haven't written in over a week, but you mustn't imagine that anything is wrong. Simply Min and I have been so busy having a "good time" that I haven't had a minute to spare! We had a very easy trip over from London. The children were remarkably good. The channel was rougher than either of us had ever seen it, and Florence was seasick. The babies took a nap all the way over, as did Belle. Min and I sat on deck. One wave was so big that it threw two people out of their chairs onto the deck. One went sailing onto the railing! I really thought that the boat would never right itself. The trip on to Paris was simple and comfortable. When we arrived I took the children at once to the hotel and found Mrs. P. waiting for us. She didn't like our rooms and had looked at others across the street. As they had not been able to keep the rooms promised at the Castiglione on account of an auto accident, which detained people who were leaving, we felt justified in changing hotels. This, the "Lotti," is new, very comfortable and clean. We have lovely rooms and are all happy.

The children go to the garden every morning and in the P.M. wander about looking at sights. They took the boat to St. Cloud the other afternoon, went to Notre Dame and Ste. Chapelle yesterday, and [Napoleon's] Tomb. This morning they are at the Bon Marché and this P.M. go to the Luxembourg Gardens.

Yesterday Mrs. Palmer took Min, Potter, and me to Versailles after lunch. It was too lovely out there. Potter was thrilled, and as Belle was not along, he did everything he pleased and had the time of his life. He fished in all the fountains and threw in sticks, he ran and shouted and nearly fainted with joy over the boats. When we got back to the hotel, and Mrs. P. asked if anyone would have tea, he said "yes" very decidedly. He had two cups and three extra pieces of sugar. He had an equally good time coming home and altogether the day was a great success.

I have been looking for some clothes for next winter and have ordered from Worth two lovely evening dresses. I am now looking for a party coat and found this A.M. a black velvet brocaded a little in gold, with a lovely white fox collar. The fox is not like the usual kind, in that it has a few soft brown hairs scattered down the centre that make it have more character. I saw it at Drecoll's. As you know, I have too many clothes now.

Min is deep in Chinese porcelain. He is more enthusiastic than ever if anything. He is very well and looks it. He thinks I have too many clothes and then whenever he sees anything pretty urges me to get it! We will need new trunks by the score!

The other night we went to see "Le Coeur Dispose" at the Athenée. It was excellent, and the French was a joy to hear. We've seen two or three others that weren't so successful. Tonight we see "Les Petites Femmes de Paris." It sounds giddy, doesn't it? We dine out at the little restaurants and once at a big Ciro's on the rue Vaneau. We arrived at eight and as we walked into the large, brilliantly lighted dining room, the band began to play a very stunning piece. The headwaiter snapped his fingers, and at least 40 waiters who were crowded together gossiping scattered, and with much ceremony we were shown a table. We were the only people dining in the place! Before we finished, 23 others came in, but that was all, and it was the most lonesome place. Last night we went to Café Larue on the rue Royale and had a very good dinner. We try to go to lunch at different places, too. Mrs. P. has lunched with us nearly every day. Her apartment is as lovely as ever, and the garden is heavenly. Mary Stone is here. We went shopping together this morning. She dined the other evening with Janet Scudder, who gave a large dinner. It doesn't sound like Janet, does it?

Isn't it nice that Kay's baby is doing so well. He will be almost too fat before she knows it. Kay wrote me that they were having an ideal summer. The Convention must have been very amusing and interesting, and how embarrassing for the members of the Roosevelt family present. Why did they go? It seems queer taste.

Goodbye and love,

Pauline

Hôtel Lotti
Paris, France
July 1, 1912

Mrs. Herman Kohlsaat
844 Lincoln Parkway
Chicago, Illinois

Dear Mother:

We are having a very good time. Min and I, as I told you, have wandered around to the restaurants and theatres without finding much excitement, but last Saturday night we found it. C. Ely is in town, and Min met Uncle Fred's aide-de-camp, Lieut. Howze, so we asked them to dinner and theatre. We went to Ciro's again because we didn't know where else to go. The food there is good. It was a gala night, and we saw the most wonderful sights! We would talk, and then one would interrupt on account of some marvel coming in! C. Ely was in a very nice mood, and we all got on beautifully. Then we went to Morigny's and saw things!!!! Moorish baths with nude ladies coming out of the tubs, chiffon scarf covering one spot. A Harlequin in pink tights with black lace tights over it, which gave a most startling effect. A grizzly bear all mixed up with a Bunny Hug and added to ladies undressing all very chic. A very Parisian show, but not in the least coarse. The audience was just as good, and so the evening was most amusing and very exciting.

The Pecks are here, so we expect to see a lot of them. Aunt Ida arrived yesterday and sails the 3rd of July. She seems very well and a little more cheerful, although she looks very sad indeed. Little Bertha came with her and is spending the winter with her in Florida. She has grown very fast and Julia thought the change would do her great good.

Your grandchildren are progressing. They seem to enjoy Paris tremendously! Potter's passion now is to have the model of the ocean liners displayed in the steamship offices window. They apparently go all over and see everything. Bertha tries to talk all the time and manages to say a few words more or less indistinctly. Tell Katherine that Mrs. Ely told me that Morse was getting Kay's wedding present here this summer. She said, "He didn't give her one, you know." And I said, "Yes, we all thought it was queer." I suppose Morse was hard up over his ring for Josephine. Give Father our love, and keep some yourself.

Pauline

Following pages: The draping of the bodices at the couture house of Charles Frédéric Worth, where Pauline and Bertha Palmer often shopped in Paris. (1907)

Hôtel Lotti
Paris, France
July 7, 1912

Mrs. Herman Kohlsaat
844 Lincoln Parkway
Chicago, Illinois

Dear Mother:

Today Mrs. Palmer took us all out to Versailles in the motor. Fortunately it was the day the fountains played. It was lovely: everything was so fresh and green, after a rain, and smelt so woody. Min got each child a big balloon in the shape of a cucumber. They are both crazy about them. Potter went up to his grandmother after he spied the balloon man, and with that sickly ingratiating smile of his, he said, "Haf you any money? I want a b'loon." It was killing to see him.

We went to the Moulin Rouge the other night and saw some very remarkable sights that I will tell you about when we see you, as they can't be written. Monday night we go to hear "Sigfried" with Mrs. Palmer. I am going to wear my new Worth gown, the white satin one. It's quite a daisy.

Love, Pauline

Potter in the Tuilleries Gardens. "The children go all over and see everything."

Bear Hotel
Grindelwald, Switzerland
August 25, 1912

Mrs. Herman Kohlsaat
844 Lincoln Parkway
Chicago, Illinois

Dear Mother:

Your letter in which you say you are expecting p.c.'s from the Dolomites has just come, and we are chuckling over the time when you find out that we too have not been! We have been back here nearly three weeks, and the place is beginning to "pall," to put it mildly. We go to Paris next Thursday, and we can hardly wait.

The children still continue to bloom and grow fat. If they hadn't done so well, we would have gone down to Bellagio long before this to get warm. Bertha is doing the same thing about talking that Potter did, jumping right into sentences. Tonight she took the glass and said, "See the baby?" She imitates every sound she hears, regardless of any knowledge of what she's saying. She is a whale, and her hair on top is beginning to grow!!! Potter has gone in for long words and is simply killing. He tags around after Min, and no one else will. It's really lovely to see. Belle and Florence are getting as fat as plovers. They have the most wonderful meals served in their rooms—with the children's—and consequently overeat. Min is positively bulgy and says about me that where once there were bumps there are now hollows! So you see it is doing us all a great deal of good.

We still climb the nearby hills every day and nearly die, but time goes quickly while straining uphill. I wear my hip reducers, and the work goes hurrily on. We don't know anyone here, except one man who shook hands with Min and said he knew his mother in Rome years ago. We chatted about ten minutes, then he went on his way, and we looked up the manager of the hotel to find out his name. Min is scared to death every time we see him for fear he'll stop and begin. One of our chief diversions lately is to go to the tennis court and watch a French lady play tennis. She wears the tightest known skirt, which buttons on the side to just above the knee. These buttons she is forced to undo if she takes a stop. So when playing tennis one has a fine view of fat green stockings and deep lace ruffle on the pants that are shirred around to the knee. As she wears no petticoat and runs and jumps around like wild, the effect is thrilling. Men line the courts watching and then go into hysterics of laughter. She is short and fat.

You ask when are we going to Florida. Not until sometime in December, anyway. We haven't decided on the date yet. We expect to be at home for a little while at least. I want to go up to see Kay if I can. We can go up together and stop at the hotel. Min may be able to go, but I expect he will be terribly busy on account of being away so

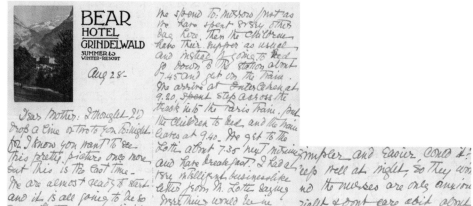

long. I haven't spoken to him about it yet.

I am not sure if the [car] is ready for use or not, but if you would like to use it, Min would love to have you do so. I'll write to Kasper to tell him, and you telephone him if you care for it anytime. He may be off at "Paw Paw Lake" with his "folks," as he was going sometime during the summer for a two weeks' vacation. The winter car is being painted. Min says you have had a perfectly fine summer with the baby and knows you have enjoyed it thoroughly. You never had much chance with our children on account of Miss Hays being there. What have your overworked servants been doing this summer? From Father's being at the Club, I presume they are vacating, at least Minnie and Frances. I have a nice second man. I think I told you. He is loafing in London at present, awaiting word to come to Paris. Taylor is going to England for a vacation, as he had a short one while we were there in June. Then he goes home earlier and gets the house in order. Thanks very much for telling me about Ross. I must write Eva that we aren't coming home until October. We'll be there by the 15th, I think.

Much love from us all, Pauline

Bear Hotel
Grindelwald, Switzerland
August 28, 1912

Mrs. Herman Kohlsaat
844 Lincoln Parkway
Chicago, Illinois

Dear Mother:

I thought I'd drop a line or two to you tonight, for I know you want to see this pretty picture once more, but this is the last time. We are almost ready to start, and it is all going to be so easy. The trunks are finished, except for a few things. Then we spend tomorrow just as we have spent every other day here. Then the children have their supper as usual and instead of going to bed go down to the station about 7:45 and get on the train. We arrive at Interlaken at 9:20, step across the track into the Paris train, put the children to bed, and the train leaves at 9:40. We get to the Lotti about 7:35 next morning and have breakfast. I had a very intelligent, businesslike letter from M. Lotti saying everything would be in readiness for us. And there you are. Nothing in the world could be so much simpler and easier, could it? Both children sleep well at night, so they won't notice the train, and the nurses are only anxious to have them all right and don't care a bit about themselves. They are both most satisfactory girls in every way and get along together like a breeze.

I don't know if I ever wrote you about the loveliness of this place, but I will do so now anyway and hope you won't be bored. Grindelwald is a little above the bottom of a valley and is enclosed on the N. and S. by high mountains, mostly snow-topped. On the E. and W. are the Big and Little Scheidegg, so that the valley is quite like a cup. A river formed by the two glaciers on the S. rushes violently along just beneath our windows and sounds like the Aarc at Thun, only not so loud. Then it follows the very narrow, twisting valley down to Interlaken. All about are lovely walks that one can go on, if one cares to climb. The fields are full of bluebells, clover and a stiff pinky stalk. Higher up there are more wildflowers than you ever dreamed of. I haven't the vaguest idea of their names, but they are lovely and every colour. The field or garden that the children play in is mowed at one end only, and at the other there are daisies, buttercups, clovers pink and white, English daisies, and the whole place is a mass of tiny colour spots. We took a very strenuous walk today up the side of a waterfall. It was rough and wet and slippery and too steep for words. We nearly melted before reaching the top, although the path led through thick woods all the way. At the top we came out on a mountainous field that was as smooth and treeless as the other had been rough and woody. It looked like England, only it was all up and down hill and always leading down into the valley, the path I mean led down. It was lovely—I think I lost five pounds, surely. This really is a heavenly place and the air is wonderful. I think you'd love it and am sorry that you haven't been here with us this summer.

The people aren't very attractive, to put it mildly. We have had a dash of English clergymen and families here the last few days. Min says that when you look at the English clergy you are discouraged, and when you look at his wife and family you think that the Roman Catholic plan of not permitting its priests to marry is an excellent one. There is an American family here named Marshall from N.Y. There are six children, the oldest about 17, then quite a gap, the next 12, and from that one a year and a half apart down to about 7. The father said that when he became 50 he would stop work and devote his life to making his wife and children happy. So he has begun by bringing them abroad for a year and a half. Last winter they spent in Munich, spring in Bavaria, six weeks here, and then slowly to Florence for three months, and then Rome for three more. The children are as lively as crickets, two boys and four girls. The parents have never had any care of them before nor the slightest responsibility, for they had a very superior German woman who took entire charge, even to ordering their clothes, etc. Now they have had to let the German go home, and they have the children to care for, with no one to help! They don't know the children, and the children are much nearer the German woman, naturally. The mother looks perfectly distracted and does everything on the run. They are always late for meals so come rushing in one by one, and finally Mrs. Marshall brings up the rear, running as if the devil were chasing her. One becomes strangely interested in trivial things when one's days are the same and the chief amusements and interests getting up, going to bed, and eating. I forgot to mention Solitaire. Min has nearly played the spots off the cards.

The children are still flourishing. Bertha has an eyetooth, discovered only by mistake! Potter is fine and still keeps at the long words. Yesterday while out walking with us he saw in the distance a trough filled with water. He looked up at Min and said, " I am interested in that puddle." He is so serious and simply killing.

I wrote a long letter the other day to Chéruit because they sent me a bill for the suit they didn't finish after untold annoyances on my part, and I have been in fear and trembling ever since about their answer. Today it came: most apologetic and everything that was nice. So I am feeling better. You will be amused to hear that the other morning when I went down to breakfast, the first thing I saw on entering the dining room was Min eating breakfast with M. Dyer, the man who said he knew Min's mother. I could scarcely go to the table. Min looked perfectly sick and just cast me a short glance! I presume M. Dyer thought me a merry sunshine at the breakfast table. It seems he has a very remarkable voice, hence is artistic. Well, this is a long, dull letter, but never mind. Much love from us all to you both.

Pauline

After reading this over, I find it duller than I thought!

Hôtel Lotti
Paris, France
September 17, 1912

Mrs. Herman Kohlsaat
844 Lincoln Parkway
Chicago, Illinois

Dear Mother:

Two nice chatty letters from you yesterday and today. It was so nice to get them. I am sorry that you have been so hot and am awfully glad we didn't come home in August, as we first intended to do. Min says he's sorry he didn't go, as it would be a fine thing to be warm again. He hasn't been so since the middle of July. Everyone here is wearing plush hats and furs! and sleeps under blankets and comforters. The leaves are off the horse chestnuts on the Champs Elysées and the second growth is sprouting. No one but Russians and South Americans in town, and North Americans, too, but not as many as usual. Mrs. P. and A.C. start off on a motor trip in a couple of days, and the Herricks go to Venice on the 19th. Mrs. Kimball is here, although I haven't seen her. Mrs. Black is getting oodles of lovely clothes, and Alice Howard is suffering from overeating green peaches, taking boiled milk, Harry said, and we all know what that means! Imagine the tragedy of being a "fixture" in Paris when clothes are in full sway!

Speaking of clothes, I ordered another dress for afternoon. Had firm intention of getting a soft brown velvet, and Min chose a blue! So I got it. The skirts aren't so dreadfully tight, and Drecoll's things are not so exaggerated, and they are the prettiest in Paris. Fur is on everything, inexpensive fur if the other fellow's getting it, and terribly expensive if you want it! Just a dab here and there. Charmeuse and velvets popular, and plush hats all the rage. If you haven't one you are not in it. I've got a daisy, tiny and sassy, even Min approves, and everyone on the streets turn to look at it with envy. Beppé and Petite are here all smiles, having the time of their lives. As yet their clothes aren't made, so they are wearing Carson Pirie things.

September 23, 1912

Just see how long this letter has been left unfinished! As I have said many times before, the time goes by without my knowing it. One does so many things that one can't keep track of everything. I heard today of Owen Aldi's engagement to a French girl of 20! She is of very fine family, most attractive, and madly in love with him. And he says that he knows everyone will think he's crazy, but he doesn't care! What will Janet say! She will probably faint away. And what do you suppose the Lathrops will think! We will all have to give them parties when they get to Chicago.

Min and I dined with the H. Howards last night (Sunday) at the Ritz, and it was quite amusing. Very queer people, wonderful clothes that weren't very pretty, and marvelous headdresses! Min saw several of his N.Y. friends and spoke to them. Mrs. Dunlop and the John Blacks were there together looking very fine and full of addresses for shopping. Now that it's nearly time to sail, I am beginning to feel that I shan't get finished in time! I tackled the hat question again today and found two beauties at Reboux, for which they asked 190 francs and 250 francs!! Perfectly good prices for Chicago, but awful when you add on 60% duty. I didn't get them. I went to Chéruit's for a suit or a dress and found a dress that I like extremely. So think I will go back tomorrow and get it. I don't ever expect to get any more clothes, as I can't resist the things I've seen here. Still, when you consider that I absolutely had nothing to wear when we left Switzerland (except lovely summer things that I have scarcely put on!) and had to get something, it isn't so awful. The dress Mrs. MacAvoy made me is a sight, as I've worn it so much. She was over here for models, so you had better go to her and see what she has. I hope never again to be in such a state as I was this summer without anything heavy.

We saw Mrs. Eames on the street the other day. She looks very thin but was as cheerful as ever. And today I saw Mrs. Field. She didn't look smart and was much thinner. We called on Mrs. Dunlop and had a chatty visit with her. The other night Gretchen Isham Shelton asked us to dinner in their apartment. No one else was there, and we had great fun. They had a grate fire, and you should have seen us cling to it! Steam is on in this hotel, and so our rooms are nice and cozy now, and we no longer shiver. It is impossible to believe that it has been so hot in U.S.A.

I tried to get you Ischekoff books and have succeeded in finding three novels, but no plays. I asked Michel what he was like, and Michel said, "Damn fool!" and also that if you believe about 50 percent of what he writes you will get nearer the truth. So apparently he exaggerates. He writes a kind of slang, which is impossible to translate. I have "Un Duel," "Le Meutre," and "Les Mougles." We have had Paris scoured for them. Michel says to read Tolstoi and you get the best "Anna Karenina." Min has read a lot here, "Old Touraine," and is now deep in the history of the Dark Ages in Italy. A Whistler book, a new novel called "Caviare," which is amusing, and I'll bring it home to you. Two books on Chinese porcelain and all the magazines. We went to the Luxembourg the other day and liked Whistler and Manet and Degas best. We had lunch at Foyots and then walked back to the river. Tonight we went to Pruniers and had crabmeat and steak. It was crowded there, and the crowd was amusing, flashy ladies in all kinds of costumes with hats. We could scarcely eat for looking. Had a letter from Joe Peck saying that little Jean Farquhar was much better. G. Shelton told me that Marion wrote that she was sending the trained nurse off, as Jean was so improved. Isn't it splendid? Goodbye, much love to you both from us all, Pauline

Children fine, B. now yells "Patrie" all the time, like the men on the streets.

Hôtel Lotti
Paris, France
October 1, 1912

Mrs. Herman Kohlsaat
844 Lincoln Parkway
Chicago, Illinois

Dear Mother:

Bertha got upset on Sunday, vomited, and was in a very high fever. She looked and acted dazed, quite unlike herself. I was able to help her a little, I am thankful to say, and the fever left after lunch and only came back a little toward bedtime. She wouldn't eat anything and passed mucous in green streams. Monday she was better and this morning a little more improved. Not caring to risk a sickish infant on the ocean, I went to the Scientist I went to here four years ago. She was out of town, but a friend was there, who must be good, for Bertha is fine tonight, much less yellow and a little pink in her cheeks. I think it is probably her stomach teeth, the last two that she has to cut of this first lot. She is the funniest youngster. This evening she was sitting on my lap before going to bed. She was playing with the things on the dressing table. I took up my comb and began to comb her "beautiful curls." She immediately stopped playing and sat perfectly still, enjoying the combing to the last degree. She is most decided on what she wants and how she wants it done. Her hair is growing in front now and is curly! Her new clothes are too lovely. Tell Kay so—it will save her the trouble of hunting up things for Roger. Mrs. Holman can easily copy these—if Kay cares for them, that is!

Kay's clothes sound lovely, I think the Callot suit and waist is the one I wanted to get, but they asked 2100 francs for it! She must get a plush or panne velvet hat, or plain velvet, black. The day hats are small, and some of the dressy ones, too. Evening ones are big and fairly flat. Aigrettes, paradise and what they call "croix" (I suppose it is spelt that way, anyway it's so pronounced) are used on the hats for dress, and any old mess on the day hats—little pompoms hanging over one ear, or a white wing. No other coloring but brown black and white, and at C. Roget they used ostrich feathers of yellow or pale mauve. Everyone has white-grey, brown, or black-and-white check tops on their shoes. Furs are enormously broad scarves. Haven't seen any muffs so far. Always a hair ornament for the evening, and I'll show Kay how the hair is done in the latest fashion. We'll show Ellen a thing or two and make her sit up and take notice!

Tell Kay that we'll all come for Thanksgiving, although I know she won't be able to manage us all, we're such a mob. It will be great fun to have all the babies together. She must take down all ornaments when ours heave in sight. They are death on them. Perhaps you and I can run up for a day or two as soon as I am settled and the children nurses and servants have swung into line. I haven't seen Kay for an awfully long time. I've really forgotten when it was. Easter, I think. She must be quite stout, if what you and she says is true. Quite out of my class, for the dressmakers all say I'm thin, so it must be true! My dresses are all home, and now I am waiting for a purse and some hatpins to come in! It'll get some pins for my hair, and then my shopping is over.

I am wondering if you will like the things we have gotten. Of the porcelain, I am sure you will like our half, and the other, will expire over. They are very nice, though. We've some furniture, and a few etchings. We are very well satisfied with things, but then Min and I generally do like our own things.

When this reaches you we will be almost in N.Y. It doesn't seem possible that two weeks from tonight we will have dinner at home. I simply can't believe it. On one hand we will be glad to get home, and on the other, we won't. We both would like to go to Touraine (!!!) and through Italy, but we wouldn't do that with the children for worlds! Min and I will have to come over alone some year and do all those things, with three trunks and a servant! Although I must say that we have no kick coming at all. Everyone has been on time, not one grumble have we heard, and everyone amiable with one another, and every face broad smiles. It has really been quite remarkable, when you think how many we are—eight people. Every trunk has been ready on time, and never once has a nurse been late. And they agree beautifully, as far as I can see. Mrs. Palmer sent Potter a postcard from Menton today. I showed it to Belle and Jennie, who were in the room at the time, and said, "We'll go there someday," and they both said quickly, "Alright, we'll go anywhere you'll take us, anytime!" And they both looked as if they'd start in the morning if they got the word to do so. A long rambling chat, but I want you to see how nicely they have all acted, trying to make it easy for us.

You see, Min is entirely buried in French history these days and hasn't a word to throw to a cat, so I must talk to someone. So you are suffering tonight. Min got started on French history by reading "Old Touraine," which was so hectic and vague that he got a history in three volumes. Very interestingly written. Well, goodnight. Billy Beale asked me what I heard from Father, and I was ashamed to say, "Not anyt'ing," as Potter says. Nevertheless, give him my best love and from all the others too, and ask him if he is one of the 500 chorus singing for T.R.? Perhaps he's leading it! "Who knowth."

Best love from all,

Pauline

Notes

June 9, 1912: "Fields" is Marshall Field's department store.

June 11, 1912: This is Pauline's thirtieth birthday. Cook's is the travel business, Thomas Cook.

June 24, 1912: Janet Scudder, an admired sculptor, had done work for Chicago's World's Fair and now lived in Paris.

July 1, 1912: Aunt Ida is Ida Grant, Bertha Palmer's sister, who is married to Frederick Dent Grant. Julia, her daughter, is married to Prince Michel Cantacuzène. Little Bertha is Michel and Julia's daughter.

August 25, 1912: Kasper is the chauffeur.

September 17, 1912: A. C. is Bertha Palmer's brother A. C. Honoré.

"Carson Pirie things" are clothes from department store Carson Pirie Scott.

September 23, 1912: Pauline mentions books by Ischekoff or Chekhov. Michel Cantacuzène is called Michel here, and later, Michael.

October 1, 1912: Pauline asks if her father is part of the "500 chorus singing for T.R."— those who want Teddy Roosevelt to run again. He was not, because he foresaw that splitting the Republican vote between two Republican candidates, the incumbent president, William Howard Taft, and his predecessor, T.R., would elect the Democrat Wilson, as happened.

"From the porch where I am writing,
I look out on the treetops.
One large live oak right before me looks like
the tree that "Peter Pan" sits in,
in the last act, and blows on his pipe."

SARASOTA, WINTER AND SPRING OF 1912-13

In these letters, written during the winter and spring of 1912-13, Pauline describes to her mother the work she and Min are doing on their place in Sarasota and their relaxed life. After a graphic account of the eventful train trip south, she reports on their arrival in Sarasota the next day, where she finds their new house, Immokalee, "simply lovely." Life is very relaxing, with five o'clock dinner parties that last until 8:30. Catching rattlesnakes is "an everyday occurrence." Food deliveries come or not. There is "no grass around the house—only sand, and a general disinclination on everyone's part to work, loafing around being the principal occupation." Some of Pauline's worries are not having a garbage pail and getting nine quarts of milk instead of sixteen from their cow.

The children by now are three-and-a-half, and one-and-a-half—both lively and full of personality and, as Pauline says, "in fine shape. Potter is fatter and looks so well...[Bertha] is the cunningest youngster. Really fascinating. Not at all in the way that Potter was and is, but in an entirely feminine manner, which is just alluring. She flirts with everyone, male or female, young or old. Nothing makes any difference so long as they are human beings to admire her."

According to Pauline, their house is relatively modest and the life they live quite simple. Bertha Palmer, however, is in the process of creating her grand establishment at Osprey Point, about nine miles farther south on Little Sarasota Bay. She remodeled the original building on the property, enlisting gardeners, landscapers, archi-

tects, engineers, and horticulturalists to help her. A Chicago architect, Thomas Reed Martin, oversaw operations. She contacted Frederick Law Olmsted, who lived at a development in Lake Wales, Florida, for landscaping advice. The final garden would include the "Duchene Lawn" with towering columns before an alleé of palms, a sunken garden, and the "Blue Garden" near the house, with a statue in the center. There was also a "Jungle Walk," and pathways of beach sand. Concrete urns were added to classical urns and sculpture to heighten the style. In the end, the property was landscaped with an artificial brook, the multiple gardens (including a rose garden), and a pavilion. As Bertha's biographer Ishbel Ross writes, "Visitors walked through rows of yellow acacias, past Chinese hibiscus, bougainvillaea and brilliant crotons." Bertha loved "the brilliant green and blue colors of sea and sky, and watching dramatic sunsets, and the great collection of birds—the cardinals and mocking birds that darted through the jungle."

The house would develop into a large and spacious mansion with a veranda that wrapped around the columned first story. It would be eventually furnished with furniture from Chicago, decorative objects including crystal, china, silver, and figurines, as well as favorite paintings by Monet, Raffaelli, Degas, and Cassatt. Upstairs guests and family could sleep in comfort in twelve bedrooms with screened porches. As the weather was warm and sultry and the landscape wild, the visitor came away with the impression of visiting a Southern plantation in earlier days.

Bertha's growing interest in Florida real

Top: Bertha Palmer and guests at a
picnic at Myakka after quail shooting.
Bottom: Model-T Ford amongst the
thick Florida undergrowth.
Right: The terrace at Bertha Palmer's
Oaks mansion, with urns and neat
landscaping looking out to the view of
the Bay.

estate has given her family reason to gather themselves in this southern setting. Cappy and Min are now involved in their mother's Sarasota–Venice real estate company. Bertha often welcomes her grandson, young Potter, at the Oaks with his nurse. She is delighted to get to know the new generation. In 1917, the year before her death, she wrote to Min about the newest arrival: "Thank you so much for sending the kodaks of the children…So pleased to have the description of the baby. She must be a wonder! Oceans of love to Pauline and kisses for the children and my heart full of loving thought."

Bertha also includes Pauline and her guests for dinners and in expeditions to Myakka, land she owned farther inland, eighteen miles away. Pauline is looking forward to visiting Myakka, saying she has heard it is wild and beautiful. Indeed, the property includes lakes, pastures, towering palms, as well as giant oaks covered with Spanish moss. Bertha created a cattle ranch called Meadow Sweet Pastures, and a camp with bungalows at the end of Upper Myakka Lake. She would visit there with friends and family, bringing along her butler, cook, and other servants to provide excellent hospitality. The Palmer family would later donate the land at Myakka to create what is now a state park.

Belle Haven Inn
Sarasota, Florida
December 26, 1912

Mrs. Herman Kohlsaat
844 Lincoln Parkway
Chicago, Illinois

Dear Mother:

We have just received Father's telegram about Mr. Shepard's death. Isn't it dreadful. I had no idea that he was so ill. Poor Roger must be heartbroken. I am so sorry for him. I see that you went to St. Paul for Xmas. It must have been a miserable day, buy Kay I know was glad enough to have you both there.

Well, my dear! Our trip was so full of tragic occurrences that it finally became ridiculous and we had to laugh. In the first place, if you remember we nearly missed getting to the train, Father being so brilliant that he averted that tragedy. Then the train didn't start until nearly 8:45! After running half an hour it stopped for a long time, as something broke. I went to bed about ten and told A.C. that I intended to stay there until three P.M. Bertha decided that she "didn't want" to travel so talked violently to herself all night, Mother not sleeping well in that account. At 8:30 Jennie brought me coffee and toast, and I remarked that the stateroom was very cold. "So's everything else," she said, and then I discovered that the break of the night before was in the steam heating! Then something went wrong in the dining car, and no one could get breakfast. Potter was in there two and a half hours! Bertha didn't get anything until nearly 10. At noon the steam was mended, so we stewed for the rest of the trip.

We were two hours late at Birmingham. The only thing that went right was that we met Min! Florence was very sick, so Belle kept the children. They got a good supper on time, and the nurses kept out toast and crackers in case we were too late for breakfast at Jacksonville. Well, we arrive there at 9:30, two hours late, and had just time to hurry to the Sarasota train without breakfast. The children had the toast, crackers, and milk, so weren't quite starving. Then we sat in that station for one hour, expecting to leave any minute. We were annoyed. Finally we started, and then got a good breakfast from the buffet in the car. The children had naps and then supper about 4:30. We were two hours late at Turkey Creek and had to change cars in the pitch dark. The next train was crowded, and no seats had been reserved in the chair car! The company paid no attention to our telegram sent two weeks ago! The car held about 30 people, and there were at least 50 in it! Hot and smelly! The children slept, thank goodness. Then the gaslights went out! They put in candles, and they went out!! And at about 10:45 we staggered into Sarasota 2 1/2 hours late. But as the train was reported due at 12, there was no motor to meet us, and we had to stand on the platform for about 15 minutes until one came. Then when we finally got into bed, the mattress was like fifteen pieces of sheet iron! And under our windows the poultry yard filled with quacking ducks, crowing roosters, and gobbling turkeys, and they squacked every other minute all night.

Next morning we went to our place, and it is simply lovely. I can't wait to get in. In spite of all these dreadful things that I've been telling you about our trip (which was all on account of its being Xmas), you must come and visit. Everything is charming and too pretty for words. Min is wild about it, and all the servants, too!

Xmas was a beautiful day, and we started early for Osprey by motor. Bertha was in fine feather and decided that she would start things going at lunch. So she got very chatty and made faces and beat the table and amused everybody. We really watched her most of the time. Grandpa Honoré said she was the "Belle of the ball." Mrs. P. gave her a doll in a buggy, and every time the wheels go round the doll moves its hands and says, "Mama!" Bertha was crazy about it and got down in front of it and talked to it with all her might and main and would have nothing to do with anything else. She'd say "Take it away!" to every other gift. We went to the house today and worked hard. I think that we'll be in sometime next week, surely. I am dead tired so won't write anymore now. Goodnight. Much love to you all from us all.

Pauline

Sarasota, Florida
January 24, 1913

Mrs. Herman Kohlsaat
844 Lincoln Parkway
Chicago, Illinois

Dear Mother:

A short note from you yesterday saying that the Kodaks had arrived. They are very poor but the best that we have been able to get so far. There are so many trees about the house that one can't get the proper distance to focus correctly. We have been doing a lot of clearing and it looks much improved. Yesterday we set out about forty plants, vines and young tress, and now I am impatiently waiting for them to grow big and blossom. I expect my patience will be tried, sure enough. Today it is lovely and cool with a strong breeze off the Bay. Yesterday morning we took the children over to the Gulf to play in the sand. It is too heavenly over there, and they had such a good time. Potter calls it "going to Mexico, Muthe-r-r-r." Your gift of the coloured paper was joyfully received. May I drop a hint to you that you would save me a near riot if you would remember that you have a granddaughter down here? Things sent to Potter do not belong to "Bertha," even if she wants them dreadfully and yells to beat the hand in her effort to convince us that she'd appreciate a peek at them. So don't be partial. Potter says, "And do my Bamma Kosat sent me these?" He is most enchanting. Bertha's hair is much longer and quite curly. She is as fat as a plover and full of sin. All the earmarks of a "belle," in fact. She is delighted with herself, and it is killing to watch her.

Tonight we are dining out, which is a great dissipation. We go to Aunt Laura's. One arrives at 5:15 here when one dines out, so as to admire the sunset. One dines at 6:30 and then says goodnight and departs no later than 8:30. If one's hosts yawn, one goes earlier. One also wears heavy high boots and a short skirt. From the porch where I am writing, I look out on the treetops. One large live oak right before me looks like the tree that "Peter Pan" sits in, in the last act, and blows on his pipe. Do you remember? You really feel as if you are sitting in the treetops yourself. It is ideal. You will see for yourself when you come down here. You will get tired of our asking you to come down, but we do want you so much. Best love to Father from us all, and the same to you.

Pauline

Sarasota, Florida
January 27, 1913

Mrs. Herman Kohlsaat
844 Lincoln Parkway
Chicago, Illinois

Dear Mother:

It is lovely down here and like summer. We are very busy with the outside of the place, clearing away trees between us and the bay and having tiles and lumber that are there moved to the back. Min is cutting a path through a jungle to the south of us, and you can't imagine how attractive he has made it. The jungle isn't very big, but the trees, palmettos, cabbage palms, and cedars, are very thick, besides a thick undergrowth of bushes, etc. Min has laid the path so that it twists and turns and you feel as if you were walking through an endless deep wood.

While the darkies were grubbing it out the other day, they ran into a rattler five fine feet, nine inches long that had 14 rattles! It was such an old one that they killed it without any trouble. It was lying just where Min had been walking about all morning! The darkies are much disappointed that they haven't found another since! and are on a constant lookout for one. It's such a different life down here that it is difficult to adjust oneself to it immediately, catching rattlers as an everyday occurrence, food coming or not, no grass around the house—only sand, and a general disinclination on everyone's part to work, loafing being the principle occupation. I think that as soon as I get used to it, I'll do very well!

"Necessity is the mother of invention" was first thought up in a wild woods like this, where you can't get anything. Did I tell you that it took the ten days to get tin candlesticks? And I haven't a garbage pail yet! It is to laugh.

The children are in fine shape. Potter is fatter and looks so well. Bertha has all her teeth —16 now—and a lot of hair. She is being broken of her bottle habit at nap time and night and is standing it very well indeed. She is the cunningest youngster. Really fascinating. Not at all in the way that Potter was and is, but in an entirely feminine manner, which is just alluring. She flirts with everyone, male or female, young or old. Nothing makes any difference so long as they are human beings to admire her. She has as much energy as Potter and is continually on the go and talk! You should hear her. No word or sentence is too much for her to tackle. Potter is most independent and getting quite well able to take care of himself. He's quite a wonder.

I had a long letter from you yesterday, besides another a day or two ago. It's very pleasant to have you pay me attention, and I hope you will keep it up. You seem to be quite gay going out so much. How does Father like it? The Shepards must have so much by now that they won't be able to realize it exactly. It seems splendid. It is a fine thing to have enough money, but generally the price for it is too high. And after it's paid, the money seems nothing and less than nothing in comparison, and still, if it had to happen anyway, I am so glad that the sweeties have it, for they are such sweeties.

Why is it that I draw maids who are about to have a change of life? I am besieged by it on all sides. As Potter said about the mosquito bites the other day, "They're a nuisance!" I shall exclude all women between the ages of 33 and 50 and cross them off my list of eligibles. Ah me! Well, this is a long ramble, and I'll bring it to a close. If you find you can come down, telegraph and come. Love to all from us all,

Pauline

Sarasota, Florida
February 2, 1913

Mrs. Herman Kohlsaat
844 Lincoln Parkway
Chicago, Illinois

Dear Mother:

I suppose it's over a week since I last wrote. The time goes so fast that it is most difficult to keep track of it. A couple of nice chatty letters from you lately. You sound very gay going to the opera so often. It is over now, and everybody must be sinking back with relief and wondering what they will do with so many evenings on their hands.

Your youngest daughter arrives on the scene tomorrow some time. I hope that the South won't be too much for her! We are so glad that she is coming. It's too bad that Roger can't come and stay longer. Grandpa Shepard has him jumping so that he probably won't be able to stay here more than one night. We were planning for ten days at the least. It will be so nice to have the Squill, though. Doesn't it seem queer to think that the first visit she makes us should be in this house, so far from anything we ever dreamed of? Life is a queer thing. Anyway, we have a great variety in ours. No dull moments! After they go home and take Roger in to St. Paul, you must come down as soon as you possibly can. I really can't imagine what you'll think of this place, and I'll bet that you can't imagine what this place will be like either. Not in your wildest moments.

Our life for the last few days has been extremely full. Min is building cowsheds and chicken miens, to say nothing of a bathroom addition to the caretaker's cottage! I have been busy doing I don't know what. We have been here six weeks! And it doesn't seem like a second. Our weather has been chillier and so more pleasant. In fact, for several days we shook with the cold. The rain finally arrived, came in torrents. It came twice and was distinctly welcome.

The children are thriving and look healthier every day. Potter is getting fat and is growing very fast, and Bertha is a chatty whale! She talks to you morning 'til night and is continually occupied. Florence is herself again and takes charge of Bertha tonight for the first time. Belle has done so beautifully with both children, but I think she is glad that she can take things easily again. Bertha has gone back to F. most naturally. No fussing for Belle. We were all wondering if she'd object to it and are much relieved that she doesn't. We went to Osprey for the day, and the children were remarkably good, in that Potter ate his lunch without a riot, and Bertha didn't get cross enough to yell her head off! They both generally cut up enough to stop a train. It was lovely down there. The place is so beautiful, and Mrs. Palmer has done a great deal to it this year.

Has Father anyone on the I.O. named Donahue who is down here? A reporter came in at Osprey saying she was from the I.O. and wanted to take some pictures, said she knew Father well, etc. I was wondering if it was another Examiner game. Mrs. P. was awfully nice to her and took her about, and the woman lost her nerve towards the end, and we couldn't make out what she was up to. I am sending some tickets to lectures that I felt it up to me to contribute to—if you want to use them. If not, throw them away. Oh! Will you get Maud some lovely Bulgaria roses from me? Do you remember the heavenly apple tree she gave me when Bertha was born? You must get something to live up to that.

Goodnight. Best love from us all to you both.

Pauline

Sarasota, Florida
February 9, 1913

Mrs. Herman Kohlsaat
844 Lincoln Parkway
Chicago, Illinois

Dear Mother:

Your youngest child has gone home, and I can't tell you how nice it was to have her here and how terribly sorry we were that they were not able to stay longer. She looked so well and so pretty in the black. Aside from any family feeling, she was a lovely person to have visit you—never late and always interested in what you did to amuse her, which is a great quality. Min and I are quite crazy about her. It was too bad that Roger couldn't stay. We met him, soaked him in the Bay, and said goodbye. He brought us some delicious quail, which Min, I have discovered, likes, and in fact it's about the only game except partridge that he does like. Your grandchildren are in fine shape. I guess Kay has told you that she was quite startled at their terribleness! She has never seen them "at home" before, and it was a surprise. Min and I want you to come down, if you want to, just as soon as you can.

Today we spent at Osprey. It has been too lovely, just cool enough and bright and sunshiny. Mrs. Palmer has planned a picnic back in the country for Tuesday and said she was very sorry that Kay and Roger were gone and so couldn't go with her. Aunt Ida said many lovely things about Kay, which I must write her. Aunt Laura, too. We are going to a part of the country called "Myakka," where I have never been and am crazy to go to. Min hates to motor, so we may not go, but I am hoping that we will. It is quite wild and uncivilized over there, and everyone says it is beautiful.

We are having our troubles with the cow. She doesn't begin to come up to specifications, gives nine quarts of milk instead of 16, and the milk is very poor instead of rich. Her calf is two weeks old, and so her milk may improve this week. If it doesn't, back she goes to the man who brought her to us. She is thin and very much underfed. Min is building quarters and mule sheds in the back lot, and what he won't know about such things when he's finished won't be worth knowing. We are working very hard on the place, and there is nothing to show for it! Which is trying, to say the least. All the orange trees are in blossom, and the air is so sweet. Spring is just beginning here now, and things are blooming. While you will be here the entire country will be one mass of wildflowers. All the vines blossom, so you will think you are in Italy when you go along the roadside. The moon will be big, too, part of the time. You must surely come. I do wish that Father could manage a couple of days. Why not drop in here for a couple of days on his way to N.Y.? It would do him good, and we'd love to have him. Much love to you both from us all.

Pauline

Sarasota, Florida
March 15, 1913

Mrs. Herman Kohlsaat
Bertolini's Palace Hotel
Naples, Italy

Dear Mother:

I am writing this with a faint idea that perhaps you didn't sail this morning, after all. But as we have heard nothing to the contrary so far, I think perhaps you did. And, as I am writing, I am sure you wish you hadn't! By the time you get this, though, you'll be more used to it all and will be glad that you are there. I hope that you are on the terrace at Bertolini's and that Capri looks very lovely and that the Bay is sparkling. I wish I could remember what I wrote about it for the Scribblers last year. You'd think that after such aging one would not be likely to forget. Still, I can remember "in the spring" and a few words about lovely yellow primroses and violets. Have you seen any, by the way?

By the time this reaches you, we will be listening to the Illinois Central Trains instead of the blue jays and mosquitoes. The blue jays have apparently been bitten to pieces by the mosquitoes and the latter have died from the effect, for neither pest seems to be around today. Min arose at the popular hour of 4:15 this morning and went to Tampa, quite against his will and better judgement, and after he was there, a telegram came here for him saying it was unnecessary to go. It was too good to keep, so I had Taylor telephone it to him. We are still planning to leave on the 22nd, if it's possible to get accommodations from here to Washington. Everybody apparently wants to go north just at this time.

Our life still goes on in its usual rut. We eat haphazardly, as to meals, and all work seems to be at a standstill on the place. Taylor breaks the monotony by being up on time for breakfast, which is a dreadful jolt in the day's machinery. We are going to Aunt Ida's to lunch tomorrow. She didn't go abroad, as you know. Potter and Bertha are flourishing. I cut P.'s hair again this morning, and once more looks human. Bertha is her same squaky, chatty, offish self. I have lost another pound, weighing 126, and am feeling very well, indeed—even better than when you were here. And I am looking much better, too. In fact, I think I could take the trip over the Central of Georgia and not notice it, so you see I am feeling better! Also, I am feeling very cheerful, more so than I've felt for a year. I haven't heard from Kay, nor in fact from anyone, since you left. I'm expecting a letter from you on Monday. Did you get letter, telegram, and oranges on the boat? I don't know why, but I have a feeling that you and the Hattly's will get friendly on the boat and take a trip together to Amalfi and Ravello, etc. when you land. Do write me often. I hope next time to give you more amusing news. Life on the farm is not conducive to interesting letters! Much love from all,

Pauline

Notes

In these letters Pauline reports seeing several members of the Honoré family: Aunt Laura, A. C. Honoré, and Ida Honoré Grant, Bertha's sister. Ida had been married to Major General Frederick D. Grant, eldest son of Ulysses S. Grant, who had a diplomatic career. Their daughter, Julia Grant, was born in June 1876, and was presented at court before their departure from Austria-Hungary. Julia was later married to Prince Cantacuzène Count Speransky of Russia, where she lived for twenty-one years. During the Russian Revolution their three children were sent to the United States to be with their grandmother Ida Grant. January 24, 1913: They took the children over to the Gulf or to one of the keys, presumably Casey's Key.

February 2, 1913: Roger's grandfather had urged him to enter the dry goods business in St. Paul, so he and Katherine left Chicago and settled there.

The I. O. is the Inter-Ocean newspaper, which Herman Kohlsaat owned at one time. February 9, 1913: Katherine Kohlsaat Shepard, who has just visited Min and Pauline in Sarasota, was wearing black because her father-in-law, Frank Parsons Shepard, has recently died. In their day, mourning customs—black or lavender for women's clothes, a black tie and armband for men—were strictly observed.

March 13, 1913: Myakka was Bertha Palmer's property inland from the coast.

Mrs. Herman Bohloaat
844 Lincoln Parkway
Chicago Ill.

"The children are fine…Potter is learning his abc's,
and Bertha is learning to cut up!
She says, 'I don't have to do it because
I don't want to,' in most convincing tones."

6

BIDDEFORD POOL, SEPTEMBER 1914

Pauline writes from Biddeford Pool, a summer place on the coast in southern Maine. It was named for the pool-shaped body of water lying in between a spit of land that curves out into the Atlantic Ocean and the mainland. Visitors to this resort at the mouth of the Saco River were constantly aware of the sea and the overreaching sky. Biddeford became popular as a summer watering spot in the nineteenth century, when its two enormous hostelries, Hussey's Mansion House and Holman's Highland House, were booked for the entire season. It was said that "Here lovers of Nature can drink in the majesty of the ocean and at the hotels . . .find intelligent and cultured companions. A quiet retreat, away from the turmoil of the city," it was not as luxurious as Cape May, Newport, or Bar Harbor. Among the recreational activities offered were bathing, boating, sailing, and deep-sea fishing. The principal industries for year-round residents were fishing and lobster-catching.

The Palmers take a cottage there and visit with the Honoré family and with Pauline's sister, Katherine, and her children, Roger and Blake. It is clear that Pauline feels mixed about being there. It is healthy for the children, and she loves the quiet and the sea air, but it is also dull and lacks interesting people. As she asks her mother later on in a letter to Biddeford Pool from France: "Are they doing just the same things, playing cards every minute and talking? And are there any attractive new people? I feel homesick for the Pool, really, and would love to be back there for a little sea air." She loves getting away to more exciting places, like the visit to New York she describes in these letters.

Much of the news here revolves around the growth of Pauline's newest arrival, Gordon, born in June, and the activities of Potter and Bertha. Daily life in Biddeford was relaxed, but social. Pauline and Min wake up late, and when Pauline is not spending time with the new baby, she is attending cocktail parties or playing cards with other vacationers. Gordon is a good-natured baby, Potter interacts more with Min, and Bertha now seems like a relatively placid child. "Potter can say his ABC's backward and forward and can spell 'dog' and knows certain letters when he sees them and is correspondingly proud of it all."

The Great War started in August 1914, and Pauline is participating in the war effort for the Red Cross, making buttonholes for pajamas and surgical shirts. Both sides predicted victory by Christmas. Instead, a bloody four-year stalemate ensued along the Western Front, a continuous line of trenches from the North Sea to Switzerland. In the United States, the upper class supported the British and French, and war relief projects became the fashion for society matrons. Some Chicago socialites, like their friend Mildred McCormick, went to France to help by becoming nurses and driving ambulances. Others raised money for the cause in many ways, including putting on theatricals.

Pauline worries that there will be some trouble between "the English and the German in the household," as Louise (the baby nurse) is of German background, but luckily she has "self-possession and dignity…to the queen's taste." She is also concerned that Mrs. Palmer, who has just returned from France, has developed a "foreign point of view," and urges her mother to "go and talk war with her."

"Potter is full of energy and up to every trick."

Biddeford Pool, Maine
September 2, 1914

Mrs. Herman Kohlsaat
844 Lincoln Parkway
Chicago, Illinois

Dear Mother:

It is queer where the time goes to down here. This week nearly finished. A month from today and we will probably be on our way home, or already there! The mornings are very short, as it is after ten before we get downstairs. Then the infant nurses at 11:30, so that breaks things up. Then there is generally a cocktail party, and your morning is over. I try to lie down after lunch and take the baby at 2:30 or three. Then we either go to someone's house to play cards or they come here, and by the time we get through it is time to go home for dinner.

The days are all alike and so pass quickly. Every woman is working for the Red Cross making pajamas and surgical shirts. They do them very well, and to date have sent in nearly 200! I make buttonholes! and do an odd job now and then such as taking out bastings. I can't use a machine and don't want to and don't want to baste the garments together. My buttonholes are beautiful. I would not have dared to offer my services if I hadn't seen some of the others' work!

The children are fine. Gordon weighs dressed and after nursing 18.15, but of course he nurses eight oz. and his clothes weigh about one pound and eight oz. He's some child, however. His hair is getting so long, and his legs. He is wearing Bertha's coats that she wore at 16 months! Min says that he thinks he is going to be tall! Easy guess. He is the most sociable little chap, always ready to smile and talk, and such a comfy armful to hold. Louise is so nice and pleasant and acts as if I had some claim on the child. So you will have an easy pleasant time holding him in October. Better get your muscle up, though. A cramp is in order after five or six minutes.

I haven't heard of any trouble so far between the English and German in the household. Louise hardly considers herself German, as she was born and brought up in this country, and her mother came over at the age of four years. And then, too, it would take a good deal to put anything over on Louise! I trust her to hold her own by quietness and silence. Even the English cannot [put] down self-possession and dignity, both of which L. has to the queen's taste. Min is so well and very much rested. He is very amusing and keeps everyone laughing.

I am so glad you are going to the Ryersons next Sunday. What would you have done if you hadn't gotten your clothes! You could not have accepted these invitations and would

"Kodaks" that Pauline sent her mother of
the children at Biddeford Pool.
Top right: Gordon in a later year on
a slide, with Granny Kohlsaat at left.
Bottom right: "Grandpa" with Roger
Shepard and his cousin Potter.
Opposite, clockwise from left: Min with
Potter and Bertha, children playing golf,
children's party in Chicago (third and
fourth from the right, are young Potter and
Eleanor McCormick, the editor's mother).

have had a miserable summer. Are you using Kasper? I hope so. Well, goodbye. Take good care of yourself, and send my love to Father.

Pauline

Now for the bills!

Biddeford Pool, Maine
September 14, 1914

Mrs. Herman Kohlsaat
844 Lincoln Parkway
Chicago, Illinois

Dear Mother:

It doesn't seem possible that so many lovely days should follow one another in succession. This morning Jennie washed my hair and then dried and brushed it on the back porch. It was so hot there in the sun—simply stewing. Then I waved it and dried the waves out there! I am lunching with Kay today. Roger and Miss Garett are coming over here.

Gordon is still continuing to grow. He gained 11 ounces last week and so weighs 17.13. Tomorrow he will be three months old, and I'll put him on the scales again. He is such a dear. Potter is so mad about him. He took him some flowers yesterday and always kisses him goodnight so gently. Bertha takes him more as a matter of course and, too, understands perfectly that he belongs to Potter, because Potter told her so, and so she doesn't dare touch him. Bertha isn't very sociable. She is polite to people now but prefers to play by herself, etc.

The Odells will be here until Oct. 10th and Mrs. Cramer until her mother lands—and if that is too late, until she hears what her mother plans to do. Min I expect to be back this week some time. I may stop off in Boston long enough to run out and see Alice for a second. But it depends on when we leave here. If we go the day before we take the Century, or if we start that A.M. and go right through. It's pleasant always to get it over with. The trip, I mean. I am trying to walk a lot these days and really feel quite lazy instead! Much love to you both. I am hoping for a letter from you today in the noon mail.

Pauline

Biddeford Pool, Maine
September 15, 1914

Mrs. Herman Kohlsaat
844 Lincoln Parkway
Chicago, Illinois

Just a note, Mother dear, to tell you that Gordon has doubled his weight at three months and now weighs 18 pounds and is 26 1/4 inches long, a growth of 4 3/4 since he was born! He is so lovely. Potter's second lower front teeth are growing in behind his first teeth, and the latter are loose and ready to come out. So we feel very much grown up and awfully proud. He won't have the gap in his lower jaw quite so long a time now, fortunately. Bertha and I are very well, and nothing thrilling has happened to us. We just sit by and admire.

Much love,

Pauline

Biddeford Pool, Maine
September 18, 1914

Mrs. Herman Kohlsaat
844 Lincoln Parkway
Chicago, Illinois

Dear Mother:

You will be surprised to hear that this has been the warmest day this summer! Now there is a cool breeze from the other side of the land, which is very pleasant, as Potter would say. The children and I went over to Kay's this morning and said goodbye to her. Min gets here tomorrow, and I shall be so glad to see him.

We are planning to go to New York for a few days on Monday, and I am so thrilled. I shall get a new hat and probably a new suit. I'll get a model from Bendel. They say that they have lovely models there, and everything that there is to be had. Kay and I expect to do some shopping together. She says that everything that she gets by herself you and I hate and criticize. She is very funny about it.

I feel very gay going off on a spree. Louise will take plenty of malted milk for the infant in case I haven't enough for him. If it weren't for the convenience of nursing him on the trip home I'd wean him now. He is so well and fat and has had a splendid start, as you know. He is enormous—I sent for some six-month shirts for him, and they were too small, and I was obliged to send for one-year size!

Potter is full of energy as usual and up to every trick. I have just sent him twice in to tell Taylor that I wanted him, and T. didn't believe it and didn't come. When he finally did, I had Potter ring the bell to the front door. I told him I had sent for him twice and after he had gone out, I heard Potter say to him, "Isn't it too bad that you didn't mind the first time?" The English in battle are fine, but the limit anywhere else. I, for one, am sick and tired of them. They are so arrogant and ignorant beyond what they are trained to know.

I am getting such a cunning silk coat here for Gordon, crêpe de chine with smocked yoke. He will be sweet in it. Also some smocked dresses for Bertha. She is getting tall and thin. Much love to you, Mother dear, and take care of yourself.

Pauline

Have you my extra crib? If you haven't, have Kasper bring it down for you to use while Kay is there. I have a cariole for Gordon, which I will use for the present.

Biddeford Pool, Maine
September 19, 1914

Mrs. Herman Kohlsaat
844 Lincoln Parkway
Chicago, Illinois

Dear Mother:

Your letter written Thursday has just come. Very quick time, I think. This is Saturday noon. Your description of Frances Noyes is lovely. It must seem strange to hear such a slip of a thing swear. I am glad to hear that Helen Goody's husband is at home again, even if he is wounded. It seemed too tragic a finish to think that he might be killed.

Kay's Blakie is no beauty, but will be no doubt, as soon as he gets more hair, like all the rest of the children except Gordon, who has loads and is very good-looking. I have some Kodaks of Grandpa and three of the children, which I will send on to you as soon as they are reprinted. Some of the baby are darling, but not as good as they might be. I got them last night when we went to the train.

It is quite cold today, a great change from yesterday. We are going in with Willem to meet Min this P.M., in fact in just a few minutes. There is no news. I live a very quiet life, the same things every day. Life will be a bit gayer with Min here. He likes parties, etc., when here, so we generally have people over to play cards and have tea. Our trip to N.Y. will be fun. It seems very simple to me, but everyone here apparently thinks us crazy! So much work. Gordon is no trouble, though, and as he hardly every cries, he won't disturb other people. I enthuze so about him that you will either get bored hearing about him or else be frightfully disappointed when you see him!

Much love,

Pauline

Biddeford Pool, Maine
September 27, 1914

Mrs. Herman Kohlsaat
844 Lincoln Parkway
Chicago, Illinois

Dear Mother:

You have been very badly treated as to letters from me the last few days, but I'll try to make up for it by writing you a long chatty one now. First of all, we got back here safe and sound yesterday morning. The baby was so good all of the time and doesn't look nor seem the least bit the worse for his trip. He only gained six ounces—instead of 11—but he did well at that, for it was dreadfully hot in N.Y.

The house is very draughty and the windows rattle a good deal! Today the children are in their room. Potter is painting madly and Bertha is looking over the Schwarz catalogue that I brought back with me. She has already selected 10 dollies! We brought her a dolly with "Blue rimmers" by request, some little toys, and a sweater. Potter a big speed boat, also by request, a golf club, and some small toys. Roger some small toys, and Blakie a rubber horse. Gordon a rattle. So you see we did quite a little shopping. Kay's babies look very well, especially Blakie. His cheeks were pink and he was all smiles in spite of the fact that it was naptime. Willem met us at Bid. and brought us home. Min caught such a bad cold in N.Y., so he didn't do much in the evenings. Kay and Roger dined with us the second evening we were there. They went to the theatre afterwards. Min didn't want to move, so we didn't go. Those two danced every night after the play! They certainly had a good time and looked as if they were enjoying every second.

Mrs. Palmer landed Thursday morning about noon, so we didn't do much that day. After lunch I went to my house to rest, and Min went out with his mother. I thought it just as well to loaf one day. Mrs. Palmer liked the baby, I think. She acted as if she did, anyway, and then he was so adorable and behaved so well that no one could have helped being crazy about him. He smiled and gurgled and blew bubbles just as he should do and didn't misbehave once. I sent you some Kodaks yesterday. His latest is where he is sitting on my lap out on the piazza. Isn't he a sweetie? I expect you'll see Mrs. Palmer before you get this, and she'll tell you that I am quite right about him. You must go and talk war with her. She is full of it and has all the foreign point of view about it, which is interesting.

I got myself some shoes—quite loud ones!—and stockings, also hats, and one gown, a lovely shade of blue velvet, perfectly plain draped model from Lucile. I think it will be lovely and becoming. As far as I saw, the winter styles are simply hideous, and I am very content to wear my old clothes. Kay got some lovely things from Lucile and seemed very well pleased. She got a tea gown, the prettiest one I've ever seen, and she will be lovely in it.

We saw some nice etchings and a lovely colored lithograph of Whistler's. K. and R. looked at furniture. Oh, by the way, if you want a go-cart for Blakie instead of the carriage, he can have ours. Ask Albert for the dark go-cart, and Kasper will bring it down to you. Blakie uses one here all the time. We have two, a dark stained one and a white, and don't need either, as Bertha walks now, and the baby will have his carriage.

We rented a baby carriage from the hotel in N.Y., but the baby didn't go out. Our rooms were on the N.W. corner, so it was quiet, and there was always a breeze. It was hot or dusty on the streets, and he was better off on the 8th floor. One afternoon the wind changed for a while, so Louise took the carriage and infant out in front of the big window by the lift— do you remember?—near the rooms we had, and caught the breeze there. It was lovely. She is an excellent nurse and knows her job to a T. but is painfully ignorant beyond that. As Kay said the other day, when I was talking of how dull it must be for her to do nothing, "It is wildly exciting for her to get her diapers done!" And I suppose it's true.

Potter can say his abc's backward and forward and can spell "dog" and knows certain letters when he sees them and is correspondingly proud of it all. This morning I asked him to show Min what he could do, and he proceeded to do so and finally said, "'J' stands for 'jackrabbit,' no, it stands for 'Jbix!'" It sounded so funny that we laughed until we cried, and he couldn't see the joke so looked at us in the most pitying way and ignored it!

The oil is almost burnt out of the stove, and it is getting chilly in here, so I must summon Taylor to start it up again! Oil stoves are a nuisance and a comfort. I suppose that you and Father are spending Sunday with Janet! We will be at home Saturday the 3rd at nineo'clock. Don't make any other dates on that morning! You must spend all of your time admiring my child—and children!

Much love to both,

Pauline

Min with Potter and Bertha.

Notes

September 14, 1914: "The Century" is the Twentieth-Century Limited, the train from New York to Chicago.

September 19, 1914: Willem is an African-American man who came up to St. Paul with Katherine and Roger Shepard when when they first married, helping with all sorts of tasks in and out of the house. He became part of the family and was with them for years.

Mrs Herman Kohlsaat.
844. Lincoln Parkway
Chicago Ill.

"The time slips by so quickly here that I cannot follow it.
I have been reading Horace, doing a little
knitting, chasing turkeys and chickens,
"slipping" oleanders and privet and camphor hedges."

7

SARASOTA, 1918

T he family is in Sarasota again for their winter visit with its newest member, Pauline, born January 21, 1917, whom her mother calls Baby. Potter is almost eight, Bertha about to be six, and Gordie almost three. Baby is "very fond of [Min], which also pleases him. Bertha's indifference has always hurt him, although he would never say so in so many words. The baby likes to be with him and is very cozy."

This is the first time that Pauline mentions spending much time with Julia and Michel Cantacuzène. Julia is Min's first cousin, the daughter of Frederick Dent Grant (President Ulysses Grant's son) and Bertha Honoré Palmer's sister, Ida. She had an international education in court circles, as her father served as minister to Austria-Hungary. In 1899 she married Prince Cantacuzène Count Speransky of Russia. The couple lived in Russia until the Revolution, when she and their three children, Prince Michel, Princess Ida, and Princess Bertha, went to Sarasota. In 1921 she would publish a memoir, *My Life Here and There*, and later a book on the Russian Revolution, *Revolutionary Days*. There is now more talk among the family about the war, as Julia has strong opinions on the subject.

In the spring of 1918 the Great War was reaching a climax along the Western Front, which had been fought over since 1914. Repeated Allied offensives had failed to break through the trench line, with gains measured in yards at dreadful cost. On March 21st, the German army had begun a series of "win the war" offensives which at first made extraordinary progress, advancing many miles each day. Pauline's letters reveal her anxiety over the disturbing war news as well as her familiarity with front-line geography. The March 26th letter reports that Mike Cantacuzène is "simply numb about this new offensive of the Germans" and "one feels discouraged and wants to go out and fight." The next day's letter is her analysis of the German effort. "I only hope the Germans won't make any headway at Vimy Ridge" (she did not know that Vimy Ridge had already been overrun). She discusses German battle tactics: "If the Germans can make a salient above the Arras they will make it necessary for the English to withdraw all along their north flanks above Albert." But she reckons German casualties will be too high: "Four hundred thousand men is a serious loss to the Germans, now when they are making what they themselves call their final drive." Her analysis turns out to be correct. By summer the last of the German offensives would fail, suffering "serious loss," as Pauline mentions to her mother. The Allies, British and French, reinforced by fresh American troops, would begin counter-offensives which drive back the exhausted and crippled German army over open country until Armistice Day.

Pauline confides in her mother about changes in her household during this time: "Life has gotten very simple during the war, and I find it pleasant." She has rearranged her staff, letting several servants go. Ordinarily she would have a kitchen maid, a laundress, a cook, plus a chambermaid or lady's maid, and perhaps a waitress, someone to "mend," two nurses or one tutor and one nurse for the children as well as Kasper, the

Charity work during World War I. Top: Mrs. Robert H McCormick and Mrs. George Carpenter selling tags for the blind, 1918. Bottom: Potter Palmer III (at right) and friend Gordon Kelly, 1917. Opposite: Mrs. Howard Linn (Lucy McCormick Blair) at a benefit for Children of the War Zone.

chauffeur, and a butler.

It is curious that Bertha Palmer's last illness is not mentioned in these letters. She died on May 8th of this year, about two weeks after Pauline wrote the final letter in this group. Her biographer Ishbel Ross describes how for two years Bertha had been fighting "a losing battle with cancer." She continued to work, however, directing operations at her ranch in Florida right up to the final weeks. She had previously had a mastectomy in New York. "When she no longer toured her property and her workmen saw no more of her, the story was whispered about in Sarasota that Mrs. Palmer was dying of cancer."

When Bertha Palmer died at the age of sixty-nine, her sons and their wives; her sister, Ida; her brother Adrian; and the Cantacuzènes were with her. The family gathered in Chicago for what newspapers called an "impressive but simple funeral." It was held at the Castle, where her coffin lay in the famous gallery. A blanket of orchids from her sons covered the coffin, and her English butler put a wreath of orchids at its foot as a token from the servants. Crowds gathered outside in the street to watch family members enter the house. In her will Bertha left close to $20 million, most of it in trust to Min and Honoré. Included in this were the Palmer House (valued at $5 million), the Castle, and 150 pieces of property she had inherited from her husband. She left $100,000 to each daughter-in-law, and a prime piece of Chicago property (1415-1419 Michigan Avenue) to her niece, Julia Cantacuzène. In addition, Bertha bequeathed her Sarasota cattle ranch, along with money in trust, to her brother Adrian C. Honoré, and most of her art collection to the Art Institute.

Bertha Honoré Palmer and Grace Palmer (center) standing before a procession with other prominent Chicago women: Mrs. Benjamin Carpenter, Mrs. Joseph Winterbotham, and Mrs. E. Stone.

Sarasota, Florida
February 2, 1918

Mrs. Herman Kohlsaat
844 Lincoln Parkway
Chicago, Illinois

Dear Mother:

Your first letter of the 28th came Saturday, and I was glad to have some news from you. I should feel terribly if anything interfered with your visit other than some affair of yours and Father's. We are all looking forward to it and counting on it.

Except for an attack of mosquitoes of unprecedented size and number, we are having a heavenly time. Today it is much colder, 60, with a north wind, but we do not mind, as it means death to the above-mentioned pests. Poor Gordy was stung on the eyebrow, and his eyelid began to swell so that his eye was nearly closed, only a tiny corner of blue showing near his nose. It gave him a very peculiar expression. On Saturday we planned a picnic on the beach with all the family invited. But the mosquitoes were so bad that we decided to have it at home and then send the children to the beach later.

Saturday morning the baby came down with chickenpox, so we called everything off. She has a splendid crop on her head, where they show off to every advantage. She is not ill at all. Today is her supposedly bad day, and she is in fine spirits. Bertha has overeaten and is upset. She had a little fever and no appetite but is improving now. Potter is as busy as a bee. He has been demanding the pony, so I had the animal cleaned and saddled, and P. started forth very grandly with a wave of the hand and a smile. He and the pony had trouble a little later, and Potter "jumped off," as he insists. "Anyway, he was planning to do it just before he went off, for the pony was aiming for the gate, and he knew he was going to jump it!" Min made him get on again right away, and he is going to ride again later. The pony isn't anywhere near as tall as the gate, and poor old Potter had visions of himself flying over it.

Last night it rained! Gordy was thrilled and wanted to know why the rain came down from the sky. I explained as best I could, and he said, "The clouds must be full of holes like a water can." Then he wanted to know "if the water that was drawn up from here came down salt!" What am I to do with a son like that? I wish he would put all his questions to Min. His questions never end. His curls are all come back, and he looks awfully well.

We have had great excitement chasing pigs out of the grove and off the lawn. It is great sport! They come in somewhere and grub all over. Gordy wanted to know what they grubbed for, and I told him nice juicy roots. " I should think an orange would be much juicier," he said! Min goes to Shreveport on the 6th. I go as far as Tampa with him, where we have supper with Grace and Cappy—and then he and I go visit—and I spend the night. I am going to call on Grandpa at Petersburg on my way home. This is a long letter written in bed. I am taking a day off, for reasons. I hope that you can read my scrawl and make some sense out of it.

I looked at the horoscope in the Post that Feb. is an excellent month for successful business affairs and everything connected with business. So Father may find things coming his way! Much love to you both from us all.

Pauline

Sarasota, Florida
March 26, 1918

Mrs. Herman Kohlsaat
844 Lincoln Parkway
Chicago, Illinois

I spoke to Julia about the articles, and she was delighted. She is writing now all the time apparently. I think she wanted to talk with Mike about it, and I suppose she will write Father. Every time I see her I like her better, and Mike too. He is simply numb about this new offensive of the Germans. By the time this reaches you there will be a great change in the situation, but just now, one feels discouraged and wants to go out and fight, too. I am waiting for the British report now. The Germans are claiming everything at the moment I am writing. It is awful to be away down here and get news only once a day.

Much love to you. I had a dear letter from Grandpa today. He is thinking a little of coming down here later, when his strength comes back. His letter was cheerful, and his handwriting very firm and clear.

Did I tell you that my bankbook is balanced to date? Except for three months last year that are lost, but I shan't tell Min!

P.

Sarasota, Florida
March 27, 1918

Mrs. Herman Kohlsaat
844 Lincoln Parkway
Chicago, Illinois

Dear Mother:

Your letter about Omaha came this morning. There is nothing to say, for you know how terribly disappointed I am for you and Father. Min also. We cannot understand Liph's being so unpleasant. Of course, he is going along according to business rules, but it's pretty sharp business, and a reprisal to see any moral obligation, which is there to be distinctly seen. They are a lot of crooks, the whole Omaha outfit, and the only trouble is that Father didn't take them for such when he went into the thing. Something nice has got to turn up sometime, so we'll just have to look to that, and think no more about this.

Min got back yesterday noon, looking very well and not as tired as I thought he would be. He was surprised at the baby's walking and awfully pleased. She is very fond of him, which also pleases him. Bertha's indifference has always hurt him, although he would never say so in so many words. This baby likes to be with him and is very cozy. Potter took the trouble to come in and say good morning this morning just to celebrate Min's return. The dog has come, and we are all excitement. Unfortunately it is covered with fleas, and as Potter says, "You can see them jumping." Russell is getting some flea powder, and he'll get a good wash, or succession of washes, and then we will like him better.

We are going to Myakka for a visit for overnight. I am leaving the baby at home and taking Annie and Miss Milligan and the three older children. It sounds like fun, and I hope it turns out to be.

A box from Field's came this morning for Bertha. I haven't opened it yet, as I have been busy all morning with at least two children at the elbow. We will keep most of the things for Bertha's birthday. I don't think of getting Easter things. Julia has bought up all the little stuffed chicks in town. I am going in this afternoon to see what is left for us to give them. Gordy as usual at this time is glued to my left arm. His face is hot against it, and he is asking questions and saying, "How fast you go?" "What are you doing now, thinking, why don't you talk when you think?" He is very sleepy, and I have just suggested the swing as a boat, but he refuses. As soon as I finish we are going out to see the hound, which is barking violently between howls. He is lonesome. A lovely sound he is making. I trust he doesn't resort to such doings at night. Hounds, whip poor wills, mocking birds and guinea hens will make the night quite lively.

About Josephine, I don't know that I can use her. I will talk to Gunhild and see if she thinks she'll stick it out. If she doesn't, perhaps Josephine could take her place. The war news is a little more encouraging this A.M., with the French counterattacking. I only hope that the Germans won't make any headway at Vimy Ridge. It is too horrible, all of it. I suppose they think if they can make a salient above Arras they will make it necessary for the English to withdraw all along their north flank above Albert. Four hundred thousand men is a serious loss to the Germans, now when they are making what they themselves call their final drive. They said they were willing to sacrifice 300,000 if necessary. So I should think they would not consider that they had made a great success of this drive.

I am glad that you enjoyed your Sunday at the Casino. It is a queer place. What a shame that you felt dizzy after your trip home. How nice that you didn't gain weight down here. I look thinner but have not lost any more.

The dog is almost beside himself, so we must go out and see what's up. I am sending you some Kodaks of the children, Roger, and the ponies. Much love to you both.

Pauline

Bertha's Sarasota house, the Oaks.

Sarasota, Florida
April 3, 1918

Mrs. Herman Kohlsaat
844 Lincoln Parkway
Chicago, Illinois

Dear Mother:

We had a grand rain yesterday, enough to fill the cistern for the house, and everyone is thrilled. It is lovely and cool today, just a little over 70, with a strong breeze from the north. Everybody is working hard, and all are cheerful except the cook. She asked me this morning when I was going north, and I told her. So I presume she is trying to figure out if I will let her go before I do or what. She is anxious to go home. As I have very indefinite plans—Min is vague about what we are going to do—I don't quite like to tell her to go just yet. I think that about May 1st will see my household much smaller, as a great many will want to go in time to get other places. I hope that Martha, the laundress, and the kitchen maid will prove standbys for a long time. Life has gotten very simple during the war, and I find it pleasant. We are going in town to buy some postage stamps, to look at some summer hats, and to be very busy. Later we will go to give Ida a necklace that we got her to replace one Bertha broke. Tomorrow I take a hoe in hand for the good of my country and my figger and hoe the road to the chicken yard!

Much love to you, P.

Sarasota, Florida

Dear Mother:

Julia and I are going up to Tampa for the night—without Min or Michel. We feel very gay and "frisky," as Julia calls it. How frisky we will feel after we arrive is another matter, as it is 80 by the thermometer on my porch, and it is only nine o'clock. So I may never write you again, as I shall be a grease spot by tomorrow afternoon. The time slips by so quickly here that I cannot follow it. I have been reading Horace, doing a little knitting, chasing turkeys and chickens, "slipping" oleanders and privet and camphor hedges. Eldridge is hipped on the subject of "slipping," and so I expect we will have a great profusion of plants next year. I am putting some oleanders in the corners of the formal garden and think it will be very pretty. Then we are putting them (white at the entrance gate thusly [diagram].) The gate onto the main road is so bare and ugly that it has always annoyed us, and this ought to help a lot. Then we are putting a pink (double) hibiscus hedge at the east end of the formal garden. Never having been down here as late as this, we have never seen things in bloom. They are lovely, and I think we will stay each year late just to see the flowers. I am really getting very energetic and expect to know a weed from a hibiscus by the time I leave.

Bertha's birthday was a great success. The parasol went to the right spot and the books. We had a cake, brown with white frosting, and eight pink candles on it. Miss Milligan got some paper cups in town, Ida came to lunch, and then they all went to the beach for a swim. Julia brought some china birds and a circus set. The finds pleased Bertha and the boys fell on the circus set. Bertha was thrilled over the entire day, so it just goes to show that lots of presents don't make the day. But the preparation, excitement, etc. is the thing. She was very happy. The birthday things will do very well for Potter's birthday, as he has made a mental record of everything that was done for Bertha and then said, "And I will have just the same for mine?"

I am so glad to think that you are in St. Paul. It sounds so less forlorn, and you always have such fun with Kay and at her house. Please tell Kay that I am ordering one of those bags for her, and write Frank to plant my garden? I want some annual larkspur, mignonette, snap dragon pansies, zinnias, and whatever else is pretty. I think I ordered some things last Fall, so he probably has those on hand.

Much love to you all. Pauline

I am writing Hulda "Brega" to come to me this summer. Ida the present kitchen maid will be waitress and chambermaid, Annie will mend for the older children. Potter will wash himself, and I guess Miss M. wash Bertha, and then Hulda can get her own kitchen maid. Everyone will be happy. I will keep my laundress in Chicago. She can do your washing for you if you like. She is too good to let go! I'll send certain things home for her.

Sarasota, Florida
April 10, 1918

Mrs. Herman Kohlsaat
844 Lincoln Parkway
Chicago, Illinois

Dear Mother:

As I haven't received a letter from you for four days, I judge that you were very gay in St. Paul and then went home and forgot to send me a line. Possibly the red dress reminded

The Palmer family in 1917—Pauline and Potter—wearing a black armband showing he's in mourning—with young Potter, baby Pauline, Bertha, and Gordy.

you—there are any number of reasons. But you will admit that I have every reason to be interested in the letter that was written after your visit to the dressmaker. Probably you will forget to mention the dress, and when I see you I will forget to ask and then finally will be struck dead by seeing my nice sister wear it. Do you remember the white sweater you gave Annie when you left "Immokalee?" Well, she was speaking of it last night and said that it was "dandy." It certainly went to the right spot, and that spot is still glowing. You made a great "hit," as Father says. The toys have come from Field's. I haven't opened them because I am keeping them for Potter's birthday. He is terribly pleased with the fact that a birthday is coming but has a wholesome dislike of advancing years!

We went to Bradentown yesterday to see the airplane that was supposed to come over from Arcadia for the Liberty Loan Parade at B. We took Bertha C. and Ida with us. Unfortunately the plane didn't come over, and the band and parade took place in the A.M.! But we got a soda, saw six soldiers, and came home. Julia, Mike, and A.C. came in for a cup of tea. It was cold, and tea tasted very good. Miss Milligan is putting Potter to hoeing this morning instead of lessons in lesson time. Ida is thrilled, but he will have to stick to it and not go off and play in the sand with George. We are finding George very undesirable

Julia Dent Grant, the beautiful niece of Bertha Honoré Palmer, who married Russian Prince Michel Cantacuzène at the turn of the century. Julia was the daughter of Ida Honoré, Bertha's sister and Frederick Dent Grant, a cavalry officer serving under George Armstrong Custer at the time of Julia's birth in 1876 in the White House. Her father, Frederick Grant, the eldest son of President Ulysses S. Grant took a few days off for the birth of his daughter, Julia, therefore having his life spared. All of Custer's officers were killed at the Battle of Little Bighorn by Sioux Indians on June 25th, 1876.

in a way. He is underhand sly—that is, he says "pretend you don't hear" and that sort of thing, and his language is frightful! I read some Ovid last night and was surprised to find him so lewd. I knew they were a bit free in those days but I did not realize that the writings of Ovid were so strange. Don't boys read Ovid at school and college? I shouldn't think it would be beneficial.

Much love to you all,

Pauline

Sarasota, Florida
April 23, 1918

Mrs. Herman Kohlsaat
844 Lincoln Parkway
Chicago, Illinois

Dear Mother:

This is one of those nice days when the blotters blot and the stamps stick, one's pen digs into the writing paper, and the hair fails to dry. In other words, it's damp.

Gordy got home very late for supper last night and was hungry and thirsty. Anna gave him a drink, and he shrieked out, "Everything I drink gives me a headache!" and kept on yelling. I tried to comfort him and finally asked where his head ached. "Here!" he yelled and planted his hand firmly on his nice fat tummy. It ceased aching finally, and he ate a large supper. I sometimes feel that my brains are in my tummy, too. Today Min and I go to Aunt Laura's to lunch. Afterwards Julia and I are going to Bradentown to do a little shopping. She says that there is a blue hat there that I should have before another day goes by. I am afraid Julia is wearing out all her darned stockings and gloves and oldest clothes. Like the rest of us, she has discovered that Florida is a wonderful place to wear things that are too good to throw away, not good enough to give away or to wear where you wish to look chic.

My household is quiet for a minute. The cook goes Wednesday next. Gunhild then goes into the kitchen for two weeks. Marie helps Martha with dishes in the pantry. Marie wants to stay here with me until I go East. Then she wants to go home!, which is just what I want, for I don't want her to leave before I go, nor do I want her in Biddeford. Martha was afraid that I intended to have her work alone in the future and was much upset. I calmed her, and all goes smoothly. I am hoping that Gunhild will stay on all summer. She

The sunken garden at the Oaks.

and Ida are great friends and ought to work well together.

The children go to the beach for a swim today. The tide is low in the afternoon now so that they have a fine lot of sand. Potter is swimming very well, and Bertha a little. Gordy went out quite far yesterday, a thing which he has not dared to do until now. The baby also went in swimming. Gordy's suit is very airy in a trying spot, and when he leans over the worst happens, or rather pops out. It doesn't annoy him but is disconcerting to any grownup who happens to be admiring him at that moment and calling attention to him.

Much love, P.

Notes

March 27, 1918: Pauline mentions another one of her father's business disappointments that her mother has written her about. The casino is the Casino Club—the very pretty, upscale social club where Pauline's friends meet for lunch, dinners, and dances. The Club was founded in 1914 by a number of the Palmers' friends, the McCormicks, the Blairs, the Carpenters, and Min's brother, Honoré Palmer.

April 3, 1918: The Ida who is mentioned here is the daughter of Julia and Michel Canacuzène.

"Paris, as far as we have seen it, is not gay.
Or if it is, it is only skin deep,
and a scratch shows the sorrow."

EUROPE AFTER THE WAR, 1920

Pauline and Potter sail from west to east on the Mauretania in April 1920, their first voyage since the war. Pauline reports on the journey to her mother: "Our cabins are very comfortable, but we have no warm water, and as the weather has been cold, we have either shivered in pure Atlantic or not bathed at all, like the children." While commenting on their shipboard companions she also notes several post-war happenings: Many English are returning home after the war, and a Mrs. Kip is going to France to bring back her husband's body.

"Our trip has been quiet. The children have acted beautifully. Mrs. Ryerson's sister, Miss Borie, has taken the two elder under her wing and is crazy about them. She is a dear—and such a relief after the others on board." Miss Borie plays "Sniff" with Potter and Bertha. "There are a lot of English. In fact, the heavy travel is caused by returning English, rather than gadding Americans. They take themselves so seriously…People who take themselves seriously and expect others to follow their example are ridiculous! and everyone laughs at them. . . One woman has a bowl of pet turtles!, which she takes out on deck and lets run around on her neighbors."

The family, which now consists of Pauline, Min, and their four children, now three, six, nine, and eleven, rent a house in Paris, where they stay while they divide up the belongings of Pauline's mother-in-law with Cappy and Grace. In these letters we see several interesting sides of Pauline. As usual she successfully establishes an efficient and attractive household for her family—this time, at 45 rue Cortambert, in the 16th Arrondissement near the Trocadero. She has sent her butler, Woods, along ahead to staff the house and get ready for their arrival. They settle into their house for their stay of several months and see many other Americans in Paris, including the Chauncey McCormicks and Mary Borden Spears, Ellen Borden's sister-in-law. They also see members of Michel Cantacuzène's family, including his brother Guy's children: Elizabeth, nine, and Michel, six. Cappy and Grace's sons, Honoré, now twelve, and Potter D'orsay, fifteen, are frequent visitors. Pauline describes with amusement how the younger cousins—her son, Potter, eleven, and his cousin Honoré—want to be sophisticated and imitate the older D'orsay who wears a monocle to the opera and later uses hair tonic.

Pauline's astute powers of observation show in her fashion descriptions. She reports in great detail the dramatic change of dress since the war—sometimes shocking to her good taste. It is the beginning of the 1920s, when women bobbed their hair and skirts went up and waists went down to create the "flapper" look. "But the skirts are to the knees. No corsets—perfectly plain waists with 'tummys' sticking out, and no petticoats, in fact, practically nude…Nobody has a waistline, but everyone has a 'tummy,' which makes them all look, as Katherine Adler expresses it, "as if they had a pudding in front and on behind."

Pauline also reveals her keen awareness of personality in noting how her sister-in-law, Grace, acts when they are dividing up "the things" of Bertha Palmer. Grace shows some greed and annoying frailties, and Pauline suggests this—although in an understated way. When Grace decides that "all the big stones" should be "redivided," Pauline writes: "As everything had been done according to value, and she had usually had her choice of everything, Min and I were amused." There is much valuable jewelry to be shared between them—some of which had been written about in society columns when Bertha had worn it. Pauline tells her mother that "there were enough pearls to make two very long necklaces of big pearls. They come below the waistline. They are just alike, which simplified matters a great deal. The important tiara, with standing pearls and the collar to match, fell to us. . .The flat collar of large diamonds also is ours, the ruby ring, and a very large white pearl that can be used as a pendant or a pin. Also, the diamond bow knot and a diamond wristwatch. Also, a large grey pearl ring." Another beautiful item inherited by Pauline is Bertha's toilet case, which has pieces of "chislée" or fine decorative work on metal.

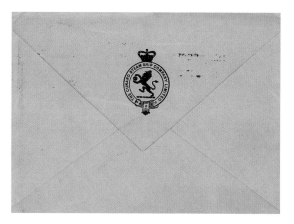

The "things" that the younger Palmers were now dividing came from Bertha Palmer's houses in Paris and London. The house in Paris on the rue Fabert had been a showcase for Bertha's Impressionist paintings. The canvases caught the light and were displayed behind artistic flower arrangements placed on low eighteenth-century tables. Also with her in Paris (in her bedroom) were the little circus girls by Renoir, plus paintings by Rafaelli of Paris, Cazin of Normandy, Diaz, and Corot. After her husband died in 1902, Bertha ceased to buy paintings, but she continued to collect: silver tankards, and a cylindrical mug

of the Charles II period dated 1677 that was particularly rare. She collected Chelsea statuettes and milk glass; she had a pair of Charles Morland's animal pictures, and 150 antique lanterns of different periods, and celadon bowls, Fabergé boxes, small jeweled clocks, and trinkets mounted in enamel and ormolu.

When war broke out in the summer of 1914, Bertha, like so many others, had been caught by surprise. She turned to protecting her large collection of artworks and had furs, etchings and household effects put in storage in Paris before she left. There were hundreds of pieces of porcelain and jade, as well as tapestries, carpets, a number of Whistler and Pennell etchings, and her favorite canopied satinwood bed, plus silver, china, and art objects. Her pearl and diamond dog collar and her favorite tiara and other pieces of jewelry were put in storage at Tiffany's Paris branch. Needing to flee the country in a hurry, she headed for Cherbourg in her Rolls Royce and the story was later told that she left the car on the dock. Since she did not return to Europe before she died, Min, Pauline, Cappy, and Grace were now left to make sense of "her things."

In mid-June Pauline's mind turns to the Republican convention in Chicago, with which her parents are very much involved. Herman Kohlsaat wrote about it in his memoirs: "It was a headless affair...the awful heat, the steaming crowds, and the strike of hotel waiters made life almost unendurable for the poor mortals compelled to live in hotels and committee rooms." He describes how Illinois governor Frank Lowden lost to Warren Harding, despite his impressive qualifi-

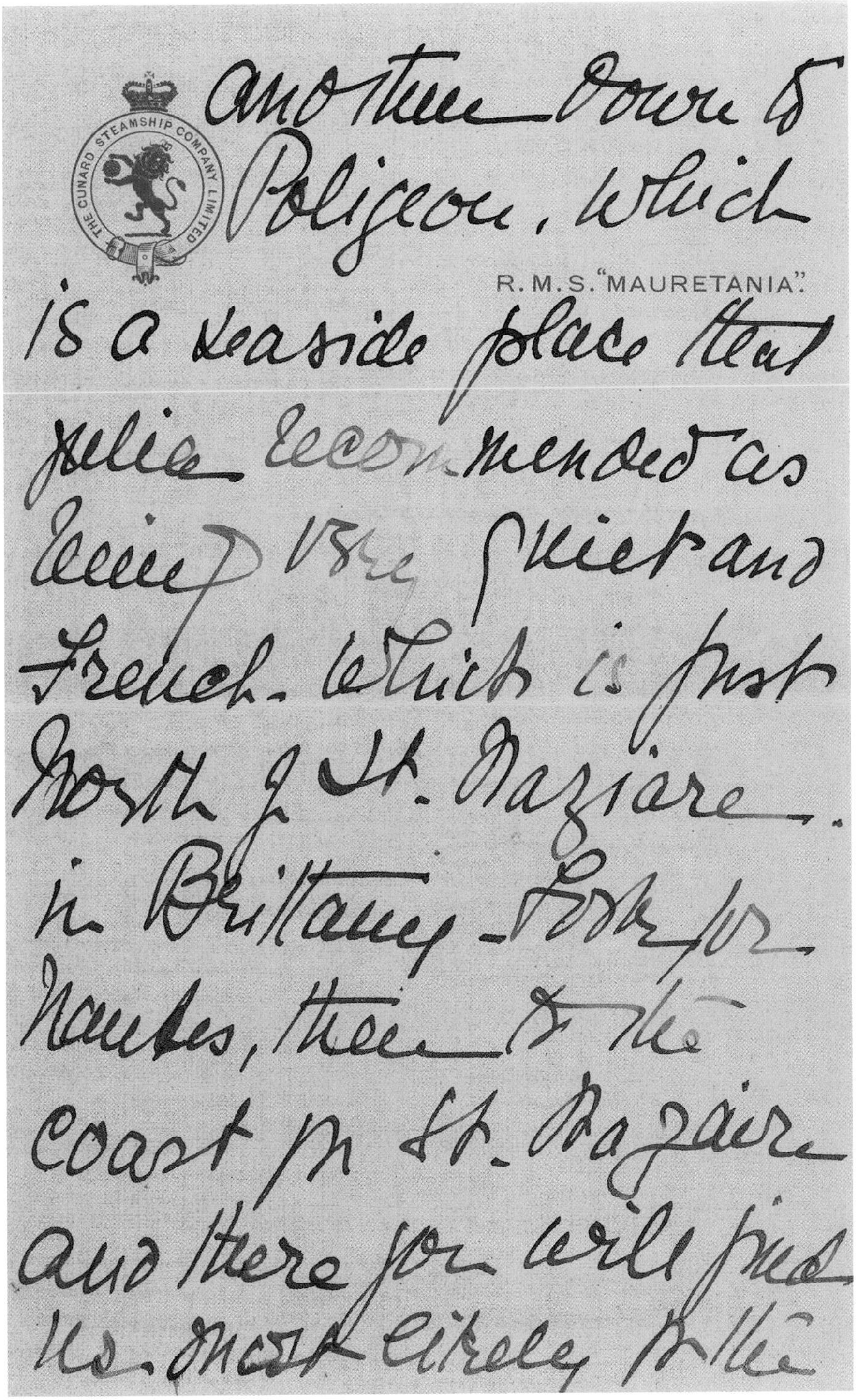

and then down to
Polizeon, which

R. M. S. "MAURETANIA".

is a seaside place that
julia recommended as
being very quiet and
French. which is just
North of St. Naziare.
in Brittany. Look for
Nantes, there to the
coast on St. Naziare
and there you will find
us. most likely billie

cations and early ballots. Pauline's concern for her parents' financial troubles is also evident. Several times in these letters, Pauline mentions sending a check to her mother—noting the transaction in the most affectionate and tactful manner.

Besides describing family events Pauline tells her mother she is horrified by the post-war changes in France. She and Min see the destruction at the battlefields when they tour in the north. She describes how towns are "all shot to pieces," and "whole blocks wiped out" and owners are "living in little wooden shacks." Over the door of one shack is written "Villa des Douceurs," which is typical of the spirit all through the country. A tour of the front line was a popular excursion for American tourists. Chateau Thierry and Belleau Wood were special attractions, as sites of victories garnered by the American Army. For a few months in 1918, shells from "Big Bertha" (which Pauline mentions), fired from within the Lumpergne Forest, had served as a German terror weapon against the people of Paris, landing indiscriminately within the city limits. Visions of the suffering make Pauline's recent acquisition of her mother-in-law's collections less appealing. When they get back to Paris to proceed with more dividing up, she senses the contrast between her situation and the suffering French, and "all the 'things' here seemed very unimportant when one looked at them again."

Pauline also reports on what is going on in the capital. As for Paris in 1920, she writes that there is "no gaiety in the city," that it is not like the old, lighthearted Paris where there was activity in the streets and fashionable clothing. She comments that there are many workers' strikes and that shops open late and close early, making shopping difficult for her.

Pauline and Min spend about five months in Europe, and it is not long before they adjust to life abroad and engage in a very busy social life. They dine with other Americans and attend lavish balls and Parisian jazz clubs. There are two particular galas that Pauline elaborates upon, calling one "a riot of flesh" and the other, which was given by Mary Borden Spears and her husband, "a circus." Mary Borden Spears, who was born in Chicago in 1886, was the daughter of a wealthy businessman. In 1918 she married Edward Spears, the head of the British Military Mission in France, whom Pauline describes as quite charming. Mary was an author who published several books between 1928 and 1950. As Pauline writes, Mary was worried that her Chicago friends would think they would be caricatured in the book she was writing.

At the end of their stay in Europe they spend a few weeks in Italy, staying at Bellagio. The exchange rate there is ideal for Americans: rooms for the ten of them, "La famiglia di dieci"—four children, Min and Pauline, and four servants—are $25 a day with food! They visit the Villa Balbianello on Lake Como, now owned by an American family, the Butler Ameses. This breathtakingly beautiful villa was perched on a promontory jutting out into Lake Como. It offered views through clipped topiary and towering cypresses out to the lake and mountains in the background. Pauline's spirits soar. "I can't see that Italy is so terribly poor after the war. Certainly the hotels are better than ever."

The Palmers' house on the Rue Cortambert.

R.M.S. "Mauretania"
[from shipboard]
April 30, 1920

Mrs. Herman Kohlsaat
1050 Lake Shore Drive
Chicago, Illinois

Dear Mother:

Your wireless reached us long after we had left New York and was a very cheery surprise. We went down to the boat very quietly about 2:45 and got on without any fuss. Father, Julia, and the two Mikes boarded with us and sat around afterwards talking. Our cabins are very comfortable, but we have no warm water, and as the weather has been cold, we have either shivered in pure Atlantic or not bathed at all, like the children. I have gotten a fine rest and feel and look much better. We land tomorrow about two P.M. and expect to motor to Caen for the night, and then to Rouen and then to Paris. And there are so many things to do and see on the way. We thought a little of going to Mt. St. Michel and then down to Poligeou, which is a seaside place that Julia recommended as being very quiet and French, which is just North of St. Nazaire in Brittany, look for Nantes, then go to the coast, and there you will find us most likely for the summer! To get there from Paris, we go through Touraine and then to Nantes, and we are planning to motor the older children to see the Chateaux, etc. and send the babies on by train with Woods. That is, this summer!

Our trip has been quiet. The children have acted beautifully. Mrs. Ryerson's sister, Miss Borie, has taken the two elder under her wing and is crazy about them. She is a dear— and such a relief after the others on board. There are a lot of English. In fact, the heavy travel is caused by returning English, rather than gadding Americans. They take themselves so seriously! There are four or five who sit at the table with Mrs. Ryerson, her sister and son, Hoytie Wiborg, Hugh Walpole, Rue, when she is up, which she hasn't been, and Sheldon Whitehouse, who is one of those Whitehouses. They all fight with the English, and we get bits of it afterwards from H. Wiborg and Whitehouse. People who take themselves seriously and expect others to follow their example are ridiculous! and everyone laughs at them. There are more long, lanky red-headed English on board. One woman has a bowl of pet turtles!, which she takes out on deck and lets run around on her neighbors! Young Ms. Henry Kip is on board. She is a dear and so sweet and pretty. She is going over to get her husband's body.

Potter and Bertha are now sitting in the Lounge playing "Sniff" with Miss Borie. You may like to know! I wonder if you are comfortable? Please make yourself so, if you are not, and please invite people in for meals, if you can bear Esther's service!

Much love from all, Pauline

45 Rue Cortambert
Paris, France
May 3, 1920

Mrs. Herman Kohlsaat
271 Summit Avenue
St. Paul, Minnesota

Dearest Mother:

Well, here we are in Paris at the 45 Rue Cortambert! Does it seem as strange to you as it does to me? The house is so different (naturally!) from what we imagined it that I can't believe we are in the right house! In the first place, it is Gothic in style, made of red brick and trimmed with grey stone; it is square and has space all around it and is quite imposing. The garden is very pretty, and there are either thrushes or mocking birds in it that sing most beautifully. And the neighborhood is very nice—in fact, quite "chic," I think. I have tried to draw the place but doubt if you can make anything of it. The bathrooms are weird but sanitary. It is quite grand, really (the house, not the plumbing!). Woods had everything ready, how he did it I don't know, for it must have been an awful job. We just walked in and had a delicious dinner and such cozy beds to sleep on. The furniture is nearly all unpacked, plants and flowers everywhere, silver polished, rugs down, everything done. He is thrilled with what he accomplished, and so are we. He told us that we could have 16 to dinner last night if we wanted to! Bed seemed like the best place to us, however. He has been talking to the Ogden Mills butler, and they entertain every minute. We have got to go out and make friends for his sake, I'm afraid!

Now for a line about our trip. We reached the harbour at Cherbourg at 12 noon on Saturday and landed at 4:30! It took an endless time to get a permit to land. Woods met us with the motor, which was very nice, and we left C. after our bags were examined. We spent the night at Bayeux in a very nice little hotel. We had dinner at nine P.M. and left the next morning at nine. Our entire bill was not over $12.00! but millions of francs. There is enough food, but not an abundance. No wheat, but very good bread.

Well, you should hear Potter on the subject of French W.C.s! He is dumbfounded and can't get over each new one. The one at Bayeux had one of those seats that spring up when you get up, and that finished him. He talks of them on all occasions. We went to see the Cathedral, which is as fine as Henry Adams says it is, and then the tapestries. They are wonderful. We have a colored series of them to show you when we get back. Then we went to Caen, to the Abbey aux Dames. Potter was thrilled over the tombs in the pavement. In fact, he is quite breathless over it all. Then we stopped at Lisieux for lunch, and then on to Paris. We had stones thrown at us, but we didn't get hurt. May 1st, you see—that was just outside of Paris, and the men were drunk. Apparently we were very smart to get through at all! The people who came down by train left at seven P.M. and got in at four

A.M. strike on and no cabs. I don't know what they did. Woods walked to the Ritz and got a cab and went back for Hannah Arthur and the bags and got here about six A.M. So we were lucky in coming by motor. Can you imagine those children on that train after seven days on the boat? Today they have played in the garden all day and had "lots of fun." Potter is enchanted with his room and for some strange reason is not afraid to sleep there.

Tomorrow I start out for clothes for us all and expect to be terribly busy. Our motor doesn't look so terribly old and out of style, and I don't expect to mind it in the least. It will be ready in two weeks. Certain things are very scarce, such as gas, coal, gasoline, butter, and bacon, but we are careful and so get along very well. Sometime I'll write more about the towns in Normandy. Tonight it is late, but I want to get this off as early as possible. We are all well. Send lots of love. How are you? Am hoping for a letter soon.

Pauline

Please give our love to the Shepards. Every picture of a baby my baby sees she calls Constance.

45 Rue Cortambert
Paris, France
May 5, 1920

Mrs. Herman Kohlsaat
1050 Lake Shore Drive
Chicago, Illinois

Dear Grandmother:

We have had a good time. I have a little room all of my own and little desk and I am writing to you on it. Gordon and Pauline sent their love to you. When we were driving home a drunk man got a stone and threw it at us and we were going along we ran over a dog. Potter is sent his love to you.

Love from,

Bertha Palmer

45 Rue Cortambert
Paris, France
May 9, 1920

Dear Mother:

We have been in Paris a week today. It hardly seems possible, and on the other hand, we feel as if we had never been anywhere else! It is quite cold, but we manage to keep fairly warm with the furnace and fires. No "beautiful May in Paris" so far! Paris, as far as we have seen it, is not gay. Or if it is, it is only skin deep, and a scratch shows the sorrow. Nearly everyone is in black, and all the faces are sad. You never hear anyone singing as they walk along the streets the way we used to. It is just as difficult to get anything here as at home. Everything is "out." There is plenty of food if you can pay for it, and plenty of everything else for living, if you have the money. Things seem frightfully high—1000s of francs—which melt to very little when changed into American money. We pay the chef 500 francs a month—a little over $35.00! The "valet de pied" 150 with extra for washing and wine! I haven't had the bill for the food for a week but expect that to be a shock—really large, much higher than at home, but not worse than the Biltmore!

The clothes are much less expensive. I am getting a lovely crêpe de chine, embroidered $1800.00=$112.00, and another without embroidery for 1400, about $90.00. The same for a long coat and 1800 for a black lace evening gown! The clothes so far are so hideous that one is not tempted and one only buys to be clothed. No one is gayly dressed. I cannot wear my coral hat! I would look like a sunset. But the skirts are to the knees. No corsets—perfectly plain waists with "tummys" sticking out, and no peticoats, in fact, practically nude. And everybody made-up! I have hardly seen anyone who looked smart. The "mode" isn't smart, nor can it be made to be, as far as I can see. Tailor suits in the morning, one-piece gabardine in the P.M., a semi décolleté for teas and receptions that serve also with a hat for dinner in a restaurant, and only two or three "grande robes" have I seen, for opera or ballet! I am going to Callot tomorrow—they have moved to the Rond Point—to see if I can find anything pretty. Worth and Cheruit were quite bad, especially Worth. Nothing begins before 10:30—everything closes from 12 to two and closes again at five. So if you live in the country as we do, you have an awful time getting to places while they are open. The working class does just what it d— pleases, and that's all there is to it.

We have an extremely nice young Russian for Potter, whom we like very much. Potter also likes him! We have met Julia's family, and they are charming, the brother very gay, and the sister a dear but horribly gloomy, simply bowed down by events, nor does one wonder at it. The children are spending the P.M. with Guy's [Cantacuzène] children, and Min and I are trembling! We are asking them here on Thursday, and I hope that after that they will be friends. There is a girl of nine and a boy of six.

We still like our house and garden. It is very quiet. In the garden are two horse chestnuts, one pink and one white, in bloom!

We have gone over to Grace and Cappy's apartment. It is on the top floor (3rd) of the building next to Mrs. Palmer's—is quite small, but I imagine will be quite comfortable. The kitchen is on the 4th floor! No "ascenseur." I don't know how Grace will like it on that account. It is being done over, the whole building remodeled, and we don't see how it can be ready in time for them. Everything moves so slowly here. We haven't decided about the summer. We are thinking of Dinard now. Everybody looks at B. in wonder and says, "Ah, Madame, elle est magnifique!" which amuses B. a good deal. They all look awfully well— even Potter is fat and has round cheeks! I am hoping for a letter from you soon.

Love,

Pauline

Tell Kay that I will bring her things instead of sending them, as they would never arrive that way!

Our love to them all, P

45 Rue Cortambert
Paris, France
May 23, 1920

Mrs. Herman Kohlsaat
c/o Mrs. Roger Shepard
271 Summit Avenue
St. Paul, Minnesota

Dearest Mother:

I am sure that you must think that we've all died without letting you know. As a matter of fact, I have been going at a great rate and have been awfully tired at the end of the day. You have no idea what Paris is like, and until one gets used to it, it is awfully trying. In the first place, no one considers taking the least notice of you until 10:30 in the morning, and then they treat you like the scum of the earth. At 12 everyone rushes out for two hours, so you can do nothing until about 2:30. After five, it is too late. On Saturday at 12, everything except the big stores close, and the big stores are closed on Mondays until two P.M.! Then there are a thousand different strikes a day, each one holding up some part of everything you want done! I am now getting used to it, but at first when I was trying to dress the children and myself I nearly lost my mind. Now we are all settled and the clothes are trickling in, slowly! We are wondering what will happen to Cappy and Grace, as their apartment is not yet in order, and we doubt if it will be for another month.

We have had every box opened and unpacked, and this house looks like a curio shop. The furniture from London is on the way here, but we don't know when it will arrive! I have an English governess for the moment, who is finishing up Potter's course (did I say that the Russian fellow gave out after two hours!?), and then I am getting a French woman to teach them the French language this summer! I am determined that they shall learn to speak, and they also are keen to learn. Woods took Potter to a shooting gallery yesterday, and he hit the bull's eye three times and more or less shot up the place. So we are arranging to send him out to a shooting school in the country. It takes such a long time to do anything here! And no one knows what "being in a hurry" means. Probably a very good thing for me if I can't do it!

We went out to dinner with the Chauncey McCormicks. They have fine Deering's Villa at Neuilly. It is lovely, and so is the garden. The house is modern—at least it looks it inside. Not as attractive as this house, by any means. We went to the theatre afterwards to see "Mille Et Une Nuits," which was very well done. The McCormicks are awfully nice, much nicer than when at home. Chauncey has lost his dandified manner and is very human. We have seen Rue several times. She looks very well and is, as usual, great fun. She visited, or rather saw, a lot of Hazel in London and says she is very fat but perfectly beautiful—looks as she did when she was 17.

Last night we went to dinner at a dancing place (Morgan's) where they have fine Negroes playing jazz. We had dinner and danced—dinner at 8:30 finishing at 11, when all amusement in Paris stops on account of the electric light and coal shortage. The Roy McWilliams' gave the party. It was very amusing. Rue was there and some other Americans. Ellen's Mary Borden Spears is giving a dance on the 1st of June, to which we are going. She has a house in the rue Monsieur over on the other side of the river. She says she knows "everyone in Paris," and everybody else says she has a terrible social bee. Her husband is called "bu cocloch des dames de Paris." That means, the "whooping cough," as it is so catching! He is apparently a winner—everyone likes him. Mary is saying that she had no models for the characters in her book but is terrified for fear of what Chicagoans think of her. Goodbye, lunch is ready. Love to all,

Pauline

45 Rue Cortambert
Paris, France
June 9, 1920

Mrs. Herman Kohlssat
Biltmore Hotel
New York, New York

Dearest Mother:

I began to think that I would never get time to sit down and write. It has been two weeks since I last wrote, and you must be thinking that all sorts of terrible and awful things have happened. They haven't, however, and everything is going along quietly. There has been a terrific amount to do dividing everything. We leapt right into it the day after Grace and Cappy came, and are still at it. We hope to finish a great deal this week. It really is very difficult, but everyone is pleasant, so it goes smoothly. We haven't done the important things as yet. When that is finished, I'll write you which fell to our lot. The children claim that everything pretty has been taken away from me, and Gordy whispered to me the other day, "Mother, why don't you lock what you want up in a closet, and then Aunt Grace can't see it?" Quite an idea for a five-year-old?

On Saturday Min and I go off motoring looking for a quiet summer place along the northern coast. It has been so cold here that we have been freezing, and in the country there are slight frosts everywhere. Paris is very sad—absolutely no gaiety—and everybody looks strained and worn. Not the old Paris in any way. No singing on the streets, no shouting back and forth, no cheer of any kind. And as for the clothes! They are awful. I haven't seen anyone smart so far. We went to Mary Borden Spears' for a ball the other night, and I expected to see something fine, as she claims to know and have at her house "everyone in Paris." And I saw nothing, duchesses and princesses and all sorts of grand names flying around, but only frightful disappointment when you saw what went with them. It made me think of the circus—trapezes swinging that supported bodies that without them would fall to the ground. Mary's house and husband are charming and Mary much improved. She is terribly worried on account of her book and breaks her neck to be polite to Chicago people.

I suppose you are in the midst of conventions now. I do hope you are all comfortable at 1050. I am sending a check for July and only hope that it gives you half the pleasure to receive it that it gives us to send it. Your Biddeford plan sounds very nice. Why don't you say that you will stay as long as the food is good and will leave when the canned vegetables come on? Are you coming abroad before we go back? It would be great fun to be here together. We sail on the Olympic Oct. 20. Our house is large and comfortable, and we can make you fairly easy. Think it over!

Kay's farm sounds lovely, and I am sure they are awfully happy to be in it.

Someday I'll write details of all we have done! We all send love.

Pauline

45 Rue Cortambert
Paris, France
June 15, 1920

Mrs. Herman Kohlsaat
Biltmore Hotel
New York, New York

Dear Mother:

Your telegram came in time to be put on my breakfast tray on the 10th and made everything seem very cheerful indeed. I had a nice birthday. The children all came in with long-stemmed roses and many dewy kisses, and Min gave me a lovely box of lapis lazula and fine diamonds and a jade picture frame. Then Julia and Mike's cable came in the P.M. I had a cake with candles and gave the children a lot of small things—soldiers, miniature sandbags, etc., etc. So we all had a very happy successful day. I only wish you had been here.

Today was Gordy's birthday, and all your and Roger's letters arrived. He was distinctly thrilled, very quiet and dignified, and walked about with slow steps. Potter bought all the children gifts in honor of Gordy, and we all had an engagement to go "Au Paradis des Enfants" for toys at 11 o'clock. There being nothing from Min and me early in the morning, Gordy came very soberly to my bed and said, solemnly, "You have many things for me, Mother, that I don't know about?" So I told him we had arranged to go shopping for them. So off we all went, the four children, Min, Anna, and myself, down the rue Cortambert to the Avenue Henri Martin and onto the cab stand, our motor having to be repaired. We did some fine shopping "Au Paradis!" Gordy chose a fire engine set, something like a set of soldiers, an English ambulance, a tank, and a spotlight! I asked him what else he wanted, and he sighed, "I can't think of anything more!" He lost his first tooth a few days ago and was duly impressed. We laughed and joked about the hole and the new tooth pushing the old one out and suddenly he dropped onto the ground sobbing. I picked him up and tried to tell him that it was fine to lose a tooth and then discovered "It's not my tooth that I mind, but you are all laughing at me!" Quite a handful, to say the least.

The Villa Balbianello on Lake Como.

We still continue to divide "things," and it's most unpleasant as it is nerve-wracking. We are almost through with the things here, and tomorrow the London things come! There is no rest for the weary.

And on top of it all, we suddenly have a lot of engagements! The Pecks, Anna Jo and Bobby are here. We had them to lunch yesterday and we lunch with them tomorrow. Rue is back from Switzerland, where she went to see Edith about opera, and she is wanting to do things, and we also want to go with her. Then there are a number of people who have called and asked us to parties, so it's gay. Mrs. Bliss called, and a Mrs. Chanler has asked us to a dance, and Mrs. Whitehouse to lunch, and so you see altogether we are frisky. The Pikes are here and Mrs. Black, and I have not had time to do anything about them, and then the Hutchinson Ryerson group. We would really be having a very nice time if we weren't working so hard, but as that is what we are here for, we can't loaf! I must tell you before I forget it, what Rue said about Edith. She, Rue, went especially to Zurich to see her and found her a new person, absolutely sane and engrossed in her work, would return to Chicago but says that she would want to continue her work and can imagine how congenial it would be with all her friends coming in and rushing away again to laugh at her and talk about it, all which is, of course, exactly what they would do. Rue was much impressed with her.

On Saturday we are going to the battlefields, just where, I don't know. I must ask Mr. Ryerson, as he is awfully well up on the whole front and knows just what to do. Our car is so comfortable that it is a pleasure to ride in it. Did I tell you that Betty McWilliams wrote of an enchanting villa on the sea near Biarritz that we could rent? Awfully nice of her to take the trouble. We, however, hear that it's hot there in summer so think we won't take it but will go north. It's so cold, though, that one doesn't even think of summer.

Were you terribly uncomfortable during the convention? We keep reading of the intense heat. The convention must have been thrilling. I think they have a fine ticket. Certainly Coolidge seems a popular candidate. Harding was very fine, as I remember, at the convention four years ago. What do people think at home? Poor Lowden, what a blow, but how fine he was about it! It's better to be a fine governor than a poor president, and he is sure of being a fine governor! And "you never can tell by the looks of a toad how far he can hop," as you have always told me, and he might not hop so far in Washington! Was the house comfortable and the food and service good? We hear from Ellen occasionally, and she is much excited with her job! I kept thinking that at least you would get back to a cool house and a restful room after the heat at the Coliseum. You don't know how much pleasure I have had thinking that you were all there.

Some of my new clothes have come home, and you should see them! They would make you cross-eyed! I have on a lightening pattern foulard, in dark blue ground, with bright blue blobs and streaks of white lightening shooting through it!!! It ties on, and the skirt looks like a lot of rags. Quite fascinating and strange to say Min is keen about it. Also, I am giving up corsets and wearing a band! Very comfortable and very fat and shaky. In fact, could Kay see me, she would be sure that my hips shake! Nobody has a waistline, but everyone has a "tummy," which makes them all look, as Katherine Adler expresses it, "as if they had a pudding in front and on behind." No one tries to be chic—just cozy and at ease. There is little formality and none of the old order of things has begun to make an appearance. All the French ladies of title who can have babies are having one every ten months. This is a terribly long ramble, and I hope you've been able to read it and understand it. I love your letters about the life in St. Paul. It must be lovely. I hope that we can go out to Kay's farm next spring. Will they name the next calf for me, do you think? Loads of love from us all. Pauline

45 Rue Cortambert
Paris, France
June 28, 1920

Mrs. Herman Kohlsaat
Sea View Inn
Biddeford Pool, Maine

Dear Mother:

A nice letter from you today and a telegram last week—otherwise, the mail has been slow. We are awfully glad that you were comfortable at 1050 during convention week. We read in the paper about the heat and hoped that the reports were exaggerated, but from your letter, they apparently were not. You and Kay and Julia are all so polite about the house and servants that we almost suspect that it was terrible and you don't want us to know! It seems strange now to think of you at Biddeford, settled in the sun. Are you comfortable and how is the food? Are they all doing just the same things, playing cards every minute and talking? Who has our house? And are there any attractive new people? I feel homesick for the Pool, really, and would love to be back there for a little sea air.

Paris is lovely, but what we are doing is a little trying in more ways than one, and we long to be finished. We have not decided about the summer. As far as we have gotten in future plans is to go to London on the 15th to do the things there. I am so tired of material "things" that I never want to own anything that I can't pack away in two or three trunks. Occasionally we enjoy ourselves!

Last week we went to Soissons passing through Meaux, Essonne, Chateau Thierry, Belleau Wood, Bézu St. Germain, where the Big Bertha was hidden. Fére-en-Tardenois, and finally Soissons. From there we went on to Compiégne, Pierrefonds, Crépy-en-Valois and Senlis to Paris. At Essonne we saw the first barren trees and ruined houses. It is terrible that first sight. Chateau Thierry was of course terribly interesting. I can't describe any of it except that everywhere people are working violently to rebuild and to take away the ruins. There are ruins everywhere, but all the fields are leveled and cultivated and covered with beautiful crops. There is no trace there of war, except for the piles of barbed wire and ammunition dumps along the roadside. There are "abri" all along the way. Belleau Wood is on the top of a hill and is all cut to pieces, the new growth coming up making it look very thick and chunky. The cemetery is beautifully kept with the American flag floating above it. It is awe-inspiring, and I think that if anyone belonging to me had been killed over here, I should want them buried in the cemetery nearest the place they fell. It all seems to belong to them, somehow. At Bézu was the great gun, which took 1200 men to operate. It is now taken away, but the base is there, a giant thing surrounded by and sunk in water for some hydraulic reason. It is camouflaged in a lovely sky blue and soft green. When the Germans left they took the gun and blew up part of the base. It seemed a diabolical thing, when you thought that it shot a shell that went all the way to Paris in about 20 minutes over the same distance that it had taken us three hours to come by motor! They say that if a gun were invented that would go three times as fast and as high again that it would strike the ether in which things whirl, and the shell would never come to Earth again! I laughed at that when I heard it, and the person telling the tale said, "Don't laugh, but first think of this gun and then the assaulting guns of the 14th century! The thing may be possible." That was Julia's friend Bakmetchief. I cannot spell his name, but he is a dear, and so is his wife.

Fère-en-Tardenois was all shot to pieces, and by our men, I think—just hollow houses. At Soissons it was terrible, the Cathedral in frightful ruins, but the people hard at work rebuilding! Whole blocks were wiped out there, with the owners living in little wooden shacks. Over the door of one of these was written "Villa des Douceurs," which is typical of the spirit all through the country. The devastated country, that is. You see nothing sweet in Paris, nor do you hear it. We were deeply impressed by the cheerful faces, all smiles, and happy voices that we saw and heard all through that country. Everyone looked healthy and strong, the children much healthier than any we have seen here. We did the whole thing from ten o'clock Sunday morning to 11:30 Sunday night. Rue went with us. All the "things" here seemed very unimportant when one looked at them again.

Last Monday night we had dinner with the Owen Aldis', the Bakmetchiefs, Mrs. Griswold (Owen's former sister-in-law, I think), and her son. It was a lovely party, and we liked it better than anything we have done so far. Friday night Fanny and Wallie gave a dinner at Pré Catalan, which was interesting, if not elevating! It was a "Gala Night" after the "Jour des Drags" at the races, and there were thousands of people there. You simply cannot imagine the amount of exposed female flesh that we saw! All that women wear now consists of the following: a band around the waist, a pair of stockings, slippers, and a dress. (That is, a piece of something supposed to be a dress, usually a lace or satin skirt with a chiffon lining, a piece of something in front drawn tight across the bust and disappearing under the arms into the belt, the back either a row or two of beads or a piece of tulle to hold up the front.) One girl I saw was in thin yellow satin, perfectly simple and nice, high in front and back, and fairly long of skirt. Under it she wore only a rubber band with garters to hold up her stockings, for I saw everything, as the satin was very thin! These women were not coquettes, but the gems of society. Everyone paints and darkens their eyes! And such behavior! The demi-monde never acted so in public. It was a riot of flesh, with all feeling for anything fine entirely lost and out of place, certainly! One man dancing with a fairly fat woman and failing to find any part of a gown at the back to touch gave it up and grabbed a lump of flesh and held on and guided the female that way, and she was a lady!

Tomorrow we are lunching with Mary Borden Spears. We don't want to go, but she has been most polite asking us to do all kinds of things, so we are going. Next Sunday she is giving a party for the Queen of Roumania at Fountainbleu, and we may go to that, but I don't know. We lunched with the Whitehouses the other day, did I tell you?, and had a very nice time. In fact, if we had time, and were not so tired, we would have a delightful time here. Everyone is awfully kind and seems to like us, for some reason.

We are finishing the jewels tomorrow. We thought they were all finished the other day, and then the next morning Grace said she thought "one person had all the big stones, so we had better re-divide." As everything had been done according to value, and she had usually had her choice of everything, Min and I were amused. So tomorrow everything promises to be settled. We hope so, for they are a little trying to work with, as they never make up their mind about what they want to do "definitely" until we, thinking it is practically decided upon, make our choice, and then they decide they were not right, and so we choose all over again in order to avoid rows. They always like what we like the best! So far we've gotten on beautifully, but you may believe that some funny things have happened. Grace is as sporty a loser at this as she is at golf. If you don't understand me, ask Kay what I mean.

It is pathetic the way she thinks she is having a good time. Cappy won't take her to any of the shows because she makes up so, and neither will Min nor Wallie. So she sits quietly at home of an evening usually. The night we went to Pré Catalan she sat next to Min, who had nothing to say to her, and another man who hates any kind of makeup, and told her so, so would not talk to her. So she sat perfectly silent with an expectant expression of "now I'm having a devilish good time!" She is like a debutante, so any time out gives her a thrill. Fanny and I have managed to get the same dresses practically everywhere! and we appeared that night as twins. My dress was much the prettiest, so I didn't mind, but Fanny did, for the same reason, I think!

169

I have a French governess coming on Thursday, who seems nice. Potter has done awfully well with his English governess, who is a dear, but fails to speak enough French to talk continuously to them in that language. His examination papers are wonders of neatness, so we are expecting all "one's" when the report comes in.

I am looking better, as I have a little color in my cheeks. I am still tired, but that is to be expected. It won't last long, however, and then I shall be very well. All the children look remarkably well.

I hear Father worked hard at the convention and stood the strain beautifully. Send him love from us all when you write. It has taken me over an hour to write this!

We all send love,

Pauline

45 Rue Cortambert
Paris, France
July 11, 1920

Mrs. Herman Kohlsaat
The Biltmore Hotel
New York, New York

Dearest Mother:

We have been dividing the jewels, and the children have been keenly interested, and the girls with eyes for what they want. The baby kindly asked me the other day, "Mudder, when are you going to died-ed for I'd like a bracelet!" They have picked out everything they want, so I am expecting to "died-ed" each day. It's up to me! Potter has been swimming with Honoré and D'orsay and their tutor, Mr. Berger at Claridge's and has had a fine time. Mr. Berger has fallen for him as usual and said that he couldn't think of any greater pleasure than to always be with Potter! He wants his boys to be with P. as much as possible as they are so underdeveloped physically and so sluggish, and Potter would be such an excellent example for them. All of which he told Grace, which must have made a hit! Honoré is frightfully fat and looks heavy-eyed. D'orsay is over six feet, very handsome, and beginning to take an interest in girls. He is a dear. You ask about Grace's career. I don't know much about it except that she claims we are wonderful to do so much, as she has done nothing. Judging by what we have done, she must be dull. I think, however, she has had fun. Cappy is socially inclined, but Grace is shy. Fanny has been sick most of the time and, when well, has exhausted herself getting clothes. Wallie is really the only one who is doing anything worthwhile. He has seen everything in Paris worth seeing and has not been "loafing" on any violent scale as far as we can see. I must say that he is the yeast to leaven that loaf, wishing Grace and Cappy no harm!

The children gave some very funny plays. Also they are keen about "scuder cars," and even the baby has one. They "scud" around violently—in fact, they are very happy and are enjoying life. Gordy still takes his food very seriously and talks in a most dignified manner. He has lost another tooth, but the new ones are growing in so rapidly that the gap will be filled in another six weeks. He is getting to be quite a boy and has lost practically all of his baby looks and ways. Still, he likes to be cuddled and kissed. Bertha enjoys her pretty clothes, is trying hard to learn French, and is nice and fat.

Potter finished his Calvert School course, and his final exam paper was so neat and fairly correct that I am sure that he will get a very high percentage of marks. They wrote him, I think I told you, that his papers were so untidy that, in spite of his deserving higher marks for the correctness of his answers, they were marking him low on account of untidiness. The next exam they returned without marking it to have done over. That one, when they received it after his copying it neatly, they marked very high—five "ones" and three "twos," I think, which is excellent. His last one ought to give him all "ones," as it was a marvel of neatness with only two or three mistakes.

You will be glad to hear that there were enough pearls to make two very long necklaces of big pearls. They come below the waistline. They are just alike, which simplified matters a great deal. The important tiara, with standing pearls and the collar to match, fell to us. As I can't wear them, we are going to have some of the stones reset, the largest standing pearls to be made into earrings and pins. The flat collar of large diamonds also is ours, the ruby ring, and a very large white pearl that can be used as a pendent or a pin. Also, the diamond bow knot and a diamond wristwatch. Also, a large grey pearl ring.

Grace was much dissatisfied with the division after it was made. The values are all the same, however. She got a lovely pearl bracelet, like a string of pearls, which offset the ruby ring. She wanted the ring, Cappy the pearls, so he took the pearls, to my joy. We would have liked the bracelet but liked better the ring. Also, she got the large pearl earrings. The earrings, the pearl bracelet, and an emerald ring in one group offset the diamond collar (the one with pearl in it) and the ruby ring, as there are enough pearls in the collar to make a bracelet. I was well satisfied with the decision. She also got the swinging diamond tiara, which we regretted, but I think that we can do some swapping and get that. She got a very ugly head bandeau and ornament, which Min and I couldn't see, so we got the diamond necklace, which offset it.

171

You see, it is so much simpler to let them take their choice without our committing our-selves that we generally do it and get what we want. The times that we have let them know our choice they have immediately switched and taken our things, which we could-n't get then, without a frightful row. And, as everything is lovely and life very short, we have let it go. They lack sensibility and a certain kind of fine feeling to an extraordinary degree. We are very friendly in spite of everything and have had no rows, which consid-ering it all, is remarkable. But I can assure you that if we had acted as they have, no one would have been speaking. They have gotten almost everything they wanted but have arranged it all so badly in their apartment that it looks cheap and unimportant, while ours looks simply divine. Grace is irritated every time she comes into the house, and especially when she goes into my room, and has deliberately torn my room to pieces four separate times when we've been choosing up furniture! And never once has she said, "I'm so sorry to spoil your room." Cappy has had the grace to be a little mortified. Woods has been in such a temper and also Anna and all the children! Grace has certainly lost all character in the servants quarter and among the children. She is firing the footmen that Woods got her. She has a French butler, who naturally wants French footmen, but Woods is in a fine stew about it. In fact, he was so upset last night, when he told us that I was afraid he would say something that would make things difficult. Fortunately he held himself in check, but only with great effort. Well, so much for the family!

On our way back from London we are having the motors meet us (Grace, Cappy, Fanny, and Wallie) at Calais, and then we are going down the entire battlefront. We are anxious to see the English front in the north and also the French front beyond Rheims. There, they say, is the place where one can see the real battlefront, untouched since the war. The French haven't had time nor money to get to it. Even the bodies, or rather bones, are still there lying where they fell. It will be very terrible, but I want to see it, for we seemed to suffer so little in the war that we know nothing about it.

I wish I could walk across the links with you and Kay and see the sunset and hear the gulls, to say nothing of smelling what Min calls "rotten seaweed." I miss Biddeford terri-bly! Isn't it strange? I suppose not really, when one thinks you and Kay are there.

I am so glad you had a nice talk with Grandpa. How is Father? And what happened with his interview with Ochs? I think that Julia would write a wonderful life of Mrs. Palmer. We hope she does it. Give Kay a kiss and a hug and tell her to give you one of each for me and then a dozen from the children.

Pauline

Paris, France
August 5, 1920

Mrs. Herman Kohlsaat
Sea View Inn
Biddeford Pool, Maine

Dear Mother:

You see I am getting better about writing now, as the work is nearly finished, and I am getting back to usual routine of life. Grace and Fanny are waiting to hear of their mother's death at any minute. They had a cable several days ago saying that she was desperately ill, and Fanny was starting home. Then she had great difficulty about passports in a hurry and then a cable saying the condition was hopeless and not to come, so they are now waiting the final cable. Grace has gone to bed, and Fanny looks like death. They still expect to go to Biarritz on Saturday, but the summer will be forlorn. The rest and change, however, will do them good. D'orsay and Honoré had a fine time. He and Honoré came up to supper and Potter thinks D'orsay marvelous. He is over six feet and very good-looking—in fact, a beauty—and his wit is of the type that appeals to them strongly! They are wild about swords, daggers, and firearms, which they buy at a pawnshop near here, and have thrilling times Jewing the owner down! You should hear them talk about it. And D'orsay has a girl, a violent case, and is all spruced up. And the two younger boys now spend their time plastering down their hair like D'orsay's, Honoré with brilliantine (like D'orsay's) but Potter with water, so far! It's very becoming to Potter, I must say. Bertha gets along very well with them all, but has her own private opinion, which is always decided, clean-cut and quaint. She acts like a mother to them and as if she were detached and years older.

Today I combed the town for shoes for the bunch and finally managed to get very nice things. In fact, such nice ones for Bertha that they are the talk of the home. We have our rooms at Geneva and can go on Thursday. And now Woods has burst into drink, and we are having a fine time. I find that he has always drunk, so it is nothing new, but I must say, we are discouraged about going off and leaving him here in charge! We have spoken to him and said it couldn't happen again so are waiting to see what will occur. He has been in a frightful temper and most impertinent and insolent ever since we arrived, and we put it down to the strain of getting the house in order and the torn-up condition it has been in ever since until now. We sent him home on a vacation so that he might get rested. Last night he served dinner, dropped every knife and fork on the floor, kicked the table every time he served, and when standing still, swayed like a lily in the breeze. It was impossible for him to speak, so I had it out with him today, with Min at my elbow to support and prompt. He was very quiet and hardly flustered at all. We have not seen him since, so I imagine he is completely sound, and we'll ship him to England tomorrow. Fortunately we have Arthur, who has been working hard and has improved wonderfully, and then another Englishman, who is willing and is learning fast. I am amazed at how little I am upset by it, in fact, not at all. Woods has been so disagreeable all spring that I would be glad to get rid of him.

It has been cold and rainy all day, not in the least like August. I have worn a heavy suit. Paris is now filled with Americans—all the French are gone—and you hear only flat voices with a perfect twang. I heard an elderly woman say today in the hat store, "I am wild for a new hat. I've been wearing the worst looking old thing you ever saw!" and tramping up and down the room shouting. You felt like whispering and speaking with an accent. Is the Pool more crowded during August? It usually is. I wonder what we'll do next year. Potter says firmly "Osprey!" We may come over again. I do not know!

Much love to you all,

Pauline

45 Rue Cortambert
Paris, France
August 7, 1920

Mrs. Herman Kohlsaat
Sea View Inn
Biddeford Pool, Maine

Dear Mother:

I am feeling much better and more rested but have retired to bed again before dinner tonight in order not to get all in again. This week has been a little hectic in a way. It's really the mental strain rather than physical that upsets me. Grace got word of her mother's death on Thursday night and went to bed at the shock—also Fanny, although they had been expecting it. Today they all left for Biarritz—the illest, most worn-out looking crew you ever saw. Grace has lost pounds and is so nervous that she cries continuously and she has that awful pain in the back of her head, which comes from nerves. Just living all summer with Fanny would give me nerves, without all the sorrow and work she has had. Biarritz will do them all good, I am sure. Pretty sad end of all their gay plans. They always do miss things, though, for one reason or another. They had a memorial service at the English church this morning, with only Min and me as outsiders. It was a cheerless occasion without a bright spot. The English burial service is so cheerful and reassuring and must give such comfort to anyone in great sorrow! Well, be that as it may! I prefer the Irish.

I read Bertha and Potter your letter about Constance, and they were thrilled and are dying to see her. Our baby, as I wrote you, names everything Constance, and her rabbit now comes when called! Has she any hair, and is it pink? She must be a darling.

Woods has been sober every time we've seen him lately, but he eyes me with a glitter! He can glitter right along. I am satisfied with the arrangement. I only hope that it doesn't become a rolling glitter.

Did I tell you about my dressing bag? I don't think I did. Anyway, perhaps the letter got lost, so I'll tell you again! On the list of things in London was a "dressing bag with fitting," so we (Grace and I) were very keen to see it. There was also one in Chicago, so two made it an easy matter, and I brought the Chicago one over and took it to London. Well, that London dressing bag was too beautiful for words—an antique affair—oh, about 50 or 75 years I imagine! And fitted out for a man and his wife with the most beautiful "chislée" silver gilt and crystal things you can imagine. Six large crystal bottles with the silver gilt stoppers, each bottle about as big as this page, and everything on that scale—powder boxes, cold cream boxes, brushes—oh, I can't begin to tell you, but more than enough for us to divide and have more than we needed. We divided and I took mine to Asprey to be put in a bag. The original bag was too huge and clumsy to be used again. There was a large silver gilt mirror, which is meant to stand on your dressing table, which I got instead of the other bag. I felt sorry about the other bag, but Grace took all the fittings out and put them into a bag she is having made here for her half of the silver gilt, so I do not feel so sad! You will be thrilled over that bag, as it is simply lovely. I've always wanted a beautiful dressing table set, and now I have one—far more beautiful than any I ever imagined. Min is equally thrilled and has given me all the men's things to be made into things for me.

The English furniture was lovely. There was less of it than there was of the Paris, however. We did quite well, getting everything we wanted except two things. English furniture is much cozier than French, and also are English houses. I suppose it is the Victorian air about it all that appeals to me!, while over here everything is stiff and formal—very lovely, though. There are some lovely yellow brocade curtains over here, which fell (at the point of a sword) to us, which make a drawing room. We have some other things from here that are nice, too, but we weren't so lucky here as in London, you know, dividing things spoils a whole, and I don't think G. and C. feel that they did very well here, either. When they took all the things they got out of this house and put them in their apartment, they made absolutely no showing, while the things we got, which didn't appeal to me as much as theirs (although I wouldn't tell Min so), looked much finer here. Everything had an air about it, and the house looks important and lovely the minute you come in the door. I think it is the yellow curtains! Rue was nice enough to say it was Min and me, but then Woods arranged the house to begin with so must have much credit. Also the house lends itself to beautiful things. Their flat was unhomelike,

175

and it took them so long to get into it, and they were never comfortable—no hot water running, and up three stories without an elevator!

Another long letter! You'll begin to hire people to read them for you.

Love,

Pauline

Paris, France
August 9, 1920

Mrs. Herman Kohlsaat
Sea View Inn
Biddeford Pool, Maine

Dear Mother:

At last we are getting a little sunshine! It was so beautiful yesterday and today also, except it was very cold. It's high time the weather changed—over a month of bad. We are almost decided about the summer! We probably will go to Montreux Chammonix, being in France is so full that they can't take in one more person. Wallie is going to let us know about rooms in Biarritz either today or tomorrow, so before long we will be off somewhere.

I have been meaning to write you two things, only one of which I can remember just now, but as it is the most important, the other can wait. You write that Fanny Foster told Mrs. Griswold that I always had a doctor. As far as she knows, she was telling the truth, but she doesn't know very far. Do you remember when the children had the measles in the Ray Cottage? We called in Doctor Robbins then, but he just told us it was measles and sent for the doctor from Portland. The children had no medicine, but as you know, if Min wants a doctor, we have one! He usually shows off the children to the doctor as perfect specimens, but as patients. Then two years ago at the Pool Mikie was with us and had the flu, and we called in Robbins and the Baltimore doctor, for him—not for any of us. Still, the doctors came to the house. Then when the baby was new and needed feeding I called in Dr. Walls to prescribe a feeding for her. Also, when we were told that Potter had such tonsils, etc., Walls looked at him and young Cary also, and they both pronounced him OK. Also, when everyone said we had whooping cough, I went to Walls, who said that if they had it, it was a kind he'd never seen. Also, Frank Cary removed dirt from Potter's chin. Also, Dr. Marguis was called in by Cappy when we were in N.Y., where Potter ran a stick into the roof of his mouth. Marguis also cleaned the wax out of his ears. So you see, Fanny as far as she knows is right, but she doesn't know enough! As far as I can remember, the only child who has had medicine was Potter when he had castor oil at two months, and when Marguis painted his mouth when he ran the stick into it. So don't worry about what people say. They always love to talk.

Potter today claimed that he only hit Gordie now when Gordie needed it! Gordie rose up in terrible and dignified wrath, walked into Potter's room, and said in a deep voice, "If you say that the only time you hit me now is when I need it, I'll say you are telling some lie!" and with equal dignity turned around and walked out. Of course, Potter immediately took up the point and argued at the top of his lungs. Gordie said solemnly, "Oh, keep still," and shut Potter's door quietly! I nearly died it was so funny. Gordie was so serious. Potter opened the door quickly and saw me laughing and forgot his argument and laughed too—but not Gordie. He saw us both laughing—I couldn't hide it from him—but he was far too serious and dignified to consider it a laughing matter! If you could have heard him say, "Some lie." It was choice.

Gordie and Bertha play beautifully together and make up the weirdest things. "Lady and Maid" is one of their favorites. Bertha the Lady and Gordie the maid, and he is screamingly funny, and no one enjoys it more than he. Bertha loves to sit in front of my mirror and pin up her hair, at the same time ordering her "maid" to bring her things. Today she ordered "Tea!" and he brought her the "Ouija" board. "There's nothing on it, Gordie," she cried. "Play there are something," commanded Gordy! So they played, and she and Baby drank tea while Gordy held the tray. Yesterday when she ordered "tea," he brought her one of Potter's old sandals, a disgraceful looking thing, but he brought it with such style that Bertha thought it was really tea until she turned around and saw it, and then they rolled on the floor with glee because they thought it so funny!

Do tell Kay that during this wild passion for old swords and pistols, Potter brought in a vicious looking rapier, bent from age, and said proudly, "I'm taking this home to Roger!" It's taller than Roger and terribly dangerous for Connie's eyes, but home it goes. Potter is now intent upon his personal appearance and now uses brilliantine on his hair! I must say it is an improvement. Also he is beginning to be willing to wear his nice clothes without rowing about it. He is particular about the shape of the toes of his shoes, preferring points. I managed to get him into a very round-toed pair the other day because they were brogans and had loads of foxing on them. He toned them down to a nice brown by polish and is really taking a little care of them. His hair after half an hour looks like Jove's curls. It hangs in snaky locks, but one word of warning and he violently brushes it down. And all of this comes because D'orsay has a girl and is in love! And he, D'orsay, keeps clean and brilliant, also. As I wrote you, Potter and Honoré look up to D'orsay as all that there is of a hero. It's too bad Roger isn't here to join the group. D'orsay bought a monocle, put it in his eye, and sat in a box at the opera all evening without acting as if he were unaccustomed to such things. His tutor, M. Berger, is very human and nearly died of it, but never let on that there was anything unusual going on. He told us about it afterwards. Bertha takes to all feminine ways like a duck to water. She looks very pretty in her Paris clothes and thinks she does, too. You will find them more amusing than ever when you see them. Bertha still flirts violently with Min, and he is quite shy about it, although he eggs her on.

We're enclosing a check (with much love!), which we hope arrives safely. Next letter I'll ask if it came and, if by any chance this letter gets lost and you don't get it, will ask you to cable "repeat" or something like that, perhaps more intelligent, but I can't think of anything just now. It's bedtime, and I am sleepy. Tomorrow we start getting ready to go off. We now have to find a place to store the furniture, list it, and arrange to have it moved! To say nothing of being packed! And there's a whole house full of it! More ornaments! And glass biblots, I believe you call it! It certainly will be a job! We'll get all the preliminaries done before we leave for Switzerland and just finish when we get back. Life is one merry whirl these days! Write me your news, and don't you and Kay forget about us!

Love to you all,

Pauline

45 Rue Cortambert
Paris, France
August 14, 1920

Mrs. Herman Kohlsaat
Sea View Inn
Biddeford Pool, Maine

Dear Mother:

No letter from you for a week. However, a nice one from Kay—a cable from Kay about Mr. Shepard. I am so sorry to hear that he is gone. How he must have hated to leave this world! I suppose Kay had to rush back to St. Paul the hottest day in the year. It's usually that way. Of course, I can't imagine being even warm! It is like winter here. Today, however, it is more comfortable, and we are thawing out a little. The children have gone to Bagatelle to sail boats, Min to call on some beaux of mine!, and I am quietly sitting here writing to you and wishing that you and Kay were here, or else I there, anyway, so that we could have a chat instead of a dull letter. We have been listing the things in the house so that when we come back in Sept. we can have things crated and stored without much work. I really hate to leave this house! It is lovely and so pleasant to live in now that all the messing of Grace and Cappy is over. By that I mean the moving out of their things, or rather the moving of them into the hall and then waiting several days for them to send for them! It has been trying to a degree. Now it is quiet and peaceful, and everything runs easily, and Woods has sobered up (for how long?), so we are enjoying our life. Kay said in her letter, "You must be getting a great deal out of life this summer!" A great deal of discipline to the disposition, yes, but not much else. Next year, if we come, we hope to like it all.

Well, I have two beaux! One has a wooden leg, and the other a flow of language. They are both over 60. It certainly takes a Frenchie to pay one compliments! One is an engineer named Bunan-Varilla. He helped the Panama Canal during Roosevelt's Administration and fought in the last war (and all the proceeding ones, also, I think!) and lost his leg when a chance bomb hit the field he was in at Verdun. A perfectly enchanting creature, whose son is an aviator with 4 decorations, "who is," he said, "not because he's my son, but because he is, the finest aviator that was ever born!" And then he tells you marvelous tales of the flying coetes, etc., etc. We met him at dinner at the Chauncey McCormicks at Versailles the other night. He sent me his book this morning, and Min is calling on him this P.M.! The other is the Vicomte Mand! … a brother of the general of that name—a very good-looking old scamp, who has such a command of the French language and such a lovely voice that he and everyone else forgets other things when he begins to speak! I found myself paying the most marvelous compliments to the French and to France in exquisite French—somewhat of a nervous reaction afterwards, however, for one can say innocently the most terrible things in French! Well, anyway, Min is much amused and says it is strange that they haven't brought their wives to call (with his eyes twinkling!). He thinks it sounds like "My wife's gone to the country!" They are sweeties!

Well, I can't keep it any longer! We are going to Bellagio for three weeks, leaving next Tuesday night at 7:30! And Min and I will go to Venice for a few days! Doesn't it sound divine? I can hardly believe it. Our rooms are engaged, and everything arranged. And think how amusing! Ten of us, for $25.00 a day with bathrooms, salon, and food. The exchange makes a great difference. I suppose we will stew in the heat, but I shan't mind! When you get this, Min and I will be floating around Venice in a gondola! Now what do you know about that? I hope it isn't a Nor'easter at the Pool! Wouldn't it be nice if we were all there together—in the gondola, I mean? Well, goodbye. Hope I get a letter before we go off!

Much love to all,

Pauline

Hotel Villa Serbelloni
Bellagio
August 19, 1920

Mrs. Herman Kohlsaat
Sea View Inn
Biddeford Pool, Maine

Dearest Mother:!

Here we are, after what the children call "some trip!" It is so beautiful, though, that it's worth all the trouble and discomfort. It is not hot by any means, just very beautiful summer weather with a haze over the lakes. Up here we see both Lecco and Como. We are at the Serbelloni, as it is better for the children, especially the little ones, and the big ones can easily go down to Bellagio at any time. They are delighted with it. We have found a place to go swimming for Bertha and Potter, so if everything else fails, that will keep up the interest. We have rooms on the ground floor overlooking the lakes, and on that side quite high from the ground, as the house is built on a hillside, if you remember. Wonderful bathrooms, much finer than ours at home, a large vast salon with balcony, two double rooms for Min and me, Gordy, Baby and Anna, and three single ones and bath for the big ones and Mlle. We have a large balcony with a yellow awning and wicker chaise lounge and table and chair, where I expect to "rest" quite a good deal. The food is good, and not many people here, as it is early in the season. The few who are here, Min says, we needn't bother about one way or another, I having remarked that they were the last word in tackiness—that because last night we stayed at Villa d'Esté and saw several fiori staying at the hotel. One attacked and the others, sitting about looking for jobs. Rather a cheaptrying-to-be smart crow. The hotel was lovely and also the gardens. Gordy announced after we left, "beautiful hotel and garden, Mother, but after you have seen that, you stop," meaning nothing to do, from his standpoint.

We left at 11 this A.M. and came up here in a motorboat, which was simply lovely. The big hotel that we have all stayed at various times is not ready yet, but we could have stayed there. The manager was anxious for us to come up here, as it is in order, so we came for a look—"Veni, vide"—and I don't know how one says, "were conquered," but here we are. I can't see that Italy is so terribly poor after the war. Certainly the hotels are better than ever—all either done over or being done over. Sixty bathrooms in these hotels with tiled floors and walls and porcelain fittings, new cretonnes and wallpaper, very good food, and plenty of it. Everything much better than the Marshall House at York. Nobody looks cross, singing and whistling going on everywhere, as gay and lighthearted as before. Of course, we've only seen Milan station, Villa d'Este and here, but that is seeing a good deal of the country.

Well, you should have see us travelling! "La famiglia di dieci," they called us on the

180

train. We took up nearly a whole car. You see, all the travel between the West and the Orient, Czechoslovakia, etc., is over the Simplon Express, through Geneva, Montreux, Stresa, Milan, Venice, Trieste to Constantinople. So the trains are crowded, and everything taken weeks in advance. We had our accommodations as far as Montreux, and when we decided to come here, we couldn't get anything further than Brig. So we decided to come anyway, trusting to luck to either get seats on another train from Brig or seats in the other cars on the Simplon. Luck was with us, and the Chef de train put us into the Trieste car yesterday A.M., and we arrived at Milan at 4:45, quite a little late. It was a hot day and dirty, and I simply couldn't bear the idea of spending the night at Milan and catching a train for here (Como) at 8:40 next morning, so we took a train at six P.M.. Such talking and gesticulating as we had with the porters in the station, but finally one old creature said he could help us get tickets, recheck trunks (they would not check further than Milan, nor sell us tickets to further than M. in Paris). So he got some official, who got us our tickets (the window wasn't opened, and there was a crowd waiting and not much time) and we checked the trunks, bought water, and got into the train at 5:40. Hot? And I got a fluggi! And I had on patent leather shoes!

Well, we all lived through it, and when we got to Como, there was the porter from the Ville d'Este and a motor bus, and it was cool, so we decided then and there to go to the Villa d'E. for the night. We got very comfortable rooms, delicious food, a good night's rest, and then left this A.M. in the motor boat. You see, it is all very easy because the children travel easily, eat anything, and are keen, and anything amuses them. Potter is thrilling over "Sherlock Holmes" and Bertha with "Little Lord Fauntleroy," the other two equally easy. Mlle. is excited within an inch of her life, also Anna and the others, so we have no "saggers" along. Min and I expect to sleep until lunch every day and then walk a little in the P.M. late and really get a rest. Later we are going to Venice for a few days. Min thinks that we ought to take Potter and Bertha, so we may. Next year we think we will land at Naples and spend the greater part of the time in Italy. We'll come over April 1st after Florida. Our main trouble is that the year is too short. Why don't Kay and R. do the same, and if you come over earlier, we can all meet, or you come over with us in April? It all sounds nice. Think it over!

Much love,

Pauline

Hotel Villa Serbelloni
Bellagio
August 25, 1920

Mrs. Herman Kohlsaat
Sea View Inn
Biddeford Pool, Maine

Dear Mother:

There is not much time here—either!—for writing letters. We loaf most of the day—getting up about 11—take a walk, have lunch, and then go off somewhere for the P.M. I am feeling much better already but am not entirely rested. It has been cold, as usual! I am sitting on my balcony with a heavy coat with fur collar, and Min's coat over my feet, and am just comfortable! We all had the Swiss feather puffs over us last night. It's really extraordinary weather. The day after we arrived, it poured torrents all day. Then the next day was beautiful. During the night, however, there was a frightful wind and lightening storm. That was Saturday. That day, a man we met in Paris came up here to lunch, bringing the Butler Ames' house party with him. She is very pretty, and we thought her a dear. She asked us for tea on Sunday, which we tried to accept without undue haste, but am afraid we resembled the bird and the berry. They came back after looking at the castle on the hill, back of this villa, and had tea with us in the garden. In the meantime, Min and I descended to Bellagio to buy cakes at the little teashop where they have delicious things.

Well, we went over on Sunday to Balbianello for tea, and it is even more beautiful there than we ever dreamed of its being. Butler Ames is very nice and simple and simply wild about his villa and the views. He is so carried away by it that I don't think he thinks of anything that is not connected with it. She is the same. I don't see where K. McCormick comes into it in any way. I can't describe it. You will just have to imagine it for yourself. We went all over the house, which really is three houses, two connected at the Loggia at the top. The Loggia has a terrace through the center and a room at either end, one the old billiard room, which they use as a sitting room, and the other a library. The buildings were begun hundreds of years ago and added to by different generations. The last owner was the Marchesa Visconti, who was (and is) a very modern woman. She put it in order 40 years ago and installed a system of telephones all over the house, which work perfectly today! Also all kinds of plumbing! Running water in the bedrooms, for instance! And a marvelous Roman bath, all tiled in blue and white, not shiny tiles. When you want a bath, there is a regular pompeian furnace, which is put into action to heat the water! Also there is a shower bath with a copper bucket on top, which holds the water, and a pump at the side, which is operated to pump the same water back into the bucket, for you to use until you feel entirely clean. The Marchesa was very fair, so she had her bedroom, from which you look up the Lake to the N. end and have a wonderful view, done in black. The walls are repp and the Victorian sofa and chairs in black satin. The ceiling is heavenly blue with gold stars and in each star her coat of arms. There is a Lucca della Robbia, blue and white, Madonna and child with angels' heads all around. When she sold the Villa, she sold everything in it, Lucca della Robbia, Luino, the wonderful library, Majolica, linen, silver china and glass! So they discover some new treasure every day. We had tea in the Loggia, after we had looked over the house and grounds. Delicious American tea with huge purple figs and raspberries and honey on toasted bread with nuts and raisins in it. It was all so beautiful, Loggia tea and view, that we forgot eating for looking and then looking for eating. We stayed nearly three hours! and took pictures and talked and walked around and thought about you and how you would have enjoyed it, too. There are no words to describe it—one must be there and dream. I am sending you some P.C.'s to show you something of what it's like.

On Monday we went to Villa Carlotta. It was tame after Sunday and the view so dull! Then we went to the Hotel Bellevue in Cadenabbia to see if we could get rooms if we want to leave here. The hotel has been used as a hospital for the mutilated and is now all done over with lovely furniture and beautiful bathrooms. It must be very attractive to live there, but the view is nothing in comparison to here, and the street runs right in front of the building, and motors and motorcycles rush by continually, and it seemed very noisy. I should like to try it, I think, in spite of that, but not with the children. We can't imagine why, with the whole lake to choose from, they should have built such a nice hotel there. They say that the hotel is very well run and that the food is delicious, so I suppose the same people return year after year, knowing that they will be comfortable and see their friends and then spend all day long in a boat on the lake eating figs! I don't know whether we'll go to Venice or not but am still hoping to do so. Min is losing his enthusiasm. We have been planning for us all to come next April, yourself, the Shepards, and our crowd, and land at Naples, work north as long as the weather is comfortable, and then establish the children at the Excelsior on the Lido, and then we grownups go on a motor tour through the Hill Towns and Northern Italy, and then back to Venice, and then later, here, and then Paris, and when we can't help it, U.S.A. How does it sound? Ask Mrs. Shepard if she approves and is willing. I think that Potter can bear it one year more, and then it will dawn on him what he has been putting up with and he will refuse to come. He is consoled (unconsciously) by the thought of Roger missing him and finding Biddeford dull and Honoré reduced to writing him from Biarritz that it's fun to go in bathing when the waves are big, and H. must be pretty well put to it for amusement when he writes Potter! Potter goes swimming and fishing and down to Bellagio. This P.M. he is in Cadenabbia with Mlle. Bertha and Arthur. Min has just come up from Bellagio, where he went with the rest of the family, and brought me figs, (I've just eaten seven), a lovely pale pink and pale blue silk blanket, and a blue silk neck scarf, the children loads of toys, and so the day was a success.

The war in Poland sounds better, and the whole situation less strained, everywhere.

Goodbye. Love to you and the Shepards. Pauline

183

Paris, France
September 19, 1920

Mrs. Herman Kohlsaat
1050 Lake Shore Drive
Chicago, Illinois

Dear Mother:

Here I am in bed again, "resting!" It is a heavenly day, much more autumn than we have at home this time of year. In fact, you feel strange in thin clothes! It is freezing cold in the A.M. and lovely at noon, cold again after sundown. The town is filled with glistening Americans. They are a cheap lot, tightly corseted and "swelly" dressed. They look like the new rich French. My main effort at present is to look unlike them, in fact, almost as English as I used to look! Not quite as bad as that, however! So far I have a velvet toque and a couple of suits for the A.M. Every Frenchie wears a dark suit like your Emily suit, only a longer coat—really, just like your Mercola suit—for the morning, with a pretty blouse and a nice hat. In fact, they wear them all day and for dinner in the Bois! Then I have ordered a black velvet evening gown with diamonds on it! and a black crépe de chine for the P.M. and a fur coat! In the meantime, my teeth are chattering together in their crépe de chine summer dresses!

I have found a wonderful hat place where they make your hats on you and don't take all your income for doing it. I have ordered the Bates things, two coats and three hats, and Bertha's trousseau and Potter's and now have only to finish up Gordy's. For Connie, Rouff is making her a divine coat and bonnet, a little "expen," but Kay won't mind, as it will last all next summer, and then she can put the lace on a dress. Also I am considering a little dress. Bertha and I chose the things. Prices are pretty high here, and the dressmakers, in consequence, have not sold much to America. They admit that next year the prices will come down. They will have to, for the U.S. dressmakers bought little and the season has been a flat failure. It's a good lesson for them because the prices were abnormal. Callot asked me 4200.00 francs for a morning dress and coat with a rat skin collar! I didn't get it. I went to a place where only French go and got a dress for 800 and the evening velvet for 1800, which is a difference. All the big houses lost their heads this autumn.

Well, we had a good laugh last night. Bertha and Potter got talking Art History, and I wish you could have heard it! Potter had a photo of Pallas Athena and couldn't remember her name or what she represented. Bertha was very disdainful. "Can't you think? Why, you silly, she was the goddess de wisdom!" French aristocracy and language getting the best of her, then she said, "I don't think you know much about Art Histrophy!" Potter was trying to tell me what the picture of Satyr was. "It's a forne, you know, a kind of a deer!" and then, "He's Augusta, the King of Rome!" with great triumph. "Oh, I don't think much of him," said Bertha. "Why, I think he's terrible. He hasn't got any clothes

The Palmer children with the Cantacuzène children. The Palmers' house on the Rue Cortambert.

on!" Gales of laughter. Bertha has acquired a very French manner and speaks with great emphasis and waves her hands and eyes and she cares nothing for either Potter's or Gordy's jeering and says, "Oh! You're silly." Min is simply fascinated and looks at her as if she were something weird. Gordy is learning French and has an excellent accent. He is as nice and fat and cozy as ever. The baby is amusing and very pretty and talks a great deal. Anna, of course, thinks her peerless.

Julia's article came, and we enjoyed it very much. N.K. wrote that he was enthusiastic. Min is interested, as he says he finds that their point of view about the same event was so different! Father also sent us a copy. I hope that we get the 2nd article.

Well, goodbye for the minute. We will be at home before long! Won't it be nice to see you all again, though!

Love,

Pauline

Lago di Como - Villa Serbelloni - Giardino.

Notes

April 30, 1920: The two Mikes would be Michel Cantacuzène and his son.

May 3, 1920: When Pauline says that "every picture of a baby my baby sees she calls Constance," she is referring to Katherine Shepard's new baby, Constance, born in 1919.

May 23, 1920: Deering who has a villa in Neuilly is Deering McCormick.

June 9, 1920: Kay's farm is a property that the Shepard family owns near St. Paul.

June 15, 1920: On the Republican Convention: the Republican ticket was Harding for President and Coolidge for Vice President.

The Hutchinson Ryerson group are important persons associated with the Art Institute: Martin Ryerson and his wife, who were often in Europe collecting art, and Mr. and Mrs. Charles Hutchinson.

June 28, 1920: Fanny who is mentioned in this letter and those following is Fanny Brown Keith, sister of Grace Palmer. Another sister is Sara Brown Field, wife of Stanley Field.

July 11, 1920: Honoré and [Potter] D'orsay are Grace and Cappy Palmer's sons, ages twelve and fifteen. Ochs is Adolph Ochs, a newspaper man and business associate of Herman Kohlsaat's. He had been owner and publisher of the New York Times since 1896, and he also owned the Chattanooga Times.

August 9, 1920: Pauline's listing of doctors may have been to placate her mother, who believes in Christian Science.

September 19, 1920: Ellen is Pauline's cook.

Mrs Herman Kohlsaat
Biltmore Hotel
New York N.Y.

"Life isn't long enough to gloom over things,
and all one gets out of it is the glooming.
It isn't easy, not a bit, not to, but still you are better
off in the end if you don't."

9

Sarasota and Chicago, 1920-21

In the late fall of 1920 the family is again in Sarasota, where Pauline, Min, and the children celebrate Christmas and stay until the following April. This is the first series of letters from Florida since the death of Bertha Palmer. They are living at the Oaks, Bertha's fabulous house in Osprey.

Pauline's reactions to being in the South range from feeling gloomy to liking the relaxed atmosphere. At one point she says that she and Min are "soggy," and there is a languid feeling that comes over her from time to time in this tropical climate. We sense a lethargy and a state of unease that prompts her to stay in close touch by letter with her mother. At one point she tells her mother that she would like to go to France to help with the reconstruction. This would be good for the children too, she says, as it would "finish their French" and "polish them off."

Pauline's response to seeing family members is mixed. Apparently they are not all very good company, and she calls some "a restless, unthinking lot." There were many Honorés to visit with: Min's great aunt Laura; Bertha Honoré Palmer's sister, Aunt Ida Grant; and Cousin Julia Cantacuzène and her daughters, Ida and Bertha. Julia's son, Mike Cantacuzène, is in town for the holidays with his fiancée, Clarissa Curtis.

The first few letters anticipate Christmas Day and then describe in detail visiting family at the Acacias and the Christmas presents received. Following the holiday celebrations, Pauline, Min and the family settle down in their new Florida home for the winter months. Pauline writes often about how self-sufficient the household is—they have cows to supply them with milk and an abundance of chickens, eggs, and vegetables. The children are content there. Bertha and Potter are getting old enough to do more on their own—Potter is twelve and Bertha ten. They ride their bikes, go to movies, and Pauline has many humorous stories to tell regarding the children's interaction with each other.

Pauline again shows her two sides—she is content in the country, but she misses the excitement of the city. "I feel as if I were getting back to myself again and take an interest in the things I used to like. I have a comfortable feeling of having washed the slate clean and beginning again, which I suppose will disappear as soon as we get back to Chicago and I get into the thick of it again. It is a great feeling to have nothing more on your mind than young turkeys and clearing away shrubs to making charming vistas!" In the same letter, Pauline grows nostalgic for life in Paris, where "the bed was more comfortable, there was more interesting news, and the lunch was apt to be more exciting."

There is more talk of dividing up the possessions from Bertha's London house. Pauline has decided that if she and Min pretend not to want something, her brother- and sister-in-law won't want it either. By this strategy, they eventually manage to obtain Bertha's house at Osprey Point, the Oaks, as well as the Palmer Castle in Chicago.

The last three letters are from Chicago to Mrs. Kohlsaat in New York. Pauline and Min are busy sorting French furniture at 1350, and there is talk of buying the Castle from Cappy. Pauline is involved with upcoming exhibits at the Art Insti-

tute. Paintings from the Palmer Castle are being shown, as well as a selection of Pauline and Min's engravings. Pauline is also trying to resolve summer plans. She offers encouragement to her father regarding his newspaper articles, and there are hints that Mr. Kohlsaat's affairs are precarious. As she often keeps her personal thoughts to herself, the reader wonders whether she is truly content or if she is hiding distressing feelings. She is clearly concerned about her father's business problems. At one point she makes a comment that shows she has learned well how "big things" are decided: "All the big things that go on are based on such small things, or so easily accomplished that they look complicated to those outside. Even the greatest inventions are simple after you learn how they have been made. And one wonders why they weren't thought of before!"

Pauline gives interesting advice to her mother about her social life in Chicago, and she defines her philosophy on life: "I find that to live in comfort and at peace in this world, one must shut up within oneself all the little feelings we have of a personal nature, only allowing those to get out that are of a social order. It saves lots of worry and bother….Call it my experiment!"

Top: "Potter 1921 Sarasota." Bottom: "Pauline 1921 Sarasota." Opposite, top: "Roger, Pauline and Kay." Opposite, bottom: "Pauline (at right), Kay, Fanny, Bertha C., Mike—1921 Crescent Beach" on Siesta Key. Page 193, Top: Potter (at right) and other boys fishing in later year. Bottom: Young Pauline and Bertha (at left), and other girls in Sarasota.

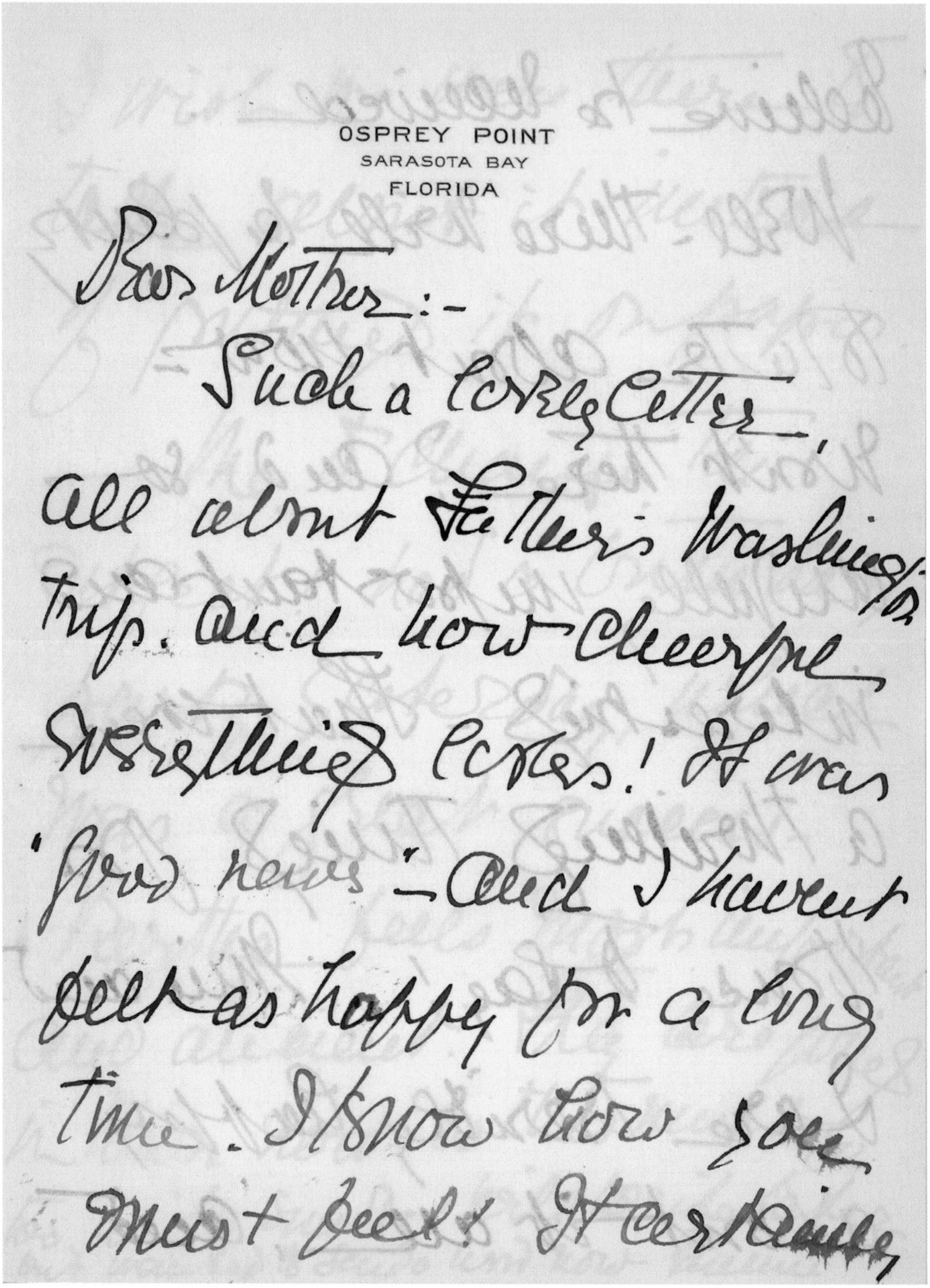

OSPREY POINT
SARASOTA BAY
FLORIDA

Dear Mother :-

Such a lovely letter —
all about Father's Washington
trip. And how cheerful
everything looks! It was
'good news' — And I haven't
felt as happy for a long
time. I know how you
must feel. It certainly

Sarasota Bay
Osprey, Florida
December 20, 1920

Mrs. Herman Kohlsaat
Biltmore Hotel
New York, New York

Dear Mother:

Well, here we are again! It is lovely and in very good order. The weather is soft and warm, and the children—well, they are in seventh heaven! The new addition is very satisfactory. Of course, there is still a good deal to do before everything is just right: shelves for bathrooms, soap dishes, etc. It won't take long, however. We had a good car coming down that brought us all the way from Chi. to Sarasota, so there was no changing at Jax. or Turkey Creek. We got off at Parrish and motored down the rest of the way. The train was late, as usual! And the servants got here about 11:15. By that time we had stopped off at the Acacias to say hello, had gotten our supper here and were in bed. Everybody is happy except Mlle., who apparently expected a Versailles and is bitterly disappointed. Somehow, no one cares if she is!

The family at the Acacias are all well. Aunt Laura looks very frail and old but seems still full of pep. Mike looks very well, also Bertha and Ida and Aunt Ida. Julia looks tired and nervous. We all go there Christmas Eve, and then they come here Xmas Day. I hope they don't expect too much, for my last week at home was busy, and it is difficult to bring Xmas tree things down here!

Your telegram about coming with Kay arrived just as I was leaving. Aren't you a dear to think of that! I only meant in my letter that you might think it strange if Kay was with you in N.Y. and leaving to come down here, that nothing had been said about your coming, too! You are to come whenever it is most convenient for you and stay as long as you can. I imagine you will be entirely guided by your trip to Naples in March!? Knowing you, I think you would like to be in N.Y. a week, at least, before the boat sails, in order to catch it? I am mean, but dare do it as I am so far away.

Try to bring Father down with you. I think he could stand it for a few days. He can have his own bath and coffee at 7:30 and everything just as he likes it. It would do him good.

Much love to you both, and see you both soon.

Pauline

Sarasota Bay
Osprey Point, Florida
December 27, 1920

Mrs. Herman Kohlsaat
Biltmore Hotel
New York, New York

Dear Mother:

As Polly would say, "You're a bad girl!" to send us the delicious candy. I have eaten a great deal, and the pounds are just rolling on. As for my Hostess Book, it is fine and will save me no end of trouble. I have tried keeping my invitations and a list of engagements as a record for indebtedness and have found it very clumsy, so this is a very welcome book. Mike gave me a "daily reminder," so I feel the family is concerned for my lack of system, etc.!

We had a lovely Xmas. Aunt Ida had all of her family, including Mike's fiancée. The fiancée, by the way, is a dear, and has made friends with all the family. On Friday, we went to the Acacias for a tree and their presents at 3:30, and we all stayed to supper—even the baby and Anna. Bertha and Potter stayed until 9:30, and we had a beautiful day. Aunt Ida gave Bertha a ring with three turquoises in a row, and she is as pleased as punch. Her gold chain is satisfactory! and her desk set. Julia gave her an ivory mirror, brush, comb, and tray with some pink and blue flowers painted in the center of each, and that is also satisfactory. Altogether, Bertha is quite puffy about Xmas! Potter got a Smith Engine for his bicycle and money for a dog, and a pair of silver brushes, among other things. Mike gave him a fine fishing rod. Gordy got a bicycle and a wagon and a circus and silver brushes and a stone from Julia. So he is satisfied. Min gave me the earrings! Kept it a secret all this time! I am so excited about them that I can hardly wait to get them. They are at Tiffany's, and we are expecting to go to Chicago by way of N.Y., so you may see us next week! Potter gave me a silver pencil. Bertha a calendar, Gordy a pack of cards and Baby a picture frame with hers and Gordy's picture in it. On Christmas Day, they all came down here for lunch, which we had in the living room, it being too cold on the porch. We had a tree first, which was a great success, then lunch, another success, and then we walked over the place in the P.M. and sat around. The three middle ones went off in the boat to Sarasota. They all stayed to supper and went home about nine. It was a lovely two days and very happy. I was afraid it would be a little gloomy, but it wasn't.

Yesterday we took Julia and Mike out in the boat and had supper with Aunt Ida at a new restaurant in town. Tomorrow we go to Myakka for the day, and on Thursday to Venice for lunch, and come back on the Gulf. We find the boat very fine this year and have a special man to run it. The Shepards are arriving Jan. 1st, a change in date, but I imagine that it may be on account of Roger. Kay didn't say so, but she may think it best for him to come down here instead of staying in the cold of St. Paul. It is lovely here, and the shooting is fine. The new house for the maids has extra rooms in it. So Kay's maids can stay there and have their own baths. We are going north either the 3rd or the 4th, so we will be here for a day with them, at least.

After lunch.

A long letter from you about your trip to Boston and Grandpa's illness. It sounds alarming, but I must say that anyone who can sign his name as he does at the end of his P.S. must have pretty strong heart action! It's really just on account of his age that one is upset. As he says, he probably will live on for a year, at least. It is, however, enough to kill him to expect it at any minute.

Clarissa has asked Bertha Palmer to be a bridesmaid at her wedding in June! Bertha and Ida! and as you can imagine, excitement is running high! So we can't go abroad until July, unless they change their plans and are married in the Autumn.

You will be amused to hear that only poinsettias are growing in the Blue Garden! Our other flower garden is fairly good, but red predominates. Well, goodbye. Write when you have time. I imagine that you are pretty busy and hope that it is great fun.

Love from all,

Pauline

Immokalee
Sarasota, Florida
February 2, 1921

Mrs. Herman Kohlsaat
844 Lincoln Parkway
Chicago, Illinois

Dear Mother:

Every paper that comes brings news of a fresh blizzard! Chicago must be completely covered by this time. Have you enough coal? And do you keep warm? Our temperature is between 78 and 80 every day, with a cool breeze and plenty of sunshine. If we hadn't had our taste of the snow we would find it impossible to picture just what you are going through. Min says that we had enough to make it an interesting experience, that more of it would become monotonous.

I am waiting to hear whether or not Kay and Roger are sitting in a snow bank at 63rd Street! We are going to lunch on the beach tomorrow. All the family is invited, and I expect that we will have a very nice party. The shelter that James built us has been taken to pieces gradually by people who needed lumber! So we are mending it this P.M., putting up the table and seats again, and patching the holes in the roof.

Our great excitement today is the arrival of a cow from Tampa! We have been scouring the country for a few quarts each day and filling out with evaporated cream and condensed milk. Another cow comes on Monday, so we should swim in milk next week.

Aunt Laura sent her love to you the other day and hopes that you'll come down soon, as she always likes to see you. Gunhill finds that the acoustics of the pantry are very good, so she is exercising her voice quite vigorously. It sounds very pretty to the jingle of silver. We are living very much off the place, chickens, eggs, vegetables all in abundance. Besides supplying everyone here, and Cappy at Tampa, I think we could send some in town. Potter is doing well in his lessons and improving very much in his writing. Bertha, also. Min goes off on Tuesday the 6th with Cappy for Shreveport, to be gone about 12 days—three there, six to stay, and three back. I hope that you are coming soon.

Much love, Pauline

I am feeling more rested today and very much better.

Sarasota, Florida
March 23, 1921

Mrs. Herman Kohlsaat
Biltmore Hotel
New York, New York

Dear Mother:

We continue along monotonously down here. It suits Min and me perfectly, but I don't know about Hope. However, the rest is doing him good. He goes either tomorrow or Saturday, depending on a telegram from Ellen saying she is in Mississippi. He is awfully nice but extremely difficult for me to get along with. Min, too, who makes a terrible effort to be polite and jolly, but knowing Min, I see the great strain! The children like him, but he doesn't draw them as Father or Roger. They like him, but they won't miss him.

Mr. Conrad came over yesterday to see the roses and was quite impressed—thought that they were doing wonderfully. The beds in front of the pond were full of flowers just for the occasion! and were very pretty. The pampas grass at the North Gate is planted, and it looks prosperous again. No cows this time! If I can get the chicken yard to operate as well, I shall feel satisfied. The roosters came yesterday, and I am going out to see them today. We had guinea fowl for dinner last night, and they were deliciously tender. One couldn't imagine a harsh squak coming from so perfect a bird! I suppose that I shall have to get some new guinea husbands! That little thought hadn't occurred to me!

It is lovely and cool, a breeze from the N.E. It's only 10 A.M., and I am up and dressed! Quite unusual for me.

We are now thinking of spending the summer in England, taking a house somewhere for the children and then touring about ourselves and perhaps going over to France through Normandy and Brittany to Paris, Reeves and Potter taking a bicycle trip somewhere. Of course, it depends on how good a governess I can get for Bertha, who will take Gordy while Reeves is away. I hope to emancipate him from Anna, but he isn't old enough for a bicycle trip. London sightseeing would be alright for him. We were figuring that there are five more weeks of our stay in Florida, if the weather permits, and Potter nearly wept. He refuses to go North! I wish you were here to go to walk with me now. It's just cool enough to exercise!

P.

Sarasota, Florida
March 24, 1921

Mrs. Herman Kohlsaat
Biltmore Hotel
New York, New York

Dear Mother:

I hope that you are not suffering from the great heat in New York that we read about in the paper. It must be terribly oppressive, it being so out-of-season.

Hope left this A.M. on the Atlantic Coast Line from Bradentown at 10:45. It took about an hour to drive up there—a very comfortable way to go if one doesn't want to spend the day at Jacksonville but takes the train to Chicago at 10 P.M. He said that he enjoyed his visit, but I am sure it was awfully dull for him after you left. Min and I are not a frisky pair! Nor does he liven up much, so we were a quiet bunch all the time. The children are having vacation. Potter caught 30 sheep head this morning and feels the day has been a success. Bertha and Gordy ride their bicycles all day and are thrilled. Gordy had a cunning letter from Blake this A.M., which he was very much delighted to get, and remarked that he thought that he wrote a better hand than Blake! Kay sent me a nice letter and told about some very pretty dresses she ordered. But she has probably written you all about them.

We are building a bathing house for the servants at the beach and a new room and bath in the Hill Cottage for Kay next winter. The roses are blooming in great style, and the whole place looks lovely. Potter has decided to stay until June 18—when we go to Nahant!—in order to have harpoon fishing.

Love to you both,

Pauline

Sarasota, Florida
March 27, 1921

Mrs. Herman Kohlsaat
Biltmore Hotel
New York, New York

Dear Mother:

Here are the first batch of Kodaks—very amusing?

My bathing suit came and fits me like the paper on the wall! It's too bad that I must put a skirt over it, as I would be such a success without it! It is just what I wanted and was afraid didn't exist. Also two pairs of stockings came from Wanamakers, just in the knick of time. I have none left. Thank you for taking so much trouble and doing it all so well.

Everything is going on quietly. The turkeys are hatching out in fine style: 40 now. I only hope that she can keep them going during the rainy season. We look in the Times every day for Father's article. Tell him to have a heart!

Well, goodbye for the moment. Much love,

Pauline

Sarasota, Florida
March 30, 1921

Mrs. Herman Kohlsaat
Biltmore Hotel
New York, New York

Dear Mother:

A nice letter from you yesterday, telling of your visiting the different exhibits with Mrs. Clark. It sounded very interesting. I don't know how I'd be now in a gallery. I've been like a squirrel in a cage for so long that I don't think I could sit quietly and enjoy anything without feeling that I was losing time and something ought to be going round. Four more weeks of Florida ought to help settle me, though!

It sounds as if you were feeling quite snappy and as if Mrs. Clark were glad to have you back. Tell Father that we think (or rather I should say "Min thinks," as it is what he said when I told him what you wrote about Father's difficulty in writing his articles)—he said it was something that people wanted. They know a lot of names superficially, but they don't know about them or where to place them or exactly what they have done, and that someone writing and explaining would fill in a big gap. Perhaps he will try now that you are there to help. It takes two to do things, I find. Whichever one is doing it, the other must act as a sort of mental clearinghouse.

Potter went fishing for gruppa the other morning, found the king fish out, got busy, and caught 89 pounds of king fish! He and Reeves were thrilled. He now has a new rifle, and they are practicing with it. We went to Immokalee Beach with Grace the other day, and Gordy got into the thick of a polo game and had the time of his life. He chewed gum violently and said that it helped him to swim! He finally swallowed it—it got all mixed up with a caramel Fannie gave him—and went down! He has gone into the movies this P.M, as he gave up going the other night when Potter and Bertha went. We are having the others in for dinner tonight. I don't know just why—they are a restless unthinking lot. Mike is coming, so that helps.

We have 50 young turkeys and five more turkey hens sitting. Their nests are very interesting. They have made them in the bushes anywhere and sit on them three days, then get off for food, to return again! It seems more than human in a way. You find the nests by following the birds after they've had food and go back to their nests. One has laid near the vegetable garden and always returns by the shore road in front of Kay's house!

All, or rather three, vanloads of the French furniture are in Chicago, and Min, I know, is itching to get up to it to take a peek. It will be another month, though, I hope before we get back. It will be great fun to open it up and see what came. I don't know what we'll do with it, as we have enough furniture at 1050. Of course, there is a white bedroom set, which we are putting in Bertha's room to make it attractive. And then there is china and silver and linen. We will have a lot to do when we get home, and not much time to do it in either.

We have had some rain—the cistern and tanks are full—so life is easier. Ellen burned her ankle with lard and is having a bad time. I am sorry that I didn't know it before I asked the crowd for tonight. She is uncomfortable with it.

This is a long scrawl. Hope you can read it. Thanks for the Easter telegram, glad mine got there. Much love to you both from all,

Pauline

Sarasota, Florida
April 3, 1921

Dear Mother:

Such a lovely letter, all about Father's Washington trip, and how cheerful everything looks! It was "good news," and I haven't felt as happy for a long time. I know how you must feel! It certainly is "a grand and glorious feeling." And it all sounds as if it had so much future. Something to work on. Father's letter sounded so cheerful and active and not so depressed at the thought of being 68! I sent him a telegram, by the way, which I don't believe he received. Well, there will be plenty to talk about, now, won't there? And so awfully important and interesting. That was a thrilling thing for House to say! Min and I are terribly happy about it all, and I wish we were there to talk about it instead of putting in on paper.

We, to change the subject!, had a birthday party yesterday, which was a great success. Bertha feels most important and ancient! They are going in town now, so this must go too, as it's Sunday! Will write later on, but wanted to send a word now.

Pauline

Sarasota, Florida
April 5, 1921

Mrs. Herman Kohlsaat
Biltmore Hotel
New York, New York

Dear Mother:

I am taking a day off in bed and feel very quiet and rested. It is a little warm in here in the middle of the day, but then I can always go out onto the balcony if it gets unbearable. It is fairly summer weather—cool at night, early in the A.M. until 10, and cool again at 6:30. Very comfortable. We take life easily, Min and I principally sogging. The children are still enthusiastic, and Potter plans to stay until June! It might not be such a bad plan after all.

Well, our party was a wild and hilarious success, Bertha perfectly satisfied and beaming with joy. Your books just hit the right spot all around, Bertha giving each one their books, and each one much impressed. I don't know if they have thanked you yet, so will do so for them in the meantime. Mlle. exerted herself at the party and kept the victor going for the dancing and went out with them when they played croquet and did all the unpleasant little jobs that make one hesitate to give a party! D'orsay came and Honoré, and they were very nice. D'orsay is very much improved, very tall—six feet, one and a half inches, and very good looking. Not too old to be polite to the family, however, kissing Min and me goodnight and thanking us for his day. They came a little after two, and the boys and tutors went swimming and to Saunders for orange crush (without the tutors). All of the family children including D'orsay took great pleasure in making fun of Honoré at every turn—nice fun, but to the point—all as a joke. I must say that H. took it all very well. "Oh, now step lively H., shake a pound" and pleasant little things of that kind. H. smiled but never "shook a pound!" D'orsay "allows" him to wait on him hand and foot. "Are we ready to start?" says D'orsay. "Very well, then, Honoré, I'll let you get my hat!" And H. hustles off to get it! It's delightful to see the change.

Gordy has now decided to swim and does 40 strokes and dives! All in this last week. Bertha lost a tooth and feels the new one in its place. Potter's hair is burned straw-colored and is as thick as a thatched roof. The Baby is the same and a dear. Oh, I must tell you Gordy has developed a passion for the Bible and how the world was made, so we started to read Genesis. Bertha came in too, and when we got to the creation of Adam Gordy said, "Well, where did Eve come from?" And Bertha said, "Oh, God took the backbone out of Adam and made her!" She is a new woman alright! Gordy said that if Adam and Eve were first made like that, where did they get their clothes? So I told him to wait for the verses where that was explained! He asked a great many interested and interesting questions. But B's remark about Adam's backbone was the high mark of the day.

Today is Tuesday, and the crowd is again here. One would think they would be gone by now, but it isn't so. The Oaks look very pretty, but the flowers are beginning to go. In their place, however, are all kinds of lovely flowering trees—wonderful things—and flowering vines that I have thought dead all winter.

Your letter about Myron Herrick has just come. How exciting. It would be great fun to go to it. Why don't you come too? Of course, he owns Paris. The President is being very clever—or rather, something with more foundation than cleverness—with the way he is going about things. I think the world is perking up a bit now—not only America. The papers seemed thrilled with Hughes' Russian note and with Harding's reply to Germany and his stand on reparations. Anyone who doubts the wisdom of it should go along the battlefront. No country or people should be allowed to do things like that to another country and get away with it. I would make Germany pay to the last farthing—not the amount "she is able." She is buying valuable things rapidly and salting them away for a future date so that she can now say she has no money.

I feel as if I were getting back to myself again and take an interest in the things I used to like. I have a comfortable feeling of having washed the slate clean and beginning again, which I suppose will disappear as soon as we get back to Chicago and I get into the thick of it again. It is a great feeling to have nothing more on your mind than young turkeys and clearing away shrubs to making charming vistas!

I refused the Fortnightly, did I tell you?, and got a letter back asking me to postpone my decision until they could arrange about suspending yours and Milly's invitation, dues, etc. Don't dream of rejoining, unless you want to. I am writing the same to Milly—the official invitation to join is their due to you and to her, and your privilege to throw them down. I wish I had done so in the beginning, but I suppose I was too confused with all that was going on then to see clearly, and then it was too late, without making a huge row, which of all things I want to keep out of. Min dictated my last answer, which was short and cold. I said I would postpone decision for two months.

I would like to go to France for a year and work in the reconstruction over there. It would be terribly interesting. Of course, there's no possibility of doing it, but I'd like to nevertheless. Min would, too. It wouldn't be a bad thing for the children, either, just now. It would finish their French, certainly, and polish them off. I am writing of it just as it comes into my head. So you see how sudden it is! I'd like to do it, anyway.

This long letter in pencil makes me think of the manuscripts I used to send you from Paris when I was in bed—only there the bed was more comfortable, there was more interesting news, and the lunch was apt to be more exciting. All of our furniture is in Chicago now, or practically all, and we would have to take a furnished apartment, but I would love it. Min hasn't heard a word of it! So when I talk of it, it will be news to him.

Cappy came down yesterday to see about dividing the places down here definitely but seemed to know so little about it and to be so vague that they didn't get far, for Min didn't want to show any preference for this place for fear they would then like it and want it. Of course, we would never go to Immokalee, and we would prefer to have all of this to ourselves. But one has to go slow and let them make all suggestions without a hint from us. Isn't it a queer world?

The sky all around looks like a storm, but the sun is shining, and it's hotter in this room. Of course, it's just a little after 12, so naturally it isn't any cooler! We have had plenty of rain, and all the banks are full again. I suppose by this time you are saying, "I do like letters from Pauline, but I do wish I could read them!"

Our love to you both,

Pauline

Sarasota, Florida
April 8, 1921

Mrs. Herman Kohlsaat
Biltmore Hotel
New York, New York

Dear Mother:

Well, I am completely bowled over by all the compliments in your last letter, and I must say that I enjoyed reading them! Thank you very much for telling me. Life down here goes on much the same. The weather is ideal—only warm in the middle of the day—and quite chilly all night. The children had supper on the beach last night. We went to the Ed Keiths, and I think that the children had the best of it! My Scribblers paper is nearly finished. It goes off tomorrow on the night train. I read it to Min, and he thinks it is fairly good, so I suppose it will do. I shall be glad to see the last of it. My bankbook is straightened out, for the first time since last April! And now I have only the Field bill on my mind, and then everything will be finished, and I shall start thinking about closing the house and going north! It has been a beautiful winter, and I, and Min too, have enjoyed it. It isn't necessary to mention the children! They won't even consider the idea of leaving. I don't know just what will be the final arrangement, and I am not worrying about it!

Your telegram came about the registered letter and Annah's book. I am anxious to hear about Ochs when he gets back and that everything is satisfactorily settled. After all, what

Father is doing with the President, House and the Times, is just what goes on all the time, only one doesn't see the inside, and to the world it is, as House puts it to Father, "How powerful you are!" All the big things that go on are based on such small things, or so easily accomplished that they look complicated to those outside. Even the greatest inventions are simple after you learn how they have been made. And one wonders why they weren't thought of before!

Well, I hope a letter comes from you in the mail this A.M. Much love,

Pauline

I hear that Ogden Armour owns the Commodore Hotel and the Manhattan and half the Biltmore! and has lately gone in a deal at Bellair. Is it true? I wish he'd do something at Venice! It would be wonderful.

Sarasota, Florida
April 9, 1921

Mrs. Herman Kohlsaat
The Biltmore Hotel
New York, New York

Dear Mother:

I think you are quite right about the Bliss dinner, and I'd get a lovely summer or spring evening gown, slippers, etc., right away so that you can go out to dinner, too. Don't wait nor hesitate. Go at once. You are very handsome, very much above the average intelligence, and a distinct additive to all parties you go to. Don't worry another minute about it or think of it again. The Mrs. Wellstone idea. Those things hurt terribly but are nine times out of ten done thoughtlessly, and now is the right moment. So be prepared. You are a most distinguished looking person. Everyone thinks so, and when you are out, forget Father belongs to you. Just pretend he is a charming person invited to the dinner and enjoy him as do the other guests. If he puts it over, let him. Don't let him see that he hasn't succeeded in doing so with you. I find that to live in comfort and at peace in this world, one must shut up within oneself all the little feelings we have of a personal nature, only allowing those to get out that are of a social order. It saves lots of worry and bother. Put all those necessary things to my account, dress, shoes, stockings, gloves, etc. Call it my experiment! Life isn't long enough to gloom over things, and all one gets out of it is the glooming. It isn't easy, not a bit, not to, but still you are better off in the end if you don't. I am speaking generally when I say "you." It tires one out, and that's all!

Potter has gone out in the speedboat for a morning's fishing, it being Saturday, thrilled stiff. Min and I go to town, he to have his haircut and I to have my Scribbler paper typed and mailed.

Much love to you, and get into action quick about that dress!

Pauline

Sarasota Bay
Osprey Point, Florida
April 17, 1921

Mrs. Herman Kohlsaat
Biltmore Hotel
New York, New York

Dear Mother:

Such reports as there are in this morning's paper of blizzards and tornadoes up north! Here we are very cozy and not too warm. Really ideal weather. It has threatened to rain all day, but one never knows, as Aunt Laura said, "It may not rain today, but I know it will eventually!" But one does not feel inclined to be patient about it. Everything is so dry and yellowing.

Well, Aunt Laura came to lunch today—much to our great surprise. Aunt Ida and A.C. were coming, and the girls were here. I asked Aunt Laura, and to her surprise, also, she came. She was so gay and chatty and more like her old self than I've seen her for a long time. She upset Woods when he was serving her by saying in a loud tone, "Woods, I've grown very old since you last saw me!" Poor Woods couldn't say, "Yes, Madam!" to that and was really quite confused. He gave her all the things she liked for lunch—hot coffee when the rest of us had iced tea, etc., and she thoroughly enjoyed it. It's the first time that she has been inside the house since before Mrs. Palmer died. We went all over in the motor afterwards, and they kept saying, "Min, I am glad that this place is yours. You and Pauline will keep it up, and it's right for you to be here!" I only hope that they don't carry on about it to Cappy like that, for he will do something terrible to us. We haven't divided up yet but are getting a survey, etc., of the amount of acreage there is here. They will make it as expensive as possible for us—you can be sure of that.

I am expecting a visit from you when you go to St. Paul. Don't forget! We will be in Chicago from the 1st of May until the 31st and are going to Monticello to visit Robert

206

about the 22nd for the weekend. We may go to St. Paul, too, perhaps all together and have a family party. Wouldn't it be fine? But don't forget to stay with us on your way, as long as you can. All of the French things ought to be there by that time, and I am sure you will find it interesting to see them. It will be great fun to show them to you. And also, I think that it will be very nice to have a little visit because probably we won't have another before we go abroad.

Much love to you both,

Pauline

Sarasota Bay
Osprey Point, Florida
April 26, 1921

Mrs. Herman Kohlsaat
Biltmore Hotel
New York, New York

Dear Mother:

The French furniture has arrived, as I wrote you, and we will have to clear that as soon as we get to Chi. It is in bond at 1350, the Custom House having allowed us to store it there, to save an extra moving, etc., which was very agreeable of them, to say the least. And then Min's engravings of early Italian, French, and German masters are to be hung in the A.I. during the first week in May to be the summer exhibit. And he wants to be there then. And then the pictures from 1350 are to be put in a gallery at the A.I., the ones given to the A.I., and he wants to see to that during the 1st week in May. So you see he will be quite busy for a few days after we get back. When the rush is over, I hope we can get off to St. Paul. That ought to be about the 13th, but "who knowth?" Anyway, I think it would be fun if you were there to see all those things, or perhaps you won't care for the confusion, etc.? You come whenever you find it most convenient, and it will be lovely to see you whenever you get there.

As for our plans in the East, don't plan accordingly, for we may change them all, have the children come up later, go direct to Boston. Lord only knows. I am sure we don't! All I know is that the wedding is June 27th, and we sail July 2nd. I told Mlle. yesterday that she would be free to do as she pleased when we got to N.Y., and also I told Annie she could leave. So I feel as if I'd done some work yesterday! Mlle. was a little surprised— Annie, too—as I think they both felt they had a life job! Mlle. has grounded the children very well. I must give her credit for that, but I simply cannot sit at table with her and watch her stuff, nor can I look at her double chin anymore. It grows rounder every day—and, too, she goes walking every night from eight until 10 with Annie, John, and Charlie, and I don't think she keeps her place. Certainly I think they are as good as she (!), but as long as she pretends to be a lady, she should be one 24 hours a day! Just now, I can't tell you how I feel about having too many people and too many possessions! Still, you can't dump everything in the Bay and let it go hang. And I do like all the news, but I hate to be responsible for it.

Bertha is doing beautifully in her music. We are delighted. I think I'm lazy. I wish that music and French, etc., just grew on trees and could be shaken off like fruit and consumed!

My love to you both, and see you soon.

Pauline

Chicago, Illinois
May 8, 1921

Mrs. Herman Kohlsaat
Biltmore Hotel
New York, New York

Dear Mother:

I have had two nice letters from you since I got back, but I haven't been overburdened with them! We saw Min for an hour the afternoon he arrived and thought that he looked awfully well and was very cheerful. He seemed vague about Green Acres, as Kay had not at that date moved up there. I wonder when we will go?
Just now we are in the midst of 1350 and the French things. I must say that it is all going quickly, but it is an enormous job, and such piles of things! Yesterday I spent clearing out the things in my storeroom, the things that last spring I thought that I might like to keep! I am sending Zula and Katherine Tandy some things and distributing the rest around generally. I am seeing daylight ahead with it all, but it's slow work. The weather is simply lovely, cool and very clear, fine for working. Today, Sunday, we are lunching at the Club with the Harry Howards. The Club has a new lease on life. It's very popular. I'll see today just what I think of it and be sure before saying I suspect it of being awfully cheap. We went up last night after dinner, and such an ordinary crowd!

We have called to a woman Evie Field knows in Sandwich for two cottages that Evie took and then gave up for this summer. She took them for her children and then decided that they would like to stay there themselves, so took a large enough home to entertain, etc. The cottages are tiny and right on the sea. The beach is wonderful, if you remember what Annah said about it. So I think everything will be fine if we get the cottages.

I am taking Hannah, as she can fit in for me in so many ways, and if I motor all summer I won't need so much maiding and can leave her with the children. I am so sick of servants and "possessions"! I envy you. It seems so simple and easy.

Much love to you both,

Pauline

1050 Lake Shore Drive
Chicago, Illinois
May 11, 1921

Mrs. Herman Kohlsaat
Biltmore Hotel
New York, New York

Dear Mother:

My pen is so poor that at any minute it may refuse to write another scratch! Well, life seems very hectic here! At any rate, I am keeping off of new committees, which I think shows at least a glimmer of sense. Slowly we are clearing up the mess of furniture at 1350, and equally slowly I am clearing my clothes, etc., here. It's a question what to take abroad. I don't want much luggage, and if I don't use my clothes this summer, they will be much too old-fashioned next winter and next spring. I think I'll give them away. Our etchings are up at the A.I. and look very well. We've never seen them hung before, and I had no idea that we had so many. They stay up all summer. Abram's paintings are being shown there, and I am terribly disappointed in them. They are so green, they make me think of Potter's teeth when they need polishing! I can't think what Abram is up to unless he is just plain crazy. It's a stunt, not art.

The paintings from 1350 are hung and have attracted a crowd. A prime psychological fact is that everyone who goes to see them puts on their best clothes! Isn't that funny?

Muriel McCormick is chairman of a committee of women to raise as many $1000.00 a year guarantors as possible for the opera and gave a large lunch yesterday to start things.

Mary was there. Nancy is giving a tea for her this P.M. In fact, between boosting Mary and running the world, the women here haven't time to call their souls their own. They don't know how to sit still. I long for my Turkey life!

Love,

Pauline

1050 Lake Shore Drive
Chicago, Illinois
May 17, 1921

Mrs. Herman Kohlsaat
Biltmore Hotel
New York, New York

Dear Mother:

The question of 1350 has come up. Cap has signified his desire to sell it, and the price at which he is willing to sell to someone else, and as long as he is willing to sell to anyone, Min thinks he might as well buy it as the next fellow. And if he is going to sell now, Min must buy now! So if he does that, we won't feel much like going abroad. There will be so much to do, moving, etc. I am awfully excited about it, and then, it will be a tremendous amount of care. So you see, I really don't know whether I am standing on my head or my heels, and I feel as if I would never be ready to think clearly again. It will probably be settled in the next two weeks, and in the meantime I must get ready to go abroad, all the time with the feeling that I am working for no use. And then if I don't do it, and we do go abroad, I will be in a fearful mess. So what little brain I have is somewhat addled.

Has Father heard from Ochs yet? I am hoping to hear that everything is satisfactorily settled. Father has done so much for the Times, and Washington, that he ought to get something out of it besides glory. I must say I think that you are having great fun in New York. The life must be exhilarating. Don't you love it all? We are having very queer weather. It has been quite cool—not at all like the middle of May! I have been walking to reduce my size—I weigh 138, isn't it awful?—so have found the weather just right!

Goodbye, and love, Pauline

All this about 1350 is a secret, as Cap would probably refuse to sell if he thought Min wanted it badly.

Notes

December 27, 1920: Clarissa Curtis, Mike Cantacuzene's fiancée, is from Boston, and is a cousin of the Wendell family. She and Mike later settle in Chicago, where they become the center of the Russian expatriate group. Pauline mentions Anna, who is the nanny of young Pauline or "Baby."

Apparently Mabel Kohlsaat visited in February or early March, as Pauline mentions it and there are no letters during this period.

March 23 and 24, 1921: Pauline mentions Hope, a mysterious guest, and how they were all quiet when he was with them. This corroborates what many have said about the two Palmers—that they were very shy, and difficult to talk to.

April 5, 1921: Pauline has refused the Fortnightly Club's invitation. It was Chicago's first prestigious women's club, its goal was to discuss intellectual concepts and its membership included women who were movers and doers.

Myron Herrick was a close friend of Pauline's father. Both were members of McKinley's inner circle and trustees of the trust set up to pay the $130,000 debt McKinley had incurred by his foolish guarantee of promissory notes. Herrick became well known in France while twice U.S. ambassador there.

Pauline is taking sides in the debate about the enormous German reparations the Versailles Treaty required. After the German economy collapsed into runaway inflation in 1923, the United States would lead in reducing German reparations payments.

April 3, 1921: Edward House was a close friend of H. H. Kohlsaat's, although in the 1912 election House was working to elect Wilson and H. H. was working to elect Taft. House became Wilson's closest advisor, particularly during the Versailles Conference negotiations among the Allied heads of state.

April 8, 1921: Pauline mentions her paper for Scribblers, which is another of her clubs. Whatever transaction H. H. was working on with "the President [Harding], House and the Times," it must have been important enough to require approval by Ochs, the publisher.

May 8, 1921: Green Acres is the farm Roger Shepard has bought not far from St. Paul.

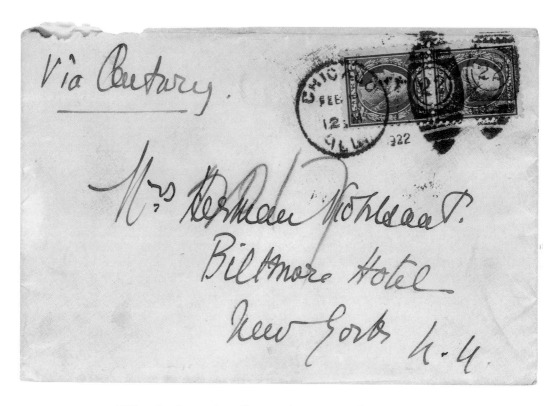

*"The Antiquarian Reception was a huge success.
Even the Martin Ryersons were enthusiastic,
so you know how well it went!"*

10

CHICAGO SOCIAL LIFE, 1922

These late winter letters of 1922 are the first since Min and Pauline are in the Palmer Castle, or "1350." Pauline and Min are making it their own—they are now using it and having great fun. In her first letter Pauline describes men coming to hang tapestries and to "do the gallery." She also describes in great detail several social events, like a "Jungle Ball" given by their friends the Noble Judahs. Everyone except Pauline and Min and the Chauncey McCormicks dresses in costume; there are feather headdresses, tiger skins, "hula girls," and "degenerate behavior!"

Although the Castle was familiar to its new owners, it was an unusual habitat, even for a family of six with a household of servants. It featured several towers, the tallest rising over eighty feet, was constructed of Wisconsin granite and contrasting Ohio sandstone, and occupied eighty-two feet of prime Lake Michigan shoreline at 1350 Lake Shore Drive. Its decoration combined Moorish and East Indian styles. It contained a Flemish Renaissance library, a Louis XV salon, and of course, the enormous gallery where Bertha's impressive art collection had lined the walls in row after row of paintings. Min and Pauline were in the process of carrying out Bertha's desire to transfer large amounts of her art to the Art Institute. They called in architect David Adler to redo some of the rooms, most importantly, the drawing room and the dining room, creating in the former what architectural historian David Lowe calls "a far more chaste English Chippendale style."

We also learn from these letters how, in accordance with an Art Institute exhibit, Pauline, who is president of their Antiquarian Society, gives a lavender and old lace party: "We got up a committee on old lace to ask various people in town to loan their laces and got together a really beautiful exhibition....We used the Egyptian Room just south of our big room for tea....We covered the walls with tapestries and had candlelight."

The Antiquarian Society had been started in 1877 as the Chicago Society of Decorative Art with the purpose of displaying the needlework of women "less fortunate than we." It had been modeled on the Society of Decorative Arts in New York founded by Candace Wheeler, an authority on home decoration, needlework, and design. Its mission was to raise the standard of women's work and create a market for it, and its members ran classes in painting, drawing, and embroidery. Playing as it did on women's creativity and enthusiasm for their own work, the Society was a smashing success from the beginning. Department stores imitated some examples of the handiwork. In 1891 the Society became an affiliate of the Art Institute of Chicago, and in 1894, as historian Celia Hilliard writes, "to underscore its shift in emphasis from amateur handicraft to works of fine art," it changed its name to the Antiquarians of the Art Institute; in 1908 it changed its name again – to The Antiquarian Society of the Art Institute of Chicago.

Now the Society's purpose was "to acquire objects of art to be presented to the Art Institute and to assist through exhibitions and lectures in stimulating interest in the Art Institute." Its members opened the exhibits with festive parties like the one Pauline describes in these letters.

The collections grew in importance, and the Society's events gave its members and friends the opportunity to mix with important artists like Mary Cassatt or English artist and designer Walter Crane. In 1919 Pauline became president, and under her tenure the Society sponsored annual shows displaying pictorial embroideries, glass, English silver, and tapestries. During and after WWI, she organized needlework sales to benefit French widows and orphans.

In accordance with her own taste and the aims of the Society, Pauline bought all kinds of artifacts herself—in 1923, a veil of Brussels lace carrying the imperial Russian coat of arms, worn by the last two czarinas, which she presented to the Society. Many members, like her older associates and friends Mrs. Martin (Carrie) Ryerson and the energetic Mrs. Chauncey J. (Mary Mitchell) Blair, were also impressive collectors. Mary Blair was the sister of Hortense Mitchell, who married Arthur Acton, the English expatriate (and father of Harold Acton) and lived at the Villa La Pietra in Florence. Mary kept an apartment in Paris, where she showed off her collection of "fine furniture, paintings, statuary, and Asian objects d'art." She was often in Italy, where she bought numerous artifacts, including all the Roman silver that was unearthed near the ancient city of Tivoli.

After her first tenure as president, which

Pauline in costume for a 1922 Antiquarian Society event.

lasted eight years, Pauline became president again in 1931 for three years. Celia Hilliard writes, "While she never attempted to match her famous mother-in-law's commanding style, Pauline Palmer won the affectionate respect of members and staff with her quiet grace and her attentive concern for the museum's welfare." Later on, in 1949, the Society opened the Antiquarian Gallery of American Decorative Arts. Gifts of Pauline over the years included *verre de Nevers* glass figures; a panel showing the Crystal Palace; French, Mexican, and American textiles; and Chinese and English needlework. She was continually interested in old needlework.

In her letter of November 17th 1925 Pauline talks about seeing Elsie McCormick, who "was full of her seeing you and her trip to Mrs. Gassettes. Apparently she got in touch with Miss. G. later and is getting some sablée through her." Elsie is Elizabeth Day McCormick, a good friend and Antiquarian Society member; her mother, Mrs. R. Hall McCormick, had been president of the Society from 1885 to 1886. Elsie collected textiles. She eventually amassed some five thousand pieces of priceless textiles including silk dress costumes, many pieces of sablée—shoes, bags, and accessories, which became an important part of the Costume Collection at the Museum of Fine Arts in Boston.

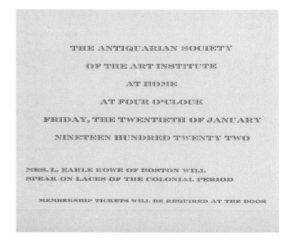

Clockwise from top: "Society Needlewomen pursue the craft at the Art Institute." Left to right: Mrs. Chauncey Borland, Mrs. Barrett Wendell, Mrs. Gustavus F. Swift, and Mrs. Charles H. Schweppe. Invitation to reception for "Laces of the Colonial Period." "Also Fashionably Late," "Two more striking costumes worn by Miss Mabel Linn as a belle of bygone days and Mrs. Howard Linn" at the Antiquarian Society Reception.

Pauline reports that "the collecting fever is flaming within her. She has added to her list of what she collects and is now after 18th-century aprons!"

Also described in detail are the happenings in the life of Edith Rockefeller McCormick. the wife of Harold McCormick, whose father started the McCormick reaper business in the 1850s. Edith is now back in Chicago after spending years in Switzerland. In Zurich she and Harold were analyzed by Carl Jung, and later she became a practicing psychoanalyst herself. Her husband, enamoured of Ganna Walska, a famous but mediocre Polish opera singer, is divorcing Edith, and Edith is frankly "washing her dirty laundry in public," much to Pauline's dismay. Their family problems of divorce, Edith's own suspicious behavior, and their children's entanglements—Muriel is having an affair at nineteen and Fowler is living with his roommate's mother—is shocking Chicago society. Pauline understands that Edith may be acting in a way consistent with a forward-looking, enlightened European manner. "[Edith] thinks whatever she has done with various men is spiritual and pure and far above the passions of ordinary men and women." Pauline feels, however, that the family's behavior "breaks the laws of civilization of the present day." Although Pauline disapproves of Edith's behavior and suggests it is a result of attitudes gained in Switzerland through Jung and his circle, many socialites continued to travel to Zurich to be analyzed by the doctor.

On February 8th Pauline tells her mother of an upcoming trip to New York, where Robert Allerton "is making arrangements for us to see these various Chinese collections, as everything is Chinese now!" Robert Allerton was a great contributor to the Art Institute, a museum trustee and

Victorian Centenary Reception, 1938.
Left to right: Miss Elizabeth McCormick, Mrs. Phillip Miller, and Mrs. James Ward Thorne.

chairman of its Decorative Arts Department. According to Celia Hilliard, he gave legendary parties at the English manor house on his estate in the country, at which guests "(a deftly composed mix of curators, visiting artists, and Chicago society figures) wander[ed] the rooms of this extraordinary treasure house set among the cornfields of the Middle West." Pauline also comments on how Evie Field (a great beauty, and wife of Marshall Field III), who has gotten fat and "lost her looks," is building two houses designed by David Adler. One was a splendid town house in New York, built in 1925, and the other an English country house in Syosset, Long Island, designed in the 1930s. Adler often went to Europe to shop for his clients, as Pauline reports here.

1050 Lake Shore Drive
Chicago, Illinois
January 10, 1922

Mrs. Herman Kohlsaat
Biltmore Hotel
New York, New York

Dear Mother:

Have had several letters from you since I wrote asking if you were ill or what? I was so sorry about the day you felt blue. It's an awful feeling, and we can never believe that the next day we may feel better. Sometimes you feel better for putting it all into a letter, so never hesitate to write me about it. It's splendid news that you are going abroad with Kay on April 8th. Our plans are very vague, and we may not go early as March—and too may not go at all! Min has a lot to do here and wants to finish it all before he goes, so that he can have a good time when he is over there. Much the best plan, I think. I hope that we can all meet somewhere over there, at any rate.

Well, this town is not without excitement! The Judahs gave a dinner the other night before the "Jungle Ball," to which everyone except the Chauncey McCormicks and our-selves went in "jungle costume," and believe me, it was "some jungle." They had their sitting room walls and ceiling covered with green vines, so that it looked like a forest. There were bunches of bananas and coconuts here and there in the green and swinging parrots (in wood) and a Hawaiian band playing sensuous music. Mrs. Judah was dressed in a costume of yellow and red feathers with a wonderful headdress of feathers. Noble was a very handsome sheik. Her brother was a cannibal in a brown union suit and a tiger skin, bear legs, and moccasins, and a wild old wig, his wife as a cannibaless—very pretty. There were 40 guests, pirates, Hula girls, Hindu princesses, [and] missionaries. Prentis Coonly was a marvelous one, with a red wig and goggles, Mary, his wife, in white skirt and waist and helmet. Mrs. Charlie Delvey was a white porcelain goddess—very wonderful—all pearls in headdress and face whitened. Katherine Jones Bennett was a tiger and lay on the floor or crawled around. Mrs. McBirney was a Hula girl, with her hair frizzed in every direction and a straw skirt—no shoes, only brown stockings to match her stained face and arms. When supper was announced everyone was feeling fine, as restraint had been thrown off with conventional dress.

The dining room was another jungle with a wooden table running around three sides and benches, painted, for seats. There was matting on the tables, electric candles stuck in coconuts, tin plates, and tin flat silver. The soup was served in wooden bowls and eaten with wooden spoons. The waiters were cannibals in black tights with a girdle of flowers and necklace of teeth—or plainclothes with wolfs heads on. It was the most carefully thought-out and beautifully done thing you can imagine. The only trouble was their choice of guests, who apparently don't know how to behave and are vulgar and ill-bred. Katherine Jones ate a live goldfish! Everybody kissed and hugged those next [to] them. Mrs. McBirney walked on the tables and fell down in my plate. Young Cyrus McCormick got-tight-along with most of the others and danced amourously all evening with the hostess' sister-in-law. One man and woman leaned across the table and kissed long and lingeringly on the mouth. Alfred Hamill got drunk, and Noble Judah nearly died of worry and distress. His wife was frantic but could do nothing. I sat next to Noble, and she came running up every few minutes and told him some new horror.

All the time the band played and sang. Joseph Ryerson, Annie Laurie, the Ralph Pirlis, the Wrigrannises, I have little opinion left of any one of them. It was a most degenerate party, and although the Judahs did have a lot for them to drink, it was no reason for their behaving like the lowest of the low. Chauncey McCormick said, "Well, Min and I may have seen parties like this before, but not in this kind of company!" A few of us were well-behaved. Prentis Coonly got tight and said funny things but behaved like a gentleman, and Mary was as she always is—quiet and nice. But the majority were awful. I was and am sorry for the Judahs, for they planned and aimed to give a beautiful party, but as Min says, "They are unfortunate in their crowd of friends."

Saturday night we went to Anne Winterbotham's to meet Margaret and Ernest Poole and had a lovely time. Sunday we went to bed early. Cappy came back for a few days, so we are not doing anything until he goes. Thursday Min starts the gallery. Robert and a gang of Art Institute men are coming up to hang tapestries and pictures. Thursday night the Hutchinsons come for dinner and the opera. Friday we go to the Chaun. McCormicks' for dinner, and then we don't do anything until the following Friday. Thursday, I mean.

Bertha is struggling with American History. Last night at dinner she said, "I must remember for my test tomorrow that sentence—'Taxation without presentation is trinity'!" Now, what do you know about that? I finally wrote it out on a bit of paper so that she couldn't forget it! We laughed ourselves sick over it. She certainly gets off some daisies. The funny part was that she knew what the sentence meant—even if she couldn't remember the words! Potter is starting French, much against his better judgement, but he must have it for his exams for St. Mark's. Gordy is plodding along pleasantly and so is the baby. The canaries are making their nest, and Gordy has bought a female bird to do likewise.

I lunched with Sara yesterday. Edith [McCormick] was there, and I must say that she was very simple and very nice. She is on such a high plane that she is able to pass over any disagreeable thing or occurrence which she considers not a part of her "destiny." I think she is quite crazy, but harmlessly so. Min says that either she is or the rest of the world is! I liked her very much. I think she thinks that whatever she has done with various men is spiritual and pure and far above the passions of ordinary men and women and thinks she is doing the right thing. Therefore, it is pure. It may be, who knows? But it's not, according to the laws of civilization of the present day. Her family have all left her—husband, children, father, and brother. I've heard nothing of her sister, and it seems strange that, without reasons, those who know her best and should love her best should desert her when she needs the greatest help. She converses of Harold freely, as if there was no break. I do not know what to make of the whole situation, and I think it is disgusting to a degree to wash one's linen so frankly in public, as she and Harold have done. Stanley and Sara are the next. Stanley is living at the Drake and Sara at the apartment, and I presume everything will be done after Katherine's wedding. I think parents have little thought for their children and the future these days.

I had an Antiquarian meeting today. I think that Mrs. Ryerson and Mrs. Hutchinson are almost at the breaking point. Mrs. Ryerson is under great distress, as she said to me today, "I have not kept up with anything that I should, but such terrible things are on my mind that I can't think of other things." I think she is getting a growth on the iris pupil of her right eye, and she may very naturally be frightfully upset. Martin is not well, and that may worry her a good deal. Anyway, she is suffering from something.

Much love from us all,

Pauline

1350 Lake Shore Drive
Chicago, Illinois
January 23, 1922

Mrs. Herman Kohlsaat
Biltmore Hotel
New York, New York

Dear Mother:

Here's another bed letter! I feel so light and airy with nothing ahead of me except my own pleasure that I hardly know what to do. The Anti Reception was a huge success. Even the Martin Ryersons were enthusiastic, so you know how well it went! We gave a lavender and old lace party. A Mrs. Rowe, whose husband is director of the Providence Museum, came on to speak on old lace form 1650 to 1800. She had slides to illustrate the different kinds. We got up a committee on old lace to ask various people in town to loan their laces and got together a really beautiful exhibition. The Edward Ayers had easily the finest collection, then I gave Mrs. Palmer's, which was 2nd best, then Mrs. M. Ryerson, Edith McCormick, Mrs. Sam Allerton, Miss Drake, the H. McB. Johnstons, and a number of others. The laces were put in cases in the big reception room and in the little room just east of it. There, Mrs. Wilkins of Salem sent on nine complete colonial costumes from the Essex Museum, which were enchanting. Then Mrs. Charlie Schweppe (Laura Shedd) took the job of collecting Georgian silver for the tea table. We used the Egyptian Room just south of our big room for tea. We sent down some of our Sheraton furniture (you remember the things they used at the Uptown Club?). George loaned his beautiful silver crichton. The Frank Logans also, and Ginevra King. So it was a lovely lot, and the room looked very beautiful. We covered the walls with tapestries and had candlelight.

Mrs. M. Ryerson, Miss Hamilton McCormick, Lucy Linn, and Mabel, Marjorie Goodman, Dodo Winterbotham and Bertha Honoré dressed in Early costumes and arranged their hair with ribbons and headdresses, and they all looked simply too lovely. Mrs. McCormick was beautiful. She wore a white wig, put on a mechlin cap with lappets and wore all her pearls. Her gown was of yellow brocade draped with the most beautiful old lace. She was a picture. Mrs. Ryerson was lovely too. I wore that blue and gold brocade Fragonard dress that Jeanne Hallie

Edith Rockefeller McCormick.

made me so many years ago, and on my head, an 18th-century "creation" of organdie with ribbons and flowers that the costume woman at the Institute copied from an old book. I really looked quite fine. All the headdresses and ideas for costumes were taken from books on colonial costumes. Miss Bennett was responsible for the idea of the party and most of the putting it over. The trustees were terribly pleased with the affair, and they nearly all came and stayed until the end! Anne Winterbotham attended to arranging to tea and that room.

The lecturer stayed with us, and we liked her a lot. I found out later that the trustees are trying to get her husband to come out as Assistant Director and Curator of classical art, so nothing could have been more opportune than her visit. She seemed very delighted with everything about the Institute. Robert has opened the large room at the right of the entrance to the A.I., where the casts used to be, as a room of Chinese Art. He has put in Mrs. Calhoun's things. Mrs. Geo. Smith had some of her things in there until she found that they were inferior to the others and then, in a rage, removed them! Miss Buckingham has given the most wonderful bronzes. Florence Crane has loaned Tang figures and Ming

Jades and two huge white porcelain Kwan gins, and Min loaned a lot of Han Jades. And then a man named Marx has loaned some lovely things, and his friend named Schwab has loaned others, so it really is a fine looking lot of cases. Robert has given many statues and carvings and paintings. It's a splendid beginning for a fine collection of Oriental Art. So much for the A.I.!

The town is now ajoy with further McCormick doings. Rue had a talk with Edith and was so overwhelmed with the tragedy of her part in all this that she was completely won over to Edith's side. It seems that Edith told her that the reason Muriel left her was because she, Edith, refused to allow Muriel to receive the attentions of an elderly married man, whom Muriel wished to receive in her sitting room, which adjoins her bedroom, at 12 o'clock at night. Harold allowed it, so Muriel rushed to him. Edith keeps writing Harold how frightful it is and claims Muriel's relations with the married man are not what they should be—a perfect picture of a broken-hearted mother looking on helplessly at her daughter going to the devil. Just about that time I had a talk with Edith, which I think I wrote you about. Just a pleasant chat, during which she was so nice and gentle and simple that I felt very differently towards her and was able to make Min feel so, also. Then when Rue heard this other, it did seem pretty tough on her—Harold planning to marry Walska, Muriel running wild, Fowler living with Fifi Stillman! It all seemed rotten, with Edith as the least rotten. Then Edith said to Ellen Borden, "I would have taken more interest in the concert you gave on the 15th if it hadn't been for Muriel's sexual relations with Muratore!" Ellen was stunned, thinking it so awful, that she kept it to herself. To explain, Muratore asked Muriel to help him with some French charities of his and said that he would sing in a concert and so forth. Muriel asked Ellen to help her, and Ellen said she would if Muriel would give some of the profits to the Illinois Children's Home and Aid. They decided on 50-50.

The concert was wonderful—Muratore Schifra-Galli-Cierci, John Carpenter, playing his songs, and Van Gordon singing them, Prokofieff playing his own things, and the Opera Ballet doing about 10 different things. It was a marvelous lot of stars and a tremendous success, but Edith naturally had nothing to do with it. It was (as I figure it out) an occasion which showed Harold and Muriel's power in the Opera Company, to swing such a thing, and made Edith one of the very lesser lights.

Edith's two subjects for insanity are sex and her will for power and first place in Chicago (why anyone should struggle for the last here!), so she took her revenge by branding Muriel for life. She told six different women that Muriel was having an affair with Muratore, and to Ellen she said "sexual relations"! The six women and one man were Chauncey McCormick, Marion McCormick, Ellen, Amy McCormick (!), Rue, Anne, and Ellen Babcock! So there was no pretense at secrecy there. Rue, of course, had not heard of the other six being taken into Edith's confidence when she left for New York, so she still thinks of her as the broken-hearted mother. But I think she's the vilest of the vile for turning on her own daughter in such a frightful way. Muriel, whether she has done those things or whether she hasn't, will have it hanging over her for the rest of her life, and the child is only 19. Everybody is terribly agitated, as you can imagine. They don't know how far Edith claims Muriel has gone. Ellen Borden has kept silent about her talk with Edith, so no one knows that she actually said that. Edith also told Florence Crane, who told Muriel what Edith was saying. Mrs. Arthur Ryerson was so wrought up over it that she gave Muriel a lunch yesterday to try to show the girl that she had some friends to stand by and help her out. Well, Min and I think that all the McCormicks of the Harold branch are perfectly crazy, and for myself, I don't believe that they care an iota what anyone thinks or feels. They are going to carry their fight to a finish and let the public be damned. We are keeping out of it all as much as we can. And all the sympathy that we felt for Edith has flown! Can you think of a more horrible thing for a mother to do? So much for the McCormicks.

Kay and Roger spent the day here yesterday and went off last night feeling very fine— sure of at least a dozen wild turkeys!

Grace and Cap arrive on the 26th with 17 people from New York and Baltimore for Bertha's dance and Katherine Field's wedding on the 28th. Grace is entertaining at luncheon and dinner every day. She called me on the telephone to order lunch at the Casino on the 26 for 22 people and to ask us to give a dinner and dance on the 28. I refused the dance but offered the dinner. She telegraphed that on second thought, as we weren't settled, she'd give the dinner, too! I think that she is crazy, too. It will certainly be gay here for a few days. Chicago will sit up and take notice, with so much style and chic coming on. I can't help but wonder if they will all come. Grace always makes such elaborate plans, which fall through. Perhaps this is the time they won't, however. Whatever she will do in Chicago with 17 visiting strangers used to N.Y. nightlife, I can't imagine! At least they will get a rest out here. This seems to be another volume!

I am so glad that your rooms look pretty. You always make your rooms pretty anyway, so it is no surprise to me to hear about the success of those you have now. I hope that we can go abroad, but it's so indefinite. I am engaging passage, so that if we can go at the last minute, we will be able to get something. I think it's fine that you are going on the 8th. Won't you have a good time all of you.

I have had a little synus, which Miss Morrison cured very quickly, and I am all well now. The children are all well, except for little colds. They are skating violently. The Baby will thank you for her books, which Roger brought on.

Much love to you both,

Pauline

1350 Lake Shore Drive
Chicago, Illinois
January 30, 1922

Mrs. Herman Kohlsaat
Biltmore Hotel
New York, New York

Dear Grandmother:

I have started to skate, and we have a nice winter. Thank you for the little book that you sent me in the letter. Please send me some funny papers and baby.

Love from Gordon and kisses to you and Grandfather.

Dear Grandmother:

Thank you for the books for my birthday.

Love from xxx

Pauline P.

xxx to Grandfather

1350 Lake Shore Drive
Chicago, Illinois
February 8, 1922

Mrs. Herman Kohlsaat
Biltmore Hotel
New York, New York

Dear Mother:

I suppose that the reason I don't hear from you is because you don't hear from me!? Well, I am sorry for both of us, for our actions, and hope we do better. We are planning to leave for New York a week from today. Min is coming with me for three days. He must get back here, as there is no one in the office to sign checks. Of course, there is no reason why Cappy couldn't come back to give Min a chance, but I suppose it would interfere with his dancing and poker parties! We are "doing" a few museums and collections on Thursday and Friday and leaving for Washington on the midnight Friday to spend Saturday and Sunday A.M. Then Min takes the Penna fast train to get here Monday A.M., and I go to N.Y. to spend a week with you. Won't it be fun? Then perhaps you will come back with me for a visit here? to see the children. Robert Allerton will be in N.Y. all next week until the 18th when he sails and is making arrangements for us to see these various Chinese collections, as everything is Chinese now! It will do Min good to get a whiff of something besides Chicago air for a couple of days. It doesn't seem possible that we are really thinking of going East. I am thrilled! We are planning to sail sometime about the end of April. The house is beginning to shake down into shape. So we are feeling more settled about it. And I hope to have it all arranged before we leave in April. It sounds queer to go away and close it as soon as we get it in order, but it will be already when we get back, and we can open it without any fuss then.

The children's vaccinations have all taken with very little trouble, Potter and Gordy having more trouble than Bertha. Gordy lost his appetite for a day and three pounds in consequence and was so pleased that he hated to get better and gain again! Potter had a little fever, but it didn't amount to much nor interfere with his pleasures by way of movies and theatre. Bertha got a little stiff in her leg, but she didn't mind. I noticed that as soon as the skating was on again that she recovered rapidly! They are a great lot and grow more amusing every day. This morning Potter and I were talking about school next year and his clothes, etc., and he said, "Of course, I will need long pants." I nearly fainted to think of that Baby in long pants!! I spoke to Min about it, and he nearly fainted, too, but said that it would be about time next year, if Potter grew during the summer. I am still breathless about it. He was not very hungry the other evening at dinner, and I mentioned casually that he wasn't eating, and Bertha said in her quiet way, "Oh well, Mother, the lovelorn, you know!" And Potter choked and stammered and helped himself so abundantly to pancakes that a little later when he had recovered he said, "Gosh, how did I ever take so many cakes, I can't eat them!" We had great fun teasing him. It seems sad to have them grow up, but it's bound to happen! Well, I want to get this on the Century, so goodbye.

Love,

Pauline

1350 Lake Shore Drive
Chicago, Illinois
March 7, 1922

Mrs. Herman Kohlsaat
Biltmore Hotel
New York, New York

Dear Mother:

I take it that you arrived safely? And I hope that you didn't catch cold! We have been busy here. The pictures are hung in the gallery and on the stairs so that we look more and more settled. The next move is to put the sofas in the gallery against the walls—and then see what is left in the middle of the room!

A nice letter from you yesterday saying that you had arrived safely and a few things about my health. I am being very quiet, hardly doing a thing really, and Anna told me last night that I was looking better, so it must be true. Min thinks so, also, and says that I am much less nervous. Certainly no cow ever led a quieter life!

Potter got off safely yesterday with every known thing in hand—tennis rackets, bathing suit, gun, and saxophone! He looked like a travelling circus. I don't know who had the broadest grin, Potter, Reeves, or John. It was a joyous party. Potter was a little leery about being homesick but is hoping for the best! Mike is there and A.C., who is here for a few days, will be there shortly, and they both think Potter grand. A.C. will pay him a lot of attention and go out to see him, besides asking him to the "acacias". So will Mike. Cappy will ask him for tennis, and later when Honoré gets there, he will have companionship at times, if he cares for it!

Saturday night we took A.C. and the children to see "The Last Walze." The children were thrilled, shrieked with laughter, and wept at the proper moments. They were better than the show, really. Potter is thrilled with his saxophone and filled the house with its groaning tones. He can play "Old Kentucky Home" and parts of "Swannee River." The latter runs wild occasionally, I am afraid. He took it on the train! Can you imagine the suffering of the other passengers? Gordy is sleeping in Mr. Reeves' room and is delighted about having his own private bathroom! He feels frightfully grown-up. I thought that he might be lonesome in the night, and Anna said, "You have the telephone away from your bed. Don't you want to move it closer in case you want to call me at night?" "Why should I call you?" he asked. Anna didn't want to put the idea of being scared into his head so said calmly, "Oh, well, you might be sick." "Well, if I am," said Gordy, "the first thing I'd do would be to go to the bathroom, not telephone!" And so that settled the matter. He is a case. Bertha is as wild as ever. I am so glad that you saw them all at this stage, for I don't suppose they will ever be quite like it again. They are so amusing and human. Pot-

Top: The Castle in the mid-1920s. Bottom: Gordy and Pauline outside the Castle.

ter and Bertha made out a list of boys and girls for a dancing party when P. gets back. So I have two parties ahead of me. Gordy wants one, too! They ought to be amusing affairs.

Love to both,

Pauline

1350 Lake Shore Drive
Chicago, Illinois
March 8, 1922

Mrs. Herman Kohlsaat
Biltmore Hotel
New York, New York

Dear Mother:

I have just had a wire from Potter saying that he had arrived safely, three hours late! His proofs taken on Saturday came this A.M. and are excellent. It is difficult to choose. There is one that looks like the baby picture that you like so much and then another very fierce and grown up! I think we'll order those two—the first for the family and the other for outsiders. I am having the other children done soon, as they haven't had a photograph for several years. I hope that they are as fine as Potter's.

It is cooly springish today—sunny and hazy. We had a very nice time at Ellen's dinner for Evie last night. Evie has grown very fat and, I think, has lost her looks. She is wildly enthusiastic about her houses and expects to have them finished a year from this summer. The city house, which David is doing, is very nice—really two houses, one on 69th Street for entertaining and the other on 70th for the family. They are connected by a gallery 50 feet long, which opens onto a court 50 x 30. Very unique idea. She thinks David a wonder. Her country house is enormous and really looks on the plan simply awful. It must be at least 300 feet long and about 75 wide. She has 18 servants' rooms, so you can imagine that it will be big. That does not include her maid's room! It is to be like a great English Estate. The house will be Georgian, the entrance one of those great two-storied square halls with the stairs running up two sides, and a gallery above, such as one sees in the books on English houses. She said both houses were absolutely flawless—perfect in every way. And every idea hers. She made a list of just what she wanted and gave it to her architect to put together. I didn't say that it took a pretty smart man to make a harmonious whole, but I thought it. She has 60 percent of the furniture for the townhouse, and David is meeting her abroad this summer to choose the rest. 1350

seemed very comfortable and established when I got home (all this about
the plans she told and showed me at
tea at Barbara Wendell's yesterday)
and all its ugly bits very restful!

Bertha and Gordy went to the dentist
yesterday with no work to be done.
B. had several teeth that were hanging by a single shred removed, and
they had their teeth cleaned. The
dentist told Gordy that he had the
cleanest, whitest teeth that he had
ever seen on a little boy. And Gordy
is now terribly cocky.

I am thrilled about Father's book
and hope everything continues to go
beautifully. Be sure and tell me anything new.

Love,

Pauline

Pauline playing outside the Castle.

Notes

January 10, 1922: Joseph and Annie Laurie Ryerson, mentioned at the Jungle Ball, are of
the Ryerson family who made their fortune in steel.

Pauline again talks of Edith Rockefeller McCormick and how her children are all siding
with her husband, Harold, in their divorce. She also mentions Mrs. Martin Ryerson and
Mrs. Hutchinson, important supporters of the Art Institute. Mrs. Martin Ryerson had
formerly been president of the Antiquarian Society (1908-1909), and Charles Hutchinson
was a founder and president of the Art Institute.

"The children are all so happy and contented
and look so well that we are very happy
and satisfied…It has been quite an experiment…"

OFF TO SCHOOL IN MASSACHUSETTS, FALL 1925

Writing from Bar Harbor, Maine, in the fall of 1925, Pauline describes taking the children to their boarding schools near Boston. Potter, now sixteen, is going to St. Marks School, and Bertha, fourteen, to Concord Academy. Later, Gordy, eleven, goes to Fessenden.

They are in the summer resort of Bar Harbor, where Bertha Palmer had previously summered and where Pauline and Min are looking for a house for the next year. The family has given up Biddeford Pool for this more upscale resort. On Mt. Desert Island off the coast of Maine, Bar Harbor had been the preferred destination for "rusticators" starting in the 1860s and 70s. They were attracted to its dramatic scenery—the mountains rising out of the sea, the rocky coast line, and brilliant golden light—for simple vacations. With the coming of the Gilded Age, Bar Harbor began to imitate Newport on a smaller scale, as large shingle-style houses and Italian villas appeared by green lawns stretching down to Frenchman's Bay. The well-heeled came to spend summers by the sea, bringing their households of many servants with them. Pauline's friends the McCormicks, avoiding the hot months in Chicago, had summered in Bar Harbor since the mid-1890s, "coming on" by train with a railroad car for their horses. Eventually Pauline and Min would buy a big house on the shore, called Hare Forest, which they enjoyed until Min's death in 1943. It burned in the Bar Harbor fire of 1947.

Herman Kohlsaat has died since the last group of letters—almost a year ago, on October 17, 1924—and Pauline is writing on black-bordered writing paper. Her father had gone to Washington to attend the World Series, and was at the home of Secretary of Commerce Herbert Hoover when he was "stricken with paralysis." His funeral was held several days later at Hoover's home. President Calvin Coolidge wrote a note of condolence to Mrs. Kohlsaat:

My dear Mrs. Kohlsaat:
It is with great sorrow that I learned of the passing away of Mr. Kohlsaat. He has been exceedingly kind to me and sympathetic with the efforts that I have been making. I wish to express to you my sincere sympathy, which I know is shared by the circle of friends and admirers which is world wide.
Very cordially yours,
Calvin Coolidge.

In a press conference Coolidge said that H. H. was prominent "for over thirty years in the journalistic life of America," and was acquainted with "prominent persons at home and abroad." Coolidge also paid tribute to his "judgment and influence in molding public opinion and directing public policy," a reference to his role as unofficial but intimate advisor to Republican presidents. H. H.'s book, *From McKinley to Harding: Personal Recollections of Our Presidents*, which contained humorous anecdotes about his political friendships, had come out in 1923.

Mabel Kohlsaat, who has been left with little money after her husband's death, recorded her sadness in a diary. She was a devout Christian Scientist, believing that physical ailments should be treated not by doctors but by practitioners who were specially trained for healing patients. She seemed to have also believed in Spiritualism, a movement that had become popular in England and America in the second half of the nineteenth century and reached its peak in England after the Great War. Believers sought to communicate with friends and family who had died. Seances were held when bereft parents tried to make contact with their dead soldier sons.

Mabel describes speaking now with her long-gone Blake ancestors who tell her "we have watched you all your life and in everything you have helped him"—presumably her husband, Herman Kohlsaat. Mrs. Palmer (who died in 1918) also appears to her. She is "very handsome and handsomely dressed in dark blue or purple with shiny things on part of [a] waist." Mabel sees her beautiful "chiseled" profile.

In her diary she also describes trips to France with her two daughters' families and visits to beautiful places in Italy, where she now lives part-time. She not only loves it, but can better afford life there, and has written Pauline about the changes for the better under Mussolini. (The subject of Mussolini is clearly controversial and of great interest to Pauline.)

Pauline is solicitous about her mother's using the family car, a fancy Hispano Suiza, and their chauffeur in Europe, and comments on her mother's penchant for action and the two-sided nature of human behavior. "If it weren't for that energetic get-up-and-go self of yours, there would not be all done in the world that has been done." She feels that "we all have the two parts and are often so chicken-hearted that we listen to the one that sits by and looks on, and then when the time for action is gone by, wish we could murder that self, as it has made us miss so many fine things that we wanted to do and could have done."

Pauline then writes from Chicago, giving a sense of the city's social life. She observes the behavior of Chicagoans in their social rituals. Commenting on an upcoming wedding, she writes: "it's a thoroughly splendid match, but not a brilliant worldly one. The Smith clan at the wedding came with the idea of looking the family over and deciding whether or not they would do, without the slightest idea that the family might be doing the same by them! As everybody approved of everybody else, it was OK. But I am sure that if they hadn't approved, they would have let Bertha's family know it!" Min is busy with the new Palmer House, which is being rebuilt on the original site. Pauline is seeing family and friends and overseeing young Pauline, now eight, who, with her siblings away, is enjoying her "single blessedness."

The Palmers go to Concord again for a stay to see the children at Thanksgiving. Pauline is very happy with the way Bertha is taking to her new school, having fun with her friends and liking her new room. The descriptions of Gordy at Fessenden School are also positive. Potter seems less successful than the others, as his mother writes: "Min has just brought Potter's marks—out of a Form of 35 he stands 32. He has been playing football very hard all autumn, so that may account for his awful standing." Although she delights in the children's progress, the detailed descriptions of their well being and their new lives at school suggest her "empty nest" anxiety. As Pauline's life has always centered on her children, it is natural that she feels the separation keenly.

At the end of the trip east Min and Pauline go to New York and shop for interesting objects, and Pauline looks for early-American furniture for an exhibit at the Art Institute. In these last letters from Chicago, there are mentions of the Palmers taking the Century, or Twentieth Century Limited—the luxurious train that brought travelers round trip between Chicago and New York. When its passengers arrived in New York, a red carpet was rolled out, and the conductor brushed off their coats.

Herman Kohlsaat's mock coat-of-arms: loaf of bread marks his bakery days. Paper delivery boy—his early career.

Bar Harbor, Maine
September 18, 1925

Mrs. Herman Kohlsaat
Hotel de Russie
Rome, Italy

Dear Mother:

This it the only pad paper that I have, and as I am in bed, I hope you don't mind my using it. Your letter came last night telling about the trip to Italy, and I just about passed away with envy. Min did, too. We think it's fine to use the Hispano, and I sent you a cable this A.M. to use it as long as you like. Min was pleased to think you'd liked it and Daniel enough to want to continue with it and him. He said to tell you that you'd better clinch Daniel because Bob McGaine is on his trail to "change" for him. Min was irritated about Bob because when Min told him that the wages were 1500 a month, Bob said "ridiculously low," and as that is 700 francs more than a chauffeur in Paris gets, and Daniel set

Mrs. R. H. McCormick

his own price, Min hated to give the address but had to, as Bob pinned him down. So he hopes you'll get hold of Daniel before Bob does, and don't spoil him as to wages! I hope that he asks you for less than us. We used to pay 1000, until Cappy gave him 1500, so we had to raise our price. If you go to Naples by motor, insist upon the shore road, as the inland road to Naples is the most awful road we ever went over. Min said to either go by train or the shore (which is rough, but beautiful and full of interest). Take someone with you, Elsie perhaps. I'm sure she'd love it. Or a St. Pauler, not for any reason except that you might get lonely on a hilltop! In Siena, go to the Pensione Santo Caterina, which is better than the hotels. In Rome, the Thorndykes, who were there three months last winter, went to the Windsor Hotel on the Via Veneto, I suppose because it was high up, or isn't it? Well, I wish I were going to be there, too!!!!!!!! I certainly do. Daniel is grand in Italy and speaks a little Italian and likes the coffee! Well, well, such is life.

Mrs. Fabbri turned down our offer as "inadequate." I, for one, am glad she did, because it meant lots of work for me and lots of responsibility for Min. So we are going to rent something else and let others do the worrying. I don't know just what as yet, but we are thinking of several places.

Such a joke on us, we gave up all invitations to dine this week to stay home with B. and P., and they've gone out every minute! Even Gordy has gone three times, and we've just sat here! They have had the best time, though, and are as happy as the day is long. The summer has been a howling success! I am afraid that Potter is going around with a very second-rate crowd, but then, he enjoys it. The others don't ask him any more. He is so rude to them. I am sorry, but perhaps he'll wake up to the fact later. Bertha's crowd is all that there is here of her age. Gordy, too. Baby won't play with anyone but the Barret child, so has no circle of friends. I am hoping that in a house next year she can invite friends and play with them. She can't invite anyone here without giving a party. I think that we are making a nice group, quite a varied one, but awfully nice, and we'll enjoy it.

Today we lunched at the Fennos and played bridge and had a very good time. They rent a lovely house that everyone thinks belongs to Mrs. Adrian Iselin, but she is very secretive about it, so no one knows. The Blairs were there, the Endicotts, the Robbins, who are cousins of Eleanor's, Eleanor, and a Mr. Putnam, Mr. Cotton, and ourselves. Eight of us played bridge afterwards, and it was amusing.

Well, it's still raining, coming down in torrents. Doesn't promise well for our trip tomorrow. I simply cannot believe that tomorrow Bertha starts on her new life! She will begin to grow up. And the old Gordy—I can't get used to the idea, and much less will I be used to the fact. But they both are thrilled about going and hate to leave Bar Harbor, no word about us!

Best love, and have a fun time with the Hispano, Pauline

Bar Harbor, Maine
September 23, 1925

Mrs. Herman Kohlsaat
Hotel de Russie
Rome, Italy

Dear Mother:

I have not written for several days, as we took the children to Boston to put them in school, and it was somewhat strenuous, and I did not have a chance to write. Now I am back. Min

Opposite top: Bar Harbor Village Green, 1920.
Bottom: Bar Harbor seen from Bar Island, at the turn of the twentieth century.
Above: "Hare Forest" built in 1899-1900, purchased by Potter Palmer II in 1926. "Hare Forest" which was on Schooner Head Road had a wonderful ocean view. It burned in the fire of 1947.

had to go on to N.Y. for the day to meet Hollis and comes here tomorrow noon. We motored down, spending the night at Biddeford. Cornelia gave us her house! We had a good trip down and arrived about seven P.M. daylight savings time. Cornelia is very well and was all excited about Howard's going to St. Mark's. We had a cocktail at Fanny's the next day and lunched at Mrs. C. Brown's and left about three P.M. for Boston. Had a good run and arrived about eight P.M. Next morning we shopped, etc., and Potter left for school. He felt very badly and looked a little weepy and actually kissed Bertha goodbye, so you can see how badly off he was! He didn't want us to go with him, so we said goodbye at the station. I am sorry to have him go, but this summer has been a hard one, and to know that he can't go out nights is a great comfort. Of course, he behaves himself, but he's late every night and has done a good deal for 16. He was so nice in Boston and not at all "crabby." It was such a relief after his disagreeableness here and abroad.

Bertha was terribly excited leaving here and wept all the way to Ellsworth. All the girls came to say goodbye, and she went to parties every night, and it was all very gay. So at the end she went to pieces. I was so sorry for her. But after Ellsworth she pulled herself together and was cheery and sweet. In Boston she got the "twillies" in her stomach from excitement! The way Baby does when she gets excited. We took her to Concord about three P.M. Everything looked so cheery there. The new house is old-fashioned and delightful. She has a corner room on the second floor. The wallpaper is white with spring flowers scattered all over it. The woodwork is painted white, the dressing bureaus with hanging mirrors are painted a lovely soft light green, also the large wicker chair, two side chairs, table and night table, new white iron beds, three windows, a fireplace, a large closet, and a sweet roommate! So we are all enchanted with it. She was so thrilled! Her roommate's name is Frances Burnett and lives in Southboro! She has been there two years. She brought in all her friends and introduced them to B., and some were old girls and some new, and when we left, five of them were sitting in her room all talking like magpies, and B. with them looking as if she were at a thrilling house party, and said "goodbye" all smiles. We left feeling very happy, no tears, nor anything but joy. Miss Hobson was so nice and everything so fresh and new and no smell of food. Miss Darling is the house matron—a nice woman.

Well, if Gordy gets along as well, I shall feel happy and start the winter with a light heart. He is thrilled at the prospect of having long pants! when the time comes for new clothes, probably a blue suit for Xmas! All smiles! I must stop now but will write again later. This must go to the P.O.

P.

Bar Harbor, Maine
September 26, 1925

Mrs. Herman Kohlsaat
Hotel de Russie
Rome, Italy

Dear Mother:

Our life is very quiet. There are a few people here, and it is quite cold but sunny. We stay as near the fire as possible, and the house is fortunately quite warm with the furnace. Yesterday we looked at houses and played bridge. Today we decide what to do about houses seen(!) and play bridge. Min can't bear "oldfarm," so that is off the map. He likes still the Fabbri place and as second choice the "Fry place," which is very nice and possible and on the hill back of Eden Street. It is a good house, but a lot would have to be done to it. I could buy some old furniture if we took it, which quite thrills me! Well, it all depends on dollars and cents, like so many things in this world. No word from either child. I suppose that they have not had time to write. I hope Potter passed his exams. He is all fed up on tutoring and says he will not fail anything in June 1926! Let's hope so. Gordy is all aquiver about his school. We go to Boston on Tuesday the 29th, and he goes to F.S. on the 30th. I shall indeed feel shorn when he is gone—it's bad enough now.

You are on the Riviera today and lucky! My last love to you,

Pauline

The Copley-Plaza
Boston, Massachusetts
October 1, 1925

Mrs. Herman Kohlsaat
Hotel de Russie
Rome, Italy

Dear Mother:

Just another line instead of a letter! We came day before yesterday, shopped yesterday A.M., put Gordy in school in the P.M. He seemed to like it a lot and was very gentle and happy—that soft little smile of his, you know it? The boys all looked very nice and healthy, and the atmosphere was right. We telephoned Bertha, and she was in a gale of laughter and delight. We had a letter from her saying she laughs so hard that she just aches, and she loves everything and everybody and it's all a success! One letter from Potter saying he passed his exams and is playing lots of football and wants to go to Philadelphia for two days on his way home at Xmas! Well, I suppose he will like it, and I don't know what Min will say!

I forgot to tell you that we passed by the house in Arlington the other day. It is beautifully kept up, same colored paint, all fresh, lawns cut, flowers in beds and gardens, and it looked homelike and inviting, just as it always did.

Love and goodbye for a day or two,

Pauline

Chicago, Illinois
October 4, 1925

Mrs. Herman Kohlsaat
Hotel de Russie
Rome, Italy

Dear Mother:

The most lovely fan arrived from you yesterday! I've never seen any so delicate and exquisite. Min and the Baby think it lovely. The latter is looking at it with a knowing eye and followed me when I put it in the glass top of the little table in my room and said, "You ought to have a glass frame made just the shape of it, to stand up." Isn't she a cutie for eight years? It is so beautifully painted and has such a lovely "feel" when one holds it. I shall carry it (when it's not in its frame) with the blue and silver brocade dress from Vionnet. It is thrilling to have such a lovely thing drop on one unexpectedly in Chicago, on a Sunday afternoon, when one is wondering whether or not one's youngest son is too young to be in boarding school and perhaps homesick. It came just at the right minute.

And speaking of my youngest son, we had a letter from him this A.M. saying he was "having a fine time at school," the only flaw being that the "crabby" teacher at his table wouldn't allow him to eat crackers before soup, nor to butter them when soup came. He took that to heart and wrote a page on it. He says that the nicest teacher in school has charge of him in his dormitory, and that is fine for Mother. I started the Baby in school this A.M. It seems like a joke to have only one child to look after! Poor Anna is struggling to find something to do to use up her time!

I love your idea of your two selves looking at each other. Of course, if it weren't for that energetic get-up-and-go self of yours, there would not be all done in the world that has been done, for I think we all have the two parts and are often so chicken-hearted that we listen to the one that sits by and looks on, and then when the time for action is gone by, wish we could murder that self, as it has made us miss so many fine things that we wanted to do and could have done. Never pay the slightest attention to it. We think what you are doing is simply splendid and I am filled with desire to do likewise. Min, too, but he for the moment is building a hotel and has just come to the finish of a nerve-wracking plasterers strike, which has held up the opening for two months, and he is not thinking of much outside Chicago. But don't you ever let anything deceive you into thinking you are not doing the best thing in the world, because you are. If you came back and sat for one day in this country, you'd know that I am right!, get a perspective on yourself, and look at what you're doing as if some other woman, such as you, were doing it. Wouldn't it seem dignified, proper, and the ideal thing to do? So send that old other self to Jericho.

Clarissa is quite big and apparently very touchy. I gave her my lovely Callot scarf, the red and gold one, and she didn't like it but tried to pretend she did in a most half-hearted way, as if she didn't like to have things given her that had anything to do with hiding her shape. Well, I'd like the scarf back, as I gave it to her because I thought she looked pathetic. So goes the world. She didn't even open it, only looked at a corner and said, "It will do perfectly to wear over an old black evening gown and cover me up," and then put it aside. I offered to take it back and give her something else, but she refused. Oh, well, you know these ladies in a family way are hard to deal with.

Here's my spinach and apple—an unappetizing lunch! But I weigh 141 and look it. It spoils one's appetite.

Love, Pauline

Chicago, Illinois
October 26, 1925

Mrs. Herman Kohlsaat
Hotel de Russie
Rome, Italy

Dear Mother:

I was starting to write you a line yesterday when the news came of Helen Bartlett's death. It was such a shock—poor Frederic, what will he do? It is all ghastly. She has been ill off

241

and on all summer with rheumatism of some sort in her legs. Last week she was very miserable and Frederic wrote Robert a terrible depressed letter about it, which he received while we were at the Farms. Then the next thing we heard was that she was dead. They are (Mrs. Field, Catherine, Mr. Birch, Frederic, and Clay) bringing her on here, arriving this morning, and the burial is to be in Graceland tomorrow, with services in the chapel out there. It seems terrible to have the same thing happen that happened with Dora. She was buried at Oakwood Cemetery. What those three men will do without her! She kept them all together and made it a beautiful existence. Young Clay is very much in love with young Barbara Wendell, which seems strange!

Gordy's marks have been coming in. Last week he stood 11th in his Form of 28 boys, and this week he stands 1st!!! So we are terribly excited about it. Hope he keeps it up. No news of Potter's marks, which should be coming in this week. I doubt if he leads his Form! Haven't heard from Bertha's marks, either.

I hear that Teresa Higginson is engaged to young Prince Caetain! Did you ever hear of such a thing! They say she is very much in love with him, but still I can't help being sorry for him! It's to be announced very soon.

Min has just brought in Potter's marks—out of a Form of 35 he stands 32. He has been playing football very hard all autumn, so that may account for his awful standing. I want this to go off, so goodbye. Hope all is well with you.

Best love,

Pauline

Chicago, Illinois
October 28, 1925

Mrs. Herman Kohlsaat
Hotel Russie
Rome, Italy

Dearest Mother:

Here we are in the midst of winter, seemingly. It is 20 degrees and covered with snow! A miniature blizzard last night. Seems a little early, but I think it much healthier than the dry frozen dirt that usually comes by this time. It is a beautiful clear day—sunny—the first we've had for some time.

I took an Italian lesson yesterday and told my teacher, who was a Lieut. Col. in the Army, a prisoner for two and a half years, and before that taught military history in the Army, all that you said about the change for the better in Italy under Mussolini, and he nearly wept, said that he knew it, but when he read the "Tribune," he felt that Italy was fast going to the dogs. The Tribune reporter is a Communist and so writes continually against Mussolini. Perugia was just the same except for the new spirit when we were there. I am surprised that the Russie is so expensive. I hope that if you decide to stay that it will be comfortable enough to pay for doing it. The food was good when we were there and the garden divine. Which side are you on? Does the morning sun come in your windows, or have you it in the evening? We had it about four A.M.—all the rooms along that side and on the corner on the second floor. You probably have the bedroom Potter had with the big bath next on one side and the sitting room with the alcove on the other cosi [a small diagram of the hotel rooms as Pauline remembers them]. That is, of course, if you are on that side of the house. What fun you will have with Mrs. Grant. She sounds very nice and a delightful companion—your trip to Nemi, etc. Sounds ideal—like a dream.

We came down from Perugia by way of Narni over the mountains and through extraordinary wild country—not at all like the road by way of Viterbo and Orvieto. You lost nothing by not lunching at Narni. Such a place—and such an "ici"! Absolutely impossible, because one had to hold their breath, and after as long a trip as that, one couldn't attend to nature without taking a breath. It is still vivid to me even now, and I don't notice odors very acutely.

Bertha and Bruce left last night and must by now be ready to start their feat in Louisville. They are a happy, vague couple! And, oh, so young! Bertha seems to have gone back two or three years and is just a little older than our Bertha. In face, Bruce represents all the youthful part of her life that she missed—the Rah-rah boy part, if you know what I mean. Being in Florida with old members of the family and then in Washington with the young diplomats, she never had that healthy period of college boys, and Bruce is of the best and finest type of that, with great promise for the future. It's just what she needs. In some ways he makes me think of Roger at that age, awfully good company with his pals, adored by them, but with a manly serious outlook on life and its responsibilities. It's a thoroughly splendid match, but not a brilliant worldly one. The Smith clan at the wedding came with the idea of looking the family over and deciding whether or not they would do, without the slightest idea that the family might be doing the same by them! As everybody approved of everybody else, it was OK. But I am sure that if they hadn't approved, they would have let Bertha's family know it!

Helen Birch was buried yesterday at Graceland. Perfectly horrible, the whole thing. Frederic sat with his eyes on her coffin and the tears running down his cheeks, and Mr. Birch's heart was beating so that it shook his body. It's a terrible thing.

I have just had a letter from Gordy saying that his Latin mark for the week was 95, and his arithmetic was 90! Some scholar. Poor old Potter! He was away at the end. I'm sure Gordy is breathless with excitement about himself.

I haven't heard anything about Bertha's work, but as Miss Harris just said, "if it were bad, I'd hear fast enough," so I'm trying to think that she is easing along comfortable. However, she has Potter's idea that to pass is sufficient. Gordy is a real student and loves to know, not so much to learn, but to know is what he is after.

I have engaged a Frenchy to come in and talk an hour every Wednesday to the Baby. It's very little, but she is busy with music twice a week and fancy dancing twice a week, and she is pretty young to force anymore. She also likes to know and also likes to be graceful! So she urged the dancing very heavily. "Birdie did it last year, and I want to do it now!" She is doing well in her music, under Anna's proud eye. In fact, I think she is enjoying her winter to the fullest extent. She's getting quite tall. I am wondering if the pictures even reached you. They should be there in about two weeks from my date of writing, as I imagine that packages go slower than letters. When I know where you are to be settled for the winter, I'll write direct, so as to save the time lost in the re-addressing in Paris. Hope you are "well and happy," as Gordy writes to me!

Love,

Pauline

The Fessenden School
October 31, 1925

Mrs. Herman Kohlsaat
Hotel Russie
Rome, Italy

Dear Granny,

I hope you are enjoying your trip to Southern France and Italy. In one of your postcards you said you were, so I trust it's so.

It snowed here some time ago, and the nights are pretty cold. Only a few nights ago I could look at the full moon from my bed. It was pretty but not as pretty as in St. Moritz.

I think that I am going to play guard on the football team. We have been playing football with two schools but were beaten both times.

I am getting along all right in studies. Last week I stood first in a tie with two other boys. I got 80 for an average and got dismissed from two study periods, once for getting clear or without any failures, and once for getting 80 or over. This week I got an average of 80 again. I think I stand about second this week.

I have not gotten any conduct marks and maybe two tardy marks.

I have lots of friends here, and I am having a very nice time.

I hope that the weather is pleasant and not disagreeable so that you will have a good time.

Much love,

Gordon

Chicago, Illinois
November 6, 1925

Mrs. Herman Kohlsaat
Hotel de Russie
Rome, Italy

Dearest Mother:

Two nice fat letters from you today, Oct. 20-22. You seem to be having a beautiful time and seeing beautiful things. The p.c. of the girl with his parted hair is charming. What fun it must be see that kind of thing again. There are marvelous new things in the Naples Musée. We didn't see them last time we were there, and I have never ceased regretting it. And what an exciting time to be in Rome, today! The papers are full of the attempted assassination of Mussolini—100,000 people packed in the square before the Chigi Palace, making history. They will probably get him someday, but let us hope it's a long way off, and in the meantime, what a thrilling time to be there now!

The Baby still continues to enjoy her single blessedness, so to speak. She has Anna just where she wants her and is doing just about as she likes. She told me this story the other day, which we think amusing: her two schoolmates were talking in the schoolroom—one named Katherine Smitty and the other Louise Frankenstein. Said Katherine Smitty to

Louise Frankenstein, "Are you a Jew?" "No," said Louise Frankenstein. "Are you?" "No!" said Katherine Smitty. "And do you know," said the Baby to me, "I thought they both were!" The way she told it was rich. You know her funny little doubting but polite manner? Mrs. Lathrop is sailing the end of Dec. for her Villa in Florence. Mrs. Owen Aldis is meeting her and staying with her for three months. So you ought to go up there and call!

Much love,

Pauline

Chicago, Illinois
November 9, 1925

Mrs. Herman Kohlsaat
Hotel de Russie
Rome, Italy

Dearest Mother:

I'm in bed for a few minutes this morning, for if I once get up, I am done for as far as letter writing goes. There's always something else that must be done at once. The Baby has just gone to school full of pep and pertness, bossing Anna like mad! Anna is amazed once in awhile at the oldish qualities the Baby has developed in the last year. The other day she was in the bathtub, and Anna went down to her supper without telling her. The Baby found her gone (not that she minded being left alone, but she minded Anna's having the nerve to go off without permissions!), she got out of the tub, called the kitchen, and gave Anna merry hell, so to speak, over the wire, and when she got upstairs, gave her more. Anna was bowled over!, and when she came to, told Pauline to get into the tub and stay until she cooled down! She's a great one!

Yesterday Julia came for the day, looking very cheerful and enjoying her lecture tour. I thought that it would be fun for her to lunch at Mrs. Arthur Ryerson's to meet Mr. and Mrs. George Porter! So up there we went, all dressed up, and discovered it was for next Sunday. So back we came—Julia and Min all smiles because they were out of it! We had a pickup lunch here, and then went to the Goodman Theatre for the Ballet. Everybody you know was there, and it was very gay and lively. The ballet was not so good and much too long, which is too bad, but as it was the first performance it may be better next time when they get more in the running. Clarissa, Mike Lazaref, Baby, and Anna went with us, and we had a nice time. The Baby likes pretty things, and especially dancing, so we took her. She also very much wanted to go.

Tomorrow is the annual meeting of the Antiquarians, which I always dread. It won't last long, however, and then it's over for another year. Mrs. George Plummer came in and gave me a lesson in how to do it, so I feel a little less vague about it. I am going downtown this morning to have her directions printed, several copies, for I tried several friends, who also have a "vague" feeling about conducting meetings, and would be grateful to know a little about it. Katherine Adler is coming to lunch, and at four o'clock I take a bridge lesson. Tonight I sort bills and then tomorrow night I go to St. Paul and Min goes to Southboro to see the Groton Game and then to N.Y. for business. It's all I can do not to go to the game, but I've promised so many times to go to St. Paul and fallen out at the last minute, and then Potter doesn't want me to watch his game. I'm staying in St. Paul until Friday night. Julia will be there for a few minutes on Wednesday, then goes to Sioux City!

Much love,

Pauline

1350 Lake Shore Drive
Chicago, Illinois
November 10, 1925

Mrs. Herman Kohlsaat
Hotel de Russie
Rome, Italy

Dearest Mother:

Well, my awful meeting is over! and I feel weak after such a strain—at least more or less so! It went along quietly enough, and now we are launched for another year, my last one, for I no longer want to be president, but to have some pleasant job at the Institute like getting up exhibitions or looking for things to add to the collections. One can have a great deal of fun that way, and much less responsibility. I don't know for how many years I have been president, but one too many, I think! We decided to buy two lovely Queen Anne chairs with needlework seats and a beautiful piece of Q. Anne embroidery, and Mrs. Joseph Adams gave the most exquisite piece of Chinese velvet—old faded turquoise blue! I've never seen anything like it, beautiful. So altogether we did very well.

I lunched at Frances Sprague's with Ginevra and then went back to the Institute to go over some costumes that needed to be sorted. That took a couple of hours, and then I came home and was glad to sit down quietly. Min went to Boston on the Century. I took him to the train. The Baby has gone to bed very happy because she has her Nany. I'm glad she has, for it makes us much freer, and she is so much happier than last winter. Well, life moves along pleasantly. Gordy continues to get high marks and stands fourth in his class, which is very good! Bertha has taken to sewing, making hats and dresses! She sent the Baby a cunning hat, much too small, but well-made and very pretty. So much for the New England atmosphere. It has been very cold and is now fortunately getting warmer.

What do you think of the franc? Isn't it awful! Friday it is worth the same as the lira.

Best love, Pauline

Chicago, Illinois
November 17, 1925

Mrs. Herman Kohlsaat
Hotel de Russie
Rome, Italy

Dearest Mother:

I had a good trip down from St. Paul and met Min, who arrived from N.Y. about an hour after I did. Potter didn't get into the Groton game, unfortunately, as the older boys (6th formers) picked up on their games and were kept in. Groton beat 13-6, I think I wrote you. Of course, they are all sick about it. Potter got three credits in his studies, which is fine. Min said Gordy looked very well, thinner and taller, and very happy. Bertha is still in a gale of happiness, and Min doesn't think she takes school very seriously! Potter was much nicer and quieter, and all three looked awfully well. Min saw each one for about 20 minutes.

Julia came on her way through on Saturday for a few hours then returned Sunday afternoon. We had supper at Clarissa's, and it was very nice, and then Monday she stayed in bed all morning and I did some errands for myself, and then we lunched at the Palmer House and went over the new building after. It is perfectly beautiful, away beyond anything that I imagined. Then we came back here and rested!, and M. and C. came to dinner, and Julia left at 7:45 P.M.

This afternoon, Elsie McC., Belle Borland, and Anne came to lunch, and we went to the new series of concerts—six of them—to be given on Tuesdays of each month. It was the most beautiful concert! Stick played encores and Brailowsky was the soloist, and he was magnificent as always. Elsie was full of her seeing you and her trip to Mrs. Gassettes. Apparently she got in touch with Miss. G. later and is getting some sablée through her.

She is going back again in January! The collecting fever is flaming within her. She has added to her list of what she collects and is now after 18th-century aprons! She says that they wore lovely aprons, taffeta, silk, brocade, etc., and worth collecting and keeping. She likes my looking glass awfully. Well, I had a fine time with them.

Your book on Mussolini sounds fine. I must tell all you say to my Italian teacher, as he likes to hear.

This looks pretty scratchy. Hope you can read it.

Love from us all, Pauline

Concord, Massachusetts
November 26, 1925

Mrs. Herman Kohlsaat
Hotel de Russie
Rome, Italy

Thanksgiving lunch here today. All the children with Honoré and Watson saw the Bridge and Bullet Hole. Now off for the movies. Love, P.

Southborough Arms, Massachusetts
November 27, 1925

Mrs. Herman Kohlsaat
Hotel de Russie
Rome, Italy

Dear Mother:

Well, here we all are! All much improved and awfully nice. A very satisfactory vacation in every way. But then I'd better begin at the beginning. I rushed like mad the last day at home, as there were so many last things to do, as usual, before going away. We went to dinner with the Pikes, the Odells, and ourselves at the Lake Shore Drive Hotel on Monday. We went to see Eddie Cantor in "Kid Books," which was as amusing as ever. Next morning Kay and Roger came from N.Y. and stayed until we left on the Century. They had an awfully good time in N.Y. and apparently bought the town out, as Kay has probably written you! They spent the day at 1350, and I hope everything went well. They are coming down on the 4th of Dec. with Helen Blair for a dinner before the young Armours' dance and I hope will stay over Sunday with us.

We went east on the train with Cornelia, the Ned Fairbanks, and Anne Winterbotham and had great fun. We played bridge a great part of the time and laughed most of it. Then we came into Boston, went to the Museum of Fine arts to see the Sargent exhibition of portraits, which like the sale at Christie's doesn't hold up as an exhibit. Isn't it strange? One would think it would be magnificent, and instead it looks messy and trivial. Some of the portraits were wonderful, but so many were mediocre that the exhibit as a whole was disappointing.

Then we went to West Newton to see Gordy and make arrangements about calling for him next day. He is quite thin for him!—114 dressed—quite freckled and much pleased with his school and his life there. We arranged to have him called for at eight A.M. Thanksgiving morning. Then we left, bought some chicken sandwiches in Waltham, and ate them on the way to Concord! B. was all ready and in fine spirits. She looks so well, is thinner and taller, and holds herself very much better, in fact very well, so does not look dumpy anymore. She is quite grown-up, not unpleasantly so, but just what I hoped she would be. Then we came over here, and Potter came in after study hour, and he looks fat and fine and is so nice and gentle, very amusing and chatty. Honoré and Watson came to supper (ink has given out!). Then Potter and Honoré came over for breakfast, and Gordy arrived about nine, so we had a fine time together. Potter was so nice to G. and took him to school and all around and treated him like a white man. Gordy was thrilled. We all wandered over to see Potter's room, and then we went to the Colonial Inn at Concord for lunch. Honoré and Watson went with us.

After lunch we went to see the Battlefield and then Bertha's room at school and her playground, and the boys were much impressed. Bertha's room is lovely, really, and looks so homelike and cozy, and fresh and young girlish. She has some plants in the window. It is charming and very warm! We went to the movies in Marlboro after and then back here for an early supper and then I went back to Fessenden with Gordy and stayed for the school entertainment, which pleased him a good deal. He showed me his room, which is as neat as a pin, and we talked about school and how much he liked it, and he was his nice cozy self, and we held hands all the way in the motor.

I came back here for the night and slept well. Bertha is doing her lessons across the table. Min is dressing slowly. Potter is coming to lunch with Tom Palmer and Tony. Tonight, some of Bertha's friends are coming, and her roommate, who lives here. We stay until Sunday afternoon and then start for Boston, dropping children on the way—Bertha first, then Gordy, and finally we have supper in Boston and take the midnight to N.Y. We stay there until Wednesday and then go home, and I hope stay there until February without taking another train! Such a hectic autumn as it has been! I have done nothing but recover from one trip and prepare to take another. The children are all so happy and contented and look so well that we are very happy and satisfied with the way things have gone. It has been quite an experiment, but it has turned out well. Min is pleased and is having a grand time with them all.

Well, I hope you can read this! We all send love, Pauline

The Ralph Waldo Emerson house in Concord, Massachusetts.

Notes

September 18, 1925: The Hispano Suiza was the Palmers' luxurious automobile. Eleanor is Pauline's Chicago friend Mrs. Robert Hall McCormick, and the editor's Grandmother.

October 4, 1925: Anna has been in the family since young Pauline was a baby and would stay on to take care of Bertha's first child, Oakleigh Thorne.

October 26, 1925: Frederic Bartlett, whose wife, Helen, has died, was an early collector of Impressionist and post-Impressionist paintings. The Helen Birch Bartlett Memorial Collection named for his wife is an important collection at the Art Institute of Chicago of modern French paintings. Barbara Wendell, the daughter of Barrett Wendell of the Higginson investment firm, was a close friend of Bertha Palmer's.

October 28, 1925: Pauline's letters have been addressed to Morgan Harjes in Paris and forwarded to Rome.

Pauline comments on the engagement of Bertha and Bruce Smith. Bertha must be Julia's daughter, Bertha Cantacuzène.

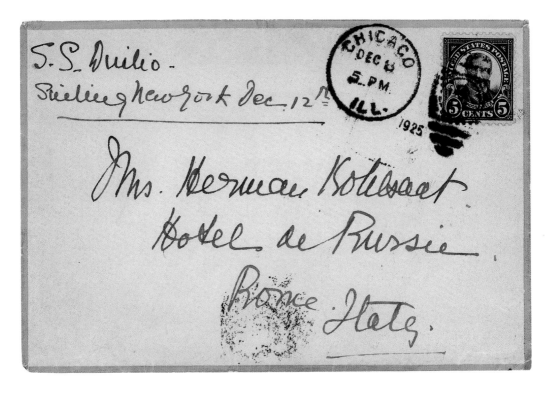

"I am trying hard to get the Gallery in order
and the South Gallery ready so that we
can have the tree there. I am selling some of
the unwanted furniture. It clutters up everything…
I'd pay them to take it away!"

CHRISTMAS HOLIDAYS IN CHICAGO, 1925–26

Pauline writes her mother, who is still living in Rome, that the children are home from school for Christmas vacation. There is great excitement on Pauline's part about their arrival from the east, and one is reminded of F. Scott Fitzgerald's description in *The Great Gatsby* of Nick Carraway's returning from school for Christmas. "I remember the fur coats of the girls returning from Miss This or That's and the chatter of frozen breath and the hands waving overhead as we caught sight of old acquaintances and the matching of invitations. . . . That's my middlewest—not the wheat or the prairies or the lost Swede towns but the thrilling, returning trains of my youth and the street lamps and sleigh bells in the frosty dark and the shadows of holly wreaths thrown by lighted windows on the snow."

After spending just a few months in boarding school, the children seem to Pauline more disciplined and mature. She describes how each one looks—Bertha and Gordy thin and Potter "fuller." Potter whose previous behavior has been that of a provocative adolescent is now "so nice you wouldn't know him." Pauline, who likes to stay attuned to her children's personalities, is not used to having a full house: "I feel very confused, and as if I were missing something of one of them when I am with the other!" But she is obviously thrilled. "It is so cheerful to have the children home again and the house gay and busy." One also senses her awareness of time moving on.

Soon after they arrive they have a Charleston party with mothers and children, and Pauline herself gets into the action. "I'm also going to learn to Charleston! Bertha has been teaching me tonight and I am sure that I can do it." Besides describing her entertaining at the Castle, she talks of shopping, theatre, and skating parties. On December 27th, Bertha and Potter go to a dinner and dance at the Casino Club, where Min and Pauline often entertain. The Club was founded in 1914 on an inspiration of Pauline's friend Lucy McCormick Blair (later Lucy Linn), along with another friend, Rue Carpenter. Min's brother, Honoré, was also a founder.

This new stage in their lives, as their children become more independent, coincides with the revamping of two Palmer properties. Pauline reports that she is "trying hard to get the Gallery in order and the South Gallery ready" and is selling unwanted furniture which "clutters up everything." The younger Palmers have created a more subdued and elegant look in Bertha Palmer's grand rooms. The renovation of the Palmer House Hotel is also a success. It is "so fine and so crowded that they turn people away, both in rooms and restaurants."

She is delighted with the success of the family's Christmas together. "The children all said it was the best yet, so I feel repaid, as it was quite strenuous." When the children leave for their next terms at school, she announces that "we have slipped back to our old way of living with such a thump! that the baby says it's just as if the others hadn't been here!" Pauline and Min are now involved with the events at the new Palmer House, which "everyone is crazy about," and Min is beginning his term as president of the Art Institute. As the letters end, the reader can envision the two Palmers beginning a new phase, having launched the children into lives of their own.

This page above: The Castle's drawing room in Pauline's
more restrained and elegant style with Chippendale
furniture. At right: Dining room in the younger Palmers'
era with portrait of Potter Palmer I by George P.A. Healy.
Opposite top: View of the Palmer castle at 1350 Lake
Shore Drive with Chicago skyline in background in 1925.
Opposite bottom: View of the Great Hall lobby from the
Empire Room of the newly refurbished Palmer House.
Pauline wrote on November 17, 1925 that the Palmer
House "is perfectly beautiful, beyond anything I had
imagined."

Chicago, Illinois
December 3, 1925

Mrs. Herman Kohlsaat
Hotel de Russie
Rome, Italy

Dearest Mother:

After a hectic trip east we are at home again—glad to be back and well satisfied with what we found. The children are fine. Bertha is so improved, stands up straight and is more reposeful and surer of herself—all of which she lacked last September—happy as a cricket and as pretty as can be. I am so pleased with her, and so is Min. We told her so, and she was pleased too. She has kept her head, which is a good thing. For studies, she is halfway between Potter and Gordy, Potter being awful and Gordy wonderful. Her friends seem devoted to her. She was met with screams of joy when she went into the girls' rooms when she got back to school. You would have thought they had been separated for months instead of three days! Gordy is much thinner and very handsome and stands so well in school.

I must tell you a joke. Perhaps I wrote it to you from Boston, but in case I didn't, I must repeat it. Bertha, Potter, Min, and I all went over to Fessenden to get Gordy on Saturday and take him to Southboro for the weekend and to see his school and room and take an interest in his affairs, as we had in the others' schools. Gordy showed off everything in great style and was pleased about it! Well, going over to Southboro afterwards, Gordy was talking about his marks, having gotten 85.6 for the week before, and said, "I'm sorry I was awfully bad this last week, I only got 81.2." Potter's face was a study and a "scream." He looked perfectly dumbfounded, never having been within ten points of such an average, he thought he was dreaming when he heard Gordy apologizing for so low a mark! Potter told Cornelia that he was going to get hold of Gordy before school next year and put a stop to such marks, as he, Potter, couldn't afford to be "shown up" in that way! Believe me, old Potter has begun to sit up and take notice! Nobody made any comparisons, nor said a thing, but Dr. Thayer and everyone else knows about Gordy's work, and it's trickled through to Potter and he told me before we left that he intended to do better work now. Well, let's hope he does. It couldn't be much worse!

Potter was lovely to Gordy, took him off with him to his rooms, showed him over school, and in general treated him like one of his own kind! G. was all smiles and excitement. I suppose that with Gordy's being at boarding school and standing well and being on the football squad that went over to Southboro to play St. Marks' 1st Form team (which beat St. Marks 13-0!), he has acquired a recognized position in Potter's mind and is worthy of notice. Also, he will be at St. Marks next year, and Potter, as all "Upper School" boys do, must look over the "Lower School" and pick out and make a fuss about the boys who are the most promising. Gordy went off with Potter, Watson, and Honoré and was thrilled!

Young Howard Gillette is doing wonderfully well at St. Marks—head of his Form, highest in "Intelligence Test," playing football and full of pep, crazy about school, gained five pounds, has pink cheeks, and has grown!, hasn't been homesick a minute, and has lots of friends. Howard and Cornelia are so excited and happy. Well, it was a fine vacation! Potter has lost all of his painful, disagreeable manner and was as sweet and gentle as he was as a little boy. I don't see how he was able to change so completely in so short a time, for frankly, I dreaded going east to see him. He was horrible in Bar Harbor—much worse than Paris—but it's all gone now, and he is enchanting. Everything went smoothly, and everyone was happy. Gordy and Bertha just fell on one another's necks, and Gordy is staying a day longer at school so he can bring Bertha home at Xmas, "so as he could come with her, as she would like it better than coming with the other girls," as he thought it up himself. And Bertha was terribly pleased. We are letting him do it, although we miss a half day of him. They are being put on the Century in Boston by their teachers and coming out in a section together. Doesn't it seem sweet to think of them and the fun they will have?

Gordy is having his first long trousers and a blue suit for Xmas. He's terribly excited, to say nothing of his mother and father being so! Well, we left Southboro Sunday afternoon and took Bertha to Concord and then Gordy to Fessenden and then went into Boston. I sent you a line from there.

We went to N.Y. on the midnight and went to the Ritz—very comfortable and very expensive! But we were both tired and the room was restful and the service and food excellent, and we had all our meals upstairs and took life very easily. I did some looking about for some Early Am. furniture for an exhibition at the A.I. but found nothing. New York is simply rolling in money. I've never seen anything like it, and people don't know how to get rid of it fast enough. The antique dealers can't keep their shops full enough. Everything is sold out, and such prices! You've never heard of such things! Min got me some needlework that was reasonable and very lovely, a small Jacobean cap from Verney, a pair of Stuart fans from Partridge, a Ralph wood vase, and a quill work picture from Norris. "Quill work" is all made of tiny strips of parchment made into designs like grill work or filigree and colored red, blue, and gold. It is a Stuart, 1670, piece and very rare and not much fuss made about it as yet, and so very cheap!

We went over to the theatre to see Leon Errol in Louis XIV—very amusing—and came home on Wednesday. Yesterday (it has taken me two days to do this letter!) Kay and Roger arrived to stay with Helen Blair for the Armours dance last night. They came to breakfast with us, and Kay and I spent the A.M. together. She looked awfully well. Min took Roger over to the Palmer House yesterday, and he seemed to like it. It really is very beautiful and unusual, and everybody in town is excited about it.

Love, Pauline

Chicago, Illinois
December 8, 1925

Mrs. Herman Kohlsaat
Hotel de Russie
Rome, Italy

Dearest Mother:

This ought to reach you in time for Christmas! So I wish you a Merry Xmas! And a Happy New Year. I hope it's a fine day in Rome. We will be thinking about you and wishing you were with us. Our tree this year is to be a small one, put onto a stand of some kind, and draped in some Christmasy way, with the presents arranged around the base. Isn't that grand? [small drawing of the tree setup] Red covering with greens and perhaps some gold stars or silver! I am trying hard to get the Gallery in order and the South Gallery ready so that we can have the tree there. I am selling some of the unwanted furniture. It clutters up everything, and there's literally no place to put it, so Williams Barker and Severns are to be invited up to take a peek and remove it. I'd pay them to take it away! I am spending the rest of the winter putting the house in order and getting it into some sort of shape.

The Palmer House is nearly done, and Min is so occupied with that that he doesn't think of anything else, and so we lead a quiet, comfortable life, and I am devoting my time from now on to getting settled! After four years. We hope to go to Florida that middle of Feb. to stay until April. Kay tells me that you are coming to her for May at the Farm. And I hope you are planning for some time with us? If you have any plans, let me know. I might come over for a little while in the spring, if you don't come home. I must be back by June 9th, as we go to Bar Harbor then.

I am now going downtown to shop for Xmas at Field's. It's early, so there won't be much of a crowd. Your life sounds lovely and just what would be the nicest thing in the world to do. And I am so happy to think that you have Mrs. Grant, Miss Risser, and your Italian lady. Mrs. Lathrop sails Dec. 29, and you will then have her!

All our love and kisses, and best wishes for a Happy Xmas!!

Pauline

Please get something for yourself with this check. I don't like to send objects!

1350 Lake Shore Drive
Chicago, Illinois
December 10, 1925

Mrs. Herman Kohlsaat
Hotel de Russie
Rome, Italy

Dearest Mother:

Just a line to tell you that we have the Fabbri house at B.H. for next summer. Only heard last night. We are delighted. Hope you'll visit us!

Best love, and a Merry Christmas, if this reaches you in time.

Love,

Pauline

Chicago, Illinois
December 21, 1925

Mrs. Herman Kohlsaat
Hotel de Russie
Rome, Italy

Dearest Mother:

We have great excitement between the children's arrivals and the big dinner for the head men who had to do with the Palmer House. I hardly know where to begin! Probably with Potter's arrival Friday morning. His train was quite late, so we spent all the morning rushing over to the station! Finally they came in—Potter, Watson, Honoré, and young Howard, and at least 600 Wellesley girls! Such sights! I could hardly wait for Bertha to come to see if she looked as awful. Fortunately she didn't, but on the contrary, very smart and English, with tweed suit, scarf inside her collar, and plain felt hat, all soft tones of brown. I was proud of her. Well, Potter looked very well—fat and rosy—and was very cheerful and pleasant—still is, in fact—and I am having a beautiful time with him. Young Howard was quite carsick, and Potter petted him, dressed him, and packed his bag, which reduced Cornelia to tears when she heard of it. There is ice, so Potter went skating after lunch and shopping with Honoré. He seems so glad to be at home and is so nice. Grace, Cappy, and Honoré came to supper, and we all went to see "Kid Boots" with

Eddie Cantor. It was very amusing, and we had a good time.

Next morning Bertha and Gordy came in on the Century looking very fit and cheerful. Gordy has grown tall and weighs 109 pounds and eats no sweets to keep thin. Bertha has lost 12 pounds and looks very well and has a lovely figure. It is fine to have them all at home, and not having had them together for so long, I feel very confused and as if I were missing something of one of them when I am with the other! They are so many, it's the queerest feeling. I'll probably get used to it by the time they go back! Well, we asked Honoré and Barbara Wendell to lunch on Saturday and to go to the movies afterwards.

Yesterday I went down to see Elsie's needlework pictures and bead pictures. They are simply superb. Then in the P.M., many mothers and their offspring came to tea, and we had the player piano going in the gallery and Charlestons going on. Bertha Charlestons very well, also Honoré, so it was very gay and lively, and about 50 came, I think. We sat around last evening worn out and went to bed early. This morning Potter and Gordy have gone to buy skates and go skating and swimming at the Racquet Club. Bertha has been trying on all her party dresses, which look lovely on her, as she is so thin, and Baby has gone to a dancing lesson. Later we are going shopping for "last things." I haven't much for Potter or Gordy, so must get something. Potter wants a set of automobile tires! and Bertha a motor and Gordy a typewriter! and the Baby, a live dog! We'll, it's a family, sure enough.

It is snowing and has been ever since night before last. Fine Christmas weather. I wonder if you are having snow? And how Christmasy it is? I am envying you all the wonderful Xmas services in St. Peters and the other churches. What a marvelous time you will have, and what an experience! I wish you were with us, just the same!, for a Christmas dinner.

Goodbye. I must dress and go "shopping."

Love,

Pauline

Chicago, Illinois
December 24, 1925

Mrs. Herman Kohlsaat
Hotel de Russie
Rome, Italy

Dearest Mother:

Your letters are rather few and far between, but I imagine you are having a fine time and doing the grandest things that you have always wanted to do. It certainly is the opportunity of a lifetime to see all the Christmas doings in Rome, and I hope that I may sometime have the chance. At just this minute I am struggling with five different points of view about "what to do, how to do it, and how to get there!" Well, it is certainly hectic! But I am pulling through, and everyone is cheerful and happy and glad to [be] home. They look so well and are so improved in every way. I sent you a cable yesterday for Xmas, hoping it would get there on time, and I had two from you about the Dec. check. I'll tell McGowan to send it earlier so that it will reach you nearer the first of the month. It takes almost two weeks from here for a letter to arrive in Rome. We can send them by airmail to catch the Saturday boats. Very quick time really.

Well, Ellen is home and trying to "make-up." I am in mood for such things, however, as I don't in the least feel angry, but just bored with her and her "problems." So in some way, we will have to be on a new footing. It will make a lot of talk if we break off completely, and I am not keen about gossip. A quiet life is all I ask, and I see it ahead of me, thank goodness. Min is so relieved that the building is finished and is fine and so crowded that they turn people away, both in rooms and restaurants! And he is hearing praise from every quarter. He is so cheerful and like his old self when abroad, and you know how nice that is. He is now going to work at the Institute and keen about that. There are many things there needing attention, and he likes it.

I am sorry that this is so hectic, but since it was started Bertha and I have arranged two theatre parties, Gordy and I one, Potter and I have decided about his trip to N.Y. for two days before school opens. The Baby has gotten money to buy "Mannie," [a] crossword puzzle book! I am in bed. It's nearly 11 o'clock, and this must be off by 11:30, so goodbye and much love,

Pauline

Chicago, Illinois
December 27, 1925

Mrs. Herman Kohlsaat
Hotel de Russie
Rome, Italy

Dearest Mother:

Another Christmas has gone by and was a success, too! The children all said that it was the best yet, so I feel repaid, as it was quite strenuous. We trimmed the tree, as usual, Christmas Eve, the children giving up invitations in order to stay at home that evening. Laseref, who is still with us, was so excited about the tree that he hung nearly all of it. Then the children finally got to bed, and we filled the stockings. Bertha slept in Baby's bed and Baby with Anna—a rare treat. Gordy slept on the sofa in Potter's room, so everything was lovely. We put the best small gift in the toe of each stocking, a ring for Potter and one for Gordy, very plain and nice, a circle of pearls with a tiny diamond bow like that [drawing] for Bertha, and a bracelet for Baby. They were all pleased. Then we put in jokes—potatoes and apples and oranges, and foolish toys. Potter likes a stocking just as well as Baby does—even if he is going on 17!

We got everything ready next morning by 10:45 and lighted the tree and had the presents. Bertha got such grown up presents! And Potter, too. Gordy got half and half, and Baby was swamped with dolls! And then the Aldis Brownes and several Wendells. Clarissa and Mike came to lunch, and later we all went to call on the Bordens and Arthur Henn. Bertha went to the concert that evening, and the rest of us went to bed as early as possible. Bertha finished the tapestry that she bought in Paris and gave it to me! It is beautifully done! She is dating it, and I am keeping it for future generations. Wasn't she a cutie to do it? I am so pleased. She made Min a pair of covers to tie around shoes when he packs! And he was so pleased. She is very clever with her fingers and has learned to use them at school. She is quite thin, which is most becoming—130— and as pretty as can be, very bright and amusing, and is having a heavenly time with all kinds of invitations.

Potter is much happier than I thought he would be, because being just between "sets," so to speak, he has no crowd of girls to go with. He's been at home a lot, which is very pleasant for us, certainly. He is going to New York on the 4th to stay with Honoré until the 7th when he goes up to school. He is quite excited about it. He is also going on an allowance for everything, except dentist and railway and motor bills! He's a cute thing and so nice this vacation that you wouldn't know him. Gordy is very happy in school and is happy to be at home for a while. He has played with his electric train all the time this vacation. We went shopping together, and he bought what he wanted, so it's all right. They certainly have a faculty of knowing what they want, these children!

Last night we had a supper party with the theatre afterwards, and it was very amusing. The girls are all pretty and fresh and young and the boys good-looking and amusing. There were about 11 of them. Min and I went with them and sat together at the theatre. After the theatre, Potter, Watson, and Sam Morse, Anne Richardson's boy, motored out to Lake Forest! It was about nine below zero! But I suspect that that made it all the more exciting. Potter stayed with Watson, and Sam went home. This morning Bertha went to lunch out there with the young Sam Walter, who gave the party for the Stanley children. Potter and Watson lunched there, too, so it was great fun. They skated and played around, and Bertha and the lunch party got home here about 7:30. Potter comes in tomorrow morning. It's been below zero all day and awfully windy—a horrible day.

Ellen is home and looks very well. She came up this P.M. and brought Dr. Siren. If you don't know about him, Mr. Sachs will. He was quite interested in our early Chinese things and is very amusing and pleasant. We had a delightful afternoon with him. Ellen and I are quite friendly, but in no way "intimate," and it works very well. I am glad to have it settled quietly and comfortably. Rows make it difficult when you both move in the same set and are hard on your friends. So it is all nicely settled, and everybody satisfied. By that, I mean Min likes the arrangement! It's a queer world, and I think that to be made like Ellen, with so many things left out of her make-up, must make life very simple and without complications.

Tomorrow Bertha and I are going shopping with her Xmas money. She wants a large seal ring. Do you remember my turquoise matrix ring that you got me at Tiffany's when I was at Dobb's? What fun I had with it and what a thrill it gave me? Well, Bertha has now reached the same stage in her career, and off we go for rings in the morning! Gordy's going too, as his ring is a little small, and he wants it enlarged. It's what Bertha called tonight "a heavy date at ten o'clock tomorrow, Mum!" I wish you were going with us.

Would it be possible for your Italian to paint miniatures of the children at this age from photos, if I send them? Let me know. I'll send wisps of hair pinned to each photo.

Min gave me so many Christmas presents. Whenever I saw anything I wanted he got it— a stump work mirror at Partridge's last summer, a needlework green and lace box, a stump work picture, and a pair of needlework fans. And then some lovely small Chinese figures! So you see, I've had a real Christmas in every way.

Next morning. It is hard to find time to write, as people, or rather children, are always coming in! Last night after Anna had locked up, upstairs Gordy appeared and asked if his "sand dredger and scoop" could be sent to Florida for Easter, as he hadn't had a minute in which to play with it here! He has been so concentrated on his tracks that he hasn't moved from his room, where it is spread out all over the floor and has been for days, to put the room in order. Ester has to step over everything! Well, he's a cute thing.

Did I tell you that in his report for the Fall Term at school he averaged 8.2 and stood 2nd in a Form of 31 boys! He would have been first, I think, except that he got so excited about coming home that he forgot all about studying the last week! They have all three improved very much. More grown-up, or at least less "cub-bish," and Bertha is really charming. Laseref, who is here, is impressed with their good manners, which I suppose means that he hasn't seen much evidence of such things in children over here.

I didn't tell you that we had the tree in the South Gallery, in front of the steps. It was lovely and looked well there.

It's still cold—zero just this morning. I am about to find out how many for lunch and dinner, just to cheer Ellen a bit and make her think I'm trying to help her. Of course, everyone by the time mealtime comes around, will either be going somewhere or else bringing home someone unexpectedly. But by no chance will there be the number I will tell Ellen to prepare for.

Wolcott Blair is engaged to a Mrs. Ellen Yuille Sturgis of New York, and she is here now visiting Mrs. Blair. I wonder how Alice feels? We haven't been asked to meet her, although I see by the paper that Mrs. Blair is entertaining for her. Perhaps she isn't very pleased and is letting Wolcott do the whole thing and not asking her friends. Well, I must say, the girl has a hard nut to crack, if Mrs. Blair doesn't like her! What fun it must be to visit in that house under those circumstances!

Tonight Ginevra and Fran Sprague are giving a dance at the Casino, and Dorothy Ranney is giving a dinner beforehand, to which B. and P. are going. Gordy is going to Howards to dinner and then to the dance, they having asked the younger boys especially for Garfield. Baby will have to conduct herself with Nannie, as we are going to dinner and the theatre with the Lawrence Armours.

This is like a manuscript! Hope you can read it!

Much love,

Pauline

Chicago, Illinois
December 30, 1925

Mrs. Herman Kohlsaat
Hotel de Russie
Rome, Italy

Dearest Mother:

My quiet moments are few and far between these days, and so when one comes around, I either take a nap or write to you, depending on my state of wakefulness. And just there I was interrupted and only now am able to write again! The Cantacuzène baby arrived last night, or rather this morning at one A.M. Clarissa apparently suffered very little, as they gave her a kind of gas at each pain and finally ether at the end. I just called her on the telephone, and she answered the ring! Her voice was strong and very happy—said she had just had a visit from her daughter, offered her lunch, which the daughter went right at and had to be dragged away, "and I feel so flattered," said Clarissa! They are thinking of calling her "Irena", pronounced short "i" and "en" like "n", making it much prettier than our Irena. She is very dark and Clarissa says "looks more like Gordy than anyone else, with big blue eyes and dark hair." I sent you a cable this morning about it and trust it arrives safely.

 Later, Bertha and I went to Mrs. Pickering's for a dress and found just what we wanted, so now she has all she needs for school. Yesterday we got a green velvetine from Emily to wear on cold evenings and today a grey crêpe to wear warmer evenings and on Sundays in the spring with a dark coat. Very nice, because she has a green felt hat, which she can wear with both. Mrs. Pickering is looking ahead, as she ought, and is making "Jeune fille" prices, which will be fine, for it's so much simpler to get one or two nice things from her than to struggle with a lot of questionable middle-priced ones. This dress is $100.00—not too cheap, one might say!, but very smart and simple, all made, and just what we want. And it took ten minutes to get it. How "expensive" all this must sound to you over there, with all the exchange, which makes American buying pleasant!

My love to you,

Pauline

Chicago, Illinois
January 3, 1926

Mrs. Herman Kohlsaat
Hotel de Russie
Rome, Italy

Dearest Mother:

The big children are off in the morning, Bertha to school and Potter to Philadelphia for the day to see his friends there and then to N.Y. to stay two days with Honoré. They are very well and look the picture of health, so to speak. Bertha has been lovely, and everyone has spoken about it. Potter is quite heavy, and so his face is full and he looks very handsome. Gordy goes on Tuesday and says, "it's awful now, but it won't be bad when I get there." He has loafed to his heart's content—breakfast every morning about ten o'clock, on a tray while he sits on the sofa in Baby's room in his pajamas and wrapper. And Baby has hers on a tray in her bed at the same time, and Bertha has hers in her bed at the same time. And Anna stands around, and everybody talks. He has eaten every fattening thing, and in a word, has thoroughly enjoyed himself. I think that he has gained several pounds but feels that it's worth it! I think it's all been a success, but it's been very short. I expect to go on to see them before we go to Florida, and then they come down about the middle to the end of March.

My life will certainly be quiet after Tuesday. Even Lasaref goes on Tuesday! But I have planned lots of things to do and so shall find the time going all too quickly. I expect to start French and Italian again and take a try at watercolors! There is a lot at Bar Harbor that would be fun to paint if I knew how to do it. I haven't much eye for the combining of colors, nor the feel for it, somehow. But I'd like to try watercolors and pastels to see what I can do with them. There are a number of people at B.H. who paint, and I'd like to try it with them. One can't spend the summer every year playing bridge and going to parties— certainly it's not my idea of a good summer.

Well, I'm also going to learn to Charleston! Bertha has been teaching me tonight, and I am sure that I can do it, and if I wear rubber corsets at the same time, I can lose tons. It's strenuous exercise. I simply cannot keep from eating, and I am too fat for comfort, and this dance seems to be the solution of my troubles.

We went over to see Clarissa's baby on Saturday, yesterday, and it is a cunning thing—no new baby, except Gordy, looks pretty!—all very soft and cuddly and sweet, but not awfully pretty. She weighs eight pounds, has dark hair, and will have very fair skin, as she is as red as anything. Clarissa looks remarkably well [and] doesn't remember any pains, as they gave her this new gas, which deadens everything, and the patient doesn't suffer at all. She was only sick about six hours—quite wonderful. Mike is still in a weakened state of intense excitement! According to Min's story, mother and child doing well, we hope to pull father through.

Your Christmas gift has not yet come, but I expect to hear of it this week. And in the meantime, I hope to get a letter from you, as it's been nearly ten days since the last!

Much love,

Pauline

Chicago, Illinois
January 6, 1926

Mrs. Herman Kohlsaat
Hotel de Russie
Rome, Italy

Dearest Mother:

We have slipped back to our old way of living with such a thump! that the baby says it's just as if the other hadn't been here!, which is quite true. She talked all through dinner last night, as usual, and then we played cards, and she went to bed about 8:15. The house was closed about 9:15, and we sat and read until 11 and then went to bed, too. And this morning Baby had her breakfast on a tray in here, and now here I am, writing to you, in bed, at 8:30 A.M. So it goes, very quiet and pleasant.

Bertha and Potter got off safely on Monday, and then yesterday morning Gordy left. He was fairly gloomy but kept saying, "I'm gloomy here because it's the end of vacation, but I'll be alright as soon as I get to school." Baby and he and Anna all slept in Baby's room, and they had their last breakfast on trays before they got up. Then Baby and Anna went to the train with us. He wept a little when they kissed him goodbye. In fact, I think all of us wept, even Min. But after that, and before the train finally left, he got off onto the platform with us and was quite cheerful and smiley. He went on with young Leeds Nutchell and an Arthur Orr boy, who felt just about as cheerful as he did. So that helped matters a good deal. He took his typewriter and was planning to write us letters on the train, and then he bought three books on the way to the train, and Min got him some magazine and some gum, so he was prepared to be occupied during the trip. They send a master up from Fessenden to meet them and take them back to school.

Today we are having about 30 people to lunch. Dinners don't work out with us, somehow, so we have luncheons. It's as gloomy a day as ever you saw, so it will be difficult to light the dining room cheerfully. I am having a number of small tables and a buffet lunch, which is most informal and really great fun and very short. It only lasts about half an hour, so with everything, the whole party is over by 2:15 or 2:30. Tonight Marion McFadden is giving a dinner dance in the red lacquer room at the Palmer House. We are going and are much excited, as it's the first time we've been to a party at night there. Everything is going so much better and bigger than anyone dreamed of. You can't imagine it. Yesterday there were more than 2,000 people there for luncheon! Everything is crowded, and people are crazy about it, for it is certainly beautiful, and the food is delicious. It is amazing. You, without seeing it, cannot possibly imagine what it's like. It's more like a huge civic institution than a hotel.

I have started a book called "The Cenci," but it's so horrible that I don't believe I'll finish it. I suppose it's true to the 16th Century in Italy, but usually we have the beautiful side and not the horrible, sordid side that this book gives. After reading of those times, one wonders how all the beauty that we now have managed to last through it. What wonders must have been destroyed! And what a quiet, protected life we lead nowadays, by comparison. We fuss about bandits, but when anybody wanted anything in those days, they took it, and if the owner made a loud sound, they laid his head open with a stick! Well, well.

I must now pen a few lines to my offspring. I've just had word that Bertha arrived safely and was met by Miss Darling and taken to Concord, and also that Potter arrived at Grace's in N.Y. after his stay in Philadelphia. I had a wild telegram from Honoré just now. "Potter not yet arrived wire information." So for a few minutes I had "visions" and then realized that Honoré hadn't received Potter's telegram saying that he would arrive about four P.M., and his telegram was sent about seven P.M. Then in a few minutes a message came from Grace saying that Potter was there. As Grace and Cappy are used to dealing in vagueness, I don't feel as if Potter has been vague, although I don't know at what hour he finally reached N.Y. But he is vague and always thinks everybody knows by second sight just what he is doing! Such a comfortable way to be for Potter! He's a dear, anyway.

I must telegraph Gordy to telegraph me that he has arrived. He likes to find telegrams and letters in his box, to say nothing of packages. So we send him something every day. Why don't you send him [a post card] of views. He loves views.

Lots of love,

Pauline

Pauline Palmer outside the Castle

Notes

December 21, 1925: Elsie is Elizabeth Day McCormick, the costume collector; Watson is Watson Armour and Howard is Howard Gillette, friends of young Potter at St. Marks.

December 24, 1925: Besides being a luxurious hotel, the Palmer House was then the place debutante parties were held. There was exhibition dancing during dinner by a couple named Veloz and Yolanda, who did jazz, tango, and Latin dancing.

December 27, 1925: The Ellen mentioned early in the letter is Ellen Borden, mother of Ellen Borden, who married Adlai Stevenson. Laseref was a colonel in the White Russian Army who came to Chicago and became a member of Mike Cantacuzène's expatriate group. Pauline comments that Ellen Sturgis may have had a hard time if her future mother-in-law doesn't like her. Ginevra is Ginevra King, who had once been a celebrated Chicago debutante, and in 1915 had carried on a brief love affair with F. Scott Fitzgerald. She is said to be the inspiration for Daisy Buchanan in The Great Gatsby. Dorothy Ranney later became Mrs. Gaylord Donnelly.

Potter Palmer II

EPILOGUE

THE END OF THE "PALMER LEGEND"

When Pauline died in 1956, her style was compared to that of her famous mother-in-law. Her entertainments were known for being done "in impeccable taste rather than on a grand scale." The writer concluded that "the Potter Palmer legend was said to have begun with Bertha Honoré Palmer, but there are many who believe it was the gracious lady, Pauline, who in her own quiet way, kept the legend alive."

Today the Palmer name brings forth the image of the enormous Palmer House Hotel, built by Potter I before the 1871 fire and rebuilt soon after. The family no longer owns the hotel; it was sold to Hilton Hotels in 1945. More than a century and a quarter since it first opened in grand style, the hotel is still an attraction for tourists and a place for business conventions and large meetings. For decades State Street, the concept of the city's first real estate developer, Potter Palmer, was the place to go for the important retail stores, and although many have departed, the original Marshall Field's and Carson Pirie Scott still remain. Today State Street has been upstaged as the chic shopping district by Michigan Avenue's "Magnificent Mile" —about a mile-and-a-half north across the Chicago River. There, customers can indulge in department stores like Bloomingdale's and Lord & Taylor. Chicago's famous loop, which includes State Street, is making a comeback, however. Older office buildings are being converted to residential spaces and hotels, and visitors are drawn to the popular new Millennium Park with its Frank Gehry band shell

and performing spaces for music and dance. At the nearby Art Institute, art lovers can view the glorious French paintings that Bertha Honoré Palmer purchased and which once hung in her long-gone Castle.

If Potter Palmer were alive today he would see that Chicago's center of gravity has shifted; even the venerable Marshall Field's has created a smaller spin-off of itself at Water Tower Place north of the Chicago River. The city has evolved from its beginnings as a mid-west boom town to become a thriving twenty-first-century metropolis. It is certainly second to none for fantastic architecture, as new buildings by leading designers punctuate the skyline. Full of energy and vitality, and situated so fortunately overlooking its lakefront, Chicago is more exciting than Potter Palmer could have dreamed of when he first saw the chance to make his fortune there.

POTTER PALMER II

After 1926 Potter II, or "Min," presided over the Board at the Art Institute. He guided the organization through financial challenges during the Depression, and through years of exciting expansion. Besides working in the family banking business in Florida with his brother, Honoré, he looked after his mother's estate, including the Palmer House and other Chicago properties. In July 1943 at the age of 67, a series of persistent colds complicated Min's heart condition. He died later that year in Santa Barbara, California, where he and Pauline had moved for the climate, leaving an estate of over four million dollars. In homage to the memory of its president, the Art

Mrs. Potter Palmer Serves Tea

Antiquarians Hold Reception

Institute flew its flag at half-mast. Min's Institute colleagues Chauncey McCormick, Joseph T. Ryerson, and Russell Tyson, wrote affectionately of his accomplishments: "he was modest and unassuming" and "his counsel formed our policies and directed our progress." Their words publicly recognized how much Potter Palmer meant to the Art Institute and "to the larger cause of art in Chicago and in the world."

PAULINE KOHLSAAT PALMER

After moving out of the Castle in the late 1920s, and into a large apartment at 1301 North Astor Street, Pauline continued to create charming and elegant rooms on three floors. She showed off her exquisite artworks. As Daniel Catton Rich noted: "Her husband's collection of early Chinese pottery was handsomely combined with eighteenth-century furniture." In her own rooms she enjoyed paintings from the Castle, collections of glass, and drawings and watercolors by Cézanne, Picasso, Seurat, and Henry Moore. Visitors to the apartment entered a mirrored foyer and found themselves in the dining room, where glass cases showed off Min's Chinese figures. On the second floor was an apartment for Pauline's mother, Mabel Kohlsaat, and above, the bedrooms.

Although her letters revealed her apprehension on leading the Antiquarian Society meetings, Pauline, like her husband, continued her enthusiastic involvement and patronage at the Art Institute in many positions. She was one of its governing life members, and she continued her role as honorary co-chairman of the Women's Board on the Decorative Arts Committee, a position held since 1922. She joined the Committee of Textiles in 1945, and two years later, the Committee of Prints and Drawings. She also remained committed to the Antiquarian Society, of which she had been a member since 1911.

While at her summer house in Bar Harbor, Pauline was active on the board of the Ruggles

House, a handsome merchant's house north of Bar Harbor that well-off summer residents were working to restore. She was often seen at the Bar Harbor Club's Tombola luncheons and at other events with friends. Grandchildren remember her hospitality at Hare Forest, a large shingle-style house on Ocean Drive that burned in the Bar Harbor Fire of 1947, and later, at her house on West Street near the town center. As always she made sure "the young"—her children and grandchildren—had a good time: sailing and frequenting the Bar Harbor Club, where all gathered for lunch, tennis, and swimming, and evening dances on Tuesday and Saturdays.

After Min died in the mid-forties, Pauline contemplated building a new house near Sarasota to be designed by architect and friend David Adler and influenced by the work of Mies van der Rohe. It was to be very different in style from the Mediterranean Revival mansion of her friends Sara and Stanley Field not far away. The house was never built. Instead, she continued on at the Oaks, enjoying the mild climate and the views of the sea, and cared for by her loyal staff, including Ellen, her cook, Ellen's sister, Esther, and Kasper, the chauffeur.

During the last years of her life Pauline took up painting. Floral still-lifes were her preference. Her obituary noted that "her paintings, like herself, were the epitome of good taste."

Pauline died at her home in Chicago on July 7, 1956, at the age of 74, after several months of illness. She was survived by three of her children, seven grandchildren, and her mother, who was still alive at the age of 96. Her estate, estimated at more than $500,000, was left in trust to her children and grandchildren, with many paintings, prints and drawings bequeathed to the Art Institute.

MABEL KOHLSAAT
Mabel Kohlsaat continued to live in Italy after 1926. But, in the late 1930s, after the rise of Mus- solini and the consequent problems with his government, the family persuaded her to give up her expatriate life. Back in America, Mabel divided her time between her daughters: wintering with Pauline, where she had her own rooms on the second floor of the apartment on Astor Street, and summering with Katherine Shepard and her family at their Green Acres Farm in St. Paul. Her grandchildren and her great-grandchildren remember her as "quite a character," a formidable and genial presence at Sunday lunches. As she grew older she showed her love of Italy by switching from speaking English to Italian. She died in 1959, after her daughter Pauline, at the age of 98.

HONORÉ PALMER
After the late 1920s Honoré ("Cappy") Palmer moved from Chicago to Sarasota and became known as Sarasota's pioneer developer and banker. He invested in holdings in the area: citrus groves, agriculture, and cattle. Sharing the family's civic sense, he, Min, and Prince Michael Cantacuzène founded the Palmer National Bank and Trust Company on July 20, 1929. It was a time of economic crisis in Florida, following the collapse of the land boom. Two Sarasota banks had failed. Palmer National Bank started its operations on the same premises as the failed banks. The Sarasota newspaper reported that "the new bank has added a feeling of confidence to the people of Sarasota." Under Palmer family management the bank survived the Great Depression and the bankruptcy of two other local banks. Major investments were made after World War II to modernize the bank's facilities and keep them competitive. While the Palmers managed the bank employment there was always an option for family members. In 1976, after the Palmers ceased to be involved in management, Palmer National Bank merged with Southeast Bank, a larger Florida competitor.

Potter Palmer III and his bride, Rose Saltonstall Movius, 1932.

Bertha Palmer and Pauline Palmer.

During the war Cappy joined in the effort as chairman of Sarasota's chapter of the Red Cross. He and his brother knew the value of preserving the beautiful Florida landscape. In 1934 they gave nineteen hundred acres of land to the state, which now makes up part of Myakka State Park. Cappy and his wife, Grace Brown Palmer, continued their generous philanthropy in the area by giving one million dollars to Sarasota's newly established New College in 1962. He died in 1964 at the age of 90 at "Immokalee," the house built by him and his brother. The two families had once taken turns spending alternate winters

there. Five years later, in 1966, Cappy's wife, Grace, died at her home in Sarasota at age 83.

Both of Cappy's sons died young: Honoré, Jr., on February 6, 1938, of a brain hemorrhage at the age of 29. He had been exercising at a New York gym when he passed out, and never regained consciousness. D'orsay died the following year. He had been divorced three times and had married wife number four, a former waitress at a curb-service sandwich stand, two days after his last divorce. According to the autopsy report, D'orsay died from a massive streptococcus infection, which caused broncho-pneumonia.

POTTER PALMER III

Potter Palmer, Pauline's first child, so affectionately described in her letters, went on from St.
Marks School to Harvard. In 1932, he returned to
Chicago to look after the Palmer House, the hotel
his grandfather built, as well as other business
affairs. The same year, he married Rose Movius
from Boston. They had two children, Rose Saltonstall Palmer, born in 1933, and Potter Palmer IV,
born in 1934. Rose, known as Posy, married John
H. O'Neil, Jr. in 1959 and they had three children. She died in 1978. Potter Palmer IV lives in

Opposite: Bar Harbor Club in the 1940s. Above: Gordon Palmer and Arthur Wood at the Bar Harbor Club.

Chicago where he has served on local civic boards, and is currently on the board of the Chicago Historical Society. He was formerly on the board of the Palmer First National Bank in Sarasota. He is a great sports fan and formerly part owner of the Harlem Globetrotters and the Atlanta Braves.

In 1942 Potter Palmer III enlisted as a lieutenant in the navy and served as a naval air intelligence officer in the Pacific. By the time he was discharged in November of 1945 he had been promoted to lieutenant commander. Potter and Rose were divorced in 1943. On October 3, 1946, at the age of 37, Potter Palmer III died of a heart attack at his home near Sarasota. Like his grandfather, he dreamed of opening a hotel, and is said to have been negotiating a deal for one in Sarasota just before his death.

BERTHA PALMER THORNE

Following her time at Concord Academy, Bertha Palmer, Pauline's feisty first daughter spent a year studying in Paris. In 1930 she married Oakleigh Lewis Thorne. They were divorced just after the War. They had three children: a son, Oakleigh Blakeman Thorne, born in 1931, and two daughters, Bertha Honoré Thorne (called Honoré), born in 1934, and Charlotte Pearsall Thorne, born in 1938. After a career in banking in New York City, her son Oakleigh retired to Millbrook, New York, and Key West, Florida. Charlotte married and divorced David Bordeaux and lives in Bar Harbor on property inherited from her mother. Honoré married Karl Wamsler and lived in Munich as well as in Osprey, Florida, near the Oaks property. She died in 2004. At the time of her death, she was a prominent patron of the New York Botanical Garden in New York City.

Bertha Palmer Thorne shared her mother's great interest in needlework. She lived in Bedford Village, New York, and then moved to Bar Harbor, Maine. She built two beautiful houses and lived there year round, enjoying the beauty of the Maine seashore at Cromwell Harbor and the paintings she inherited from her mother's and grandmother's collections. She died in 1974, at the age of 63.

GORDON PALMER

Gordon Palmer, the second son of Min and Pauline, was sent to St. Marks School in Southboro, Massachusetts. He graduated in 1932, and went on to graduate from Harvard in 1936. After college he left for Chicago, where he worked in business until he received a commission in the U.S. Navy in 1941. He was assigned a post in Washington, D.C., where he served as a lieutenant commander until 1946. In the same year he married Janis Hardage of Atlanta, Georgia. He briefly returned to Chicago for business, but in 1950 he and his wife moved to Sarasota. There

Gordon joined the family business as a director of Palmer First National Bank and Trust Company, founded by his father and uncle. He also organized the Palmer nurseries at Osprey. Gordon and Janis spent summers in Bar Harbor, where friends enjoyed the appealing personality that Pauline describes in her letters. He died in 1964 at the age of 49, following a long illness.

PAULINE PALMER WOOD
Pauline Palmer, the Palmer's second daughter, went to Concord Academy, like her sister. After traveling in Europe, she married Arthur Mac-Dougall Wood. They had two children, Pauline Palmer Wood, now Pauline Egan, born in 1948, and Arthur MacDougall Wood, Jr., born in 1950. Arthur Wood, Jr. is now the president and CEO of the Illinois North Region of the Northern Trust Company in Lake Forest, Illinois. Pauline Wood was involved with the Chicago Historical Society and the Lake Forest Garden Club. She epitomized grace and had a wonderful sense of humor. She loved music of all kinds, especially jazz, big band and pop, and even attended Rolling Stones concerts. She died in April of 1984 at the age of 67.

JULIA GRANT CANTACUZÈNE
Julia and her husband, Prince Michael Cantacuzène of Russia, who had fled the Ukraine during the Russian Revolution, (he had owned an 80,000 acre estate there), made their home in Sarasota. Julia's memoir, *My Life Here and There*, which was published in 1921, dealt with her childhood as granddaughter of President Ullysses S. Grant and her years in Russia as Princess Cantacuzène. She also wrote articles, a book about the Revolution entitled *Revolutionary Days*, and gave lectures on her past life and on contemporary world events. In 1934 she and the prince were divorced, but she continued to live in Sarasota until the late 1940s. In her later years she lost her sight, but miraculously regained it before her death. She died in Washington, D.C., on October 5, 1975 at the age of 99, where she was, according to her obituary, "one of the capital's more spirited hostesses."

Julia's son, Michael Cantacuzène, lived in Chicago, where he became the center of a Russian expatriate group.

ROGER SHEPARD
Roger Shepard's family had lived in St. Paul, Minnesota, since his grandfather David Shepard, had come west from New York State. There, he and other settlers from the East had prospered in banking and milling grain. Roger, who had been urged to enter the dry goods business by his grandfather, continued in St. Paul until the Great Depression. At that time, he moved to New York with Katherine and their children to work for Blair and Company, a Wall Street firm started by his Yale friend from Chicago, William McCormick Blair. Later on, he worked in Washington, D.C., joining a group of businessmen during Franklin D. Roosevelt's administration, but kept an apartment in New York, where his children could visit from their colleges.

KATHERINE SHEPARD
In 1929 Katherine Shepard had a fourth child, Stanley, adding to her three: Roger, born in 1911, Blake, born in 1914, and Constance, born in 1919. Katherine and her sister, Pauline, continued to be close, visiting each other regularly. Her daughter Constance Shepard Otis remembers how she and her mother would go to Aunt Pauline's apartment at 1301 North Astor Street, where her aunt would show off her new treasures. "Come see my walls," Pauline would say.

THE PALMERS' CHICAGO FRIENDS
Edith Rockefeller McCormick, whose family happenings Pauline reports to her mother, had moved back to Chicago from Switzerland in the early

Top left: Beaded drawstring bag (French, 1783) from the Elizabeth Day McCormick Collection at the Museum of Fine Arts, Boston. Bottom left: Eighteenth-century dress from the Elizabeth Day McCormick Collection.
Right: Etta McCormick Williams, Elizabeth Day McCormick, and Phoebe McCormick Ayer at the opening of Elizabeth Day McCormick Exhibition of Costumes and Costume Accessories in Boston 1945.
Page 281: The "Duchene Lawn" reminds visitors of the Palmer years at the Oaks in Osprey.

twenties. She then succeeded in replacing Bertha Honoré Palmer as the city's finest hostess, entertaining lavishly in her large and beautifully decorated house until her death in 1932. Her great interest was Chicago's Opera; it was a privilege to be asked to dine amongst her treasures before the performances. No drinks were served, however, as years ago she had promised her father, John D. Rockefeller, that she would not touch alcohol. Before her death she lost her fortune in a series of bad real estate investments, and had to sell her impressive house, a forty-one room, gray granite Romanesque mansion at 1000 Lake Shore Drive, also known as a "castle."

Elizabeth Day McCormick, who was enthusiastically involved in the Antiquarian Society with Pauline, continued to collect period needlework, textiles, laces, and costumes, traveling often to Europe to hunt for objects with Mildred, her unmarried sister. In 1943 she gave her collection to the Museum of Fine Arts in Boston, where it became the foundation of its important costume collection. The Elizabeth Day McCormick collection contains over 5,000 embroideries, textiles, and costumes from all over the world. According to a catalog from the Museum of Fine Arts' exhibit, "From Fiber to Fine Art," "especially outstanding [are] the eighteenth-century examples of men's and women's formal dress." The footwear collection contains the best examples in the country from the fifteenth century through the early twentieth century. Because of her contribution the museum possesses one of the most formidable collections of costumes in the country.

Marshall Field, one of Chicago's foremost entrepreneurs, had come to Chicago from Massachusetts in 1856. Once there, he, along with Potter Palmer and Levi Leiter, formed the dry goods store that would later become the famous Marshall Field's department store. In 1893, he funded the construction of the Field Museum, which was initially part of the World's Columbian Exposition. In the 1920s his nephew Stanley Field, himself a naturalist, and Stanley's wife, Sara, who were friends of the younger generation of Palmers, succeeded in establishing the Field Museum as it stands today on Lake Shore Drive. Stanley was president of the museum for forty-one years, as well as a generous benefactor. Today the Field Museum, along with the John G. Shedd Aquarium and the Adler Planetarium, is the place to go see its archaeological, biological, and natural history collections.

THE PALMER CASTLE

In 1928 the Lake Shore Drive mansion of the Palmers was taken over by Vincent Bendix, of the Bendix Aviation Corporation. In 1933 the Palmer estate bought back the mansion. No one lived in it and it remained for the most part vacant until 1942, when it was put to practical use by the Red Cross, which converted it into a temporary surgical dressing cener.

The Castle met its demise on February 12, 1950, when a wrecking ball demolished the majestic landmark. It was to be replaced by a "family apartment building, with units of two to five rooms (renting at forty dollars a room)." Before the demolition, the public was allowed inside briefly to view the house one last time and to gather mementos— "bits of filigree" or whatever souvenirs they could carry. In the words of one witness, the event was "like seeing the face of a haughty and elegant matriarch dissolve into tears."

THE OAKS

The Oaks, in Osprey, Florida, the mansion so enjoyed by Palmer and Honoré family members, was torn down in the early 1960s. Only the jungle garden and the sunken garden, which has been replanted according to its original design, remain to evoke Bertha Palmer's Gilded Age. The Duchene Lawn, which had been obscured by overgrowth, was restored in 1980, allowing visitors to once again view the classic portal and stately green.

In 1975 the Palmer family donated thirty acres of Oaks property to be listed in the National Register of Historic Places. The land is now known as "Historic Spanish Point" and is part of the Gulf Coast Heritage Association. Previously, an archaeological study of the estate sponsored by Gordon Palmer had established the site's significance. Found there were two prehistoric Indian shell middens, making it the largest prehistoric Indian village site on the west coast of Florida. Fortunately, its later occupants had left the land relatively undisturbed.

Today the visitor to the property comes away with a fuller historical perspective: the Native American era, which lasted from 3000 B.C. to 1000 A.D., was followed by the homestead period of the "pioneers" (1867–1910), making the Palmers occupancy there but a pause in the march of time.

Mary Cassatt famously said, "I suppose it is Mrs. Palmer's French blood which gives her her organizing powers and her determination that women should be someone and not something." Maybe her French blood also explains Bertha Palmer's partiality for the French painters of her day, whose works she bought in profusion and later gave to the Art Institute. As former president of the Institute, James N. Wood writes: "In 1922 when the collection of Mr. and Mrs. Potter Palmer was bequeathed to the museum, her foresighted choices laid the foundation for the Art Institute's preeminence in nineteenth-century art."

The Art Institute had begun in 1879 as the Chicago Academy of Fine Arts, and the Palmers, along with members of other prominent Chicago families, like the Charles Hutchinsons, the Martin Ryersons, and the Marshall Fields, supported it from the beginning. They bought European masterpieces and loaned their paintings for exhibits. Bertha presided over the Antiquarian Society and her husband, Potter, was a generous contributor until his death in 1902. After Bertha's death in 1918 her son Potter took over his parents' role, and with his brother, Honoré, donated large parts of Bertha's collections to the Institute. Potter II acted as its president for almost twenty years. With Pauline he collected as well, contributing more than five hundred prints and money to buy more. His wife, in her serene but still enthusiastic fashion, presided over the Institute's Antiquarian Society, and served on many Institute committees.

Bertha Palmer, a larger-than-life personality, enjoyed being surrounded by fine objects in the opulently decorated Palmer "Castle." Built by the senior Palmers at 1350 Lake Shore Drive in the early 1880s and designed by architects Henry Ives Cobb and Charles Sumner Frost, "the Castle" helped to transform the shorefront of Lake Michigan into a fashionable neighborhood. When it first appeared, the large house was the subject of strong reactions: it was variously described as "early English battlemented style," "castellated Gothic," "Norman Gothic," and even "a liver colored monstrosity." It cost about $1 million and was the mid-western version of the "cottages" of Newport and the Fifth Avenue mansions of New York City's *nouveaux riches*. Its decoration clearly flaunted Bertha's exuberant and eclectic taste.

Arriving at the Castle, the awed visitor found himself in an entrance hall, which, as historian Mary Blanchard writes, "opened into a large octagonal rotunda three stories high with onyx walls and a golden stained-glass cupola. This rotunda, the hub of the house, also had walls of quartersawn oak with intricately carved bas-relief and an impressive carved oak stairway." The central spiral staircase, adorned with gothic pillars and the Honoré coat of arms on the posts, was mostly decorative, since the castle boasted two private elevators, the first ever installed in a Chicago residence. As a further novelty, the white-and-gold French drawing room, with its tile floor inlaid with pink roses, was Chicago's first Louis XV salon. Bertha later embellished it with murals of roses and gold tesserae and cupids flying on the ceiling. The English dining room

Preceding page 282: Portrait of Mrs. Potter Palmer by Anders Zorn, 1893.
This page at left: The 75-foot gallery of the Palmers' Castle with Bertha Palmer's art collection displayed on the red velvet walls. Above: Jean Baptiste Camille Corot, **Interrupted Reading**, *1870.*
Following page 286, Top: Bertha Palmer's drawing room looking towards the main gallery. Bottom left: The dining room in Castle at the turn of the century. Bottom right: North corner of Palmer Castle's main gallery, around 1900. Page 287: The entry hall of the Palmer Castle, which was three stories high and welcomed the visitor with its magnificent wood carvings and entrance doors into more treasure-filled rooms.

NOTE: ALL THE ARTWORK IN THIS CHAPTER IS FROM THE ART INSTITUTE OF CHICAGO WITH THE EXCEPTION OF WHISTLER'S LITHOGRAPH, THE FAN, WHICH IS ON LOAN FROM THE ESTATE OF PAULINE K. PALMER.

Above: The Palmer Castle which drew all kinds of comments when it first appeared in the early 1880s. It was called "Castellated Gothic," "Norman Gothic" and even "a liver colored monstrosity." It was filled with treasures collected by Bertha and Potter on their many trips abroad, and led the way to making Lake Shore Drive a fashionable place to live.

Below: One of Bertha's paintings on a marine subject: James McNeil Whistler, **Grey and Silver: Old Batteresea Reach,** *1863.*

Opposite, the seventy-five foot long gallery was a later addition created in 1893 in time to show off Bertha's art collection to important visitors to the World's Columbian Expostion.

seated fifty people with ease. It featured a great mahogany-and-crystal sideboard, on either side of which hung George P. A. Healy's portraits of Mr. and Mrs. Palmer. Its Tiffany glass windows were eight feet high. The combination ballroom and picture gallery was a later addition to the house, and it served as the perfect setting for Bertha's lavish entertaining, with iridescent Tiffany glass chandeliers, red velvet covering the walls, and an overhanging balcony where the orchestra played.

The Flemish Renaissance library, with its hand-carved oak walls, murals by Gabriel Ferrier, and "six life-size oak figures over the fireplace," was the favorite retreat of Potter Palmer. Its furnishings were by the New York firm of Herter Brothers. Known for their eclectic style, their beautifully made inlaid furniture and their lavish materials, the Herter Brothers were the designers and furniture-makers of choice for American millionaires wanting to show off their social position and wealth. In the early 1880s they had just finished outfitting the Fifth Avenue mansion of railroad tycoon William H. Vanderbilt. In 1893, the Palmers would again ask the Herters for help installing the mosaic floor and the mosaic and marble border on the walls in their new gallery, using both Belgian black marble and red Numidian marble next to the wainscoting.

Bertha's bedroom was of Moorish design, in ebony and gold, with arched windows of cathedral glass copied from a palace in Cairo. Its ten-foot bed was "roomy enough for Hercules and his wife," a critic noted. Her private bathroom boasted a basin with an inlaid mother-of-pearl wreath and a sunken bathtub in the shape of a swan. Leading off the bedroom was the French sitting room, or "White Room," where intimate friends visited.

In their collecting, the Palmers followed the current vogue set by rich Bostonians like S. D. Warren, Quincy Adams Shaw, and Martin Brim-

*Top: Claude Monet, **Stacks of Wheat, End of the Summer**, 1890-91. Center: Jean Francois Millet, **In the Auvergne**, 1866-9. Bottom: Claude Monet, **Stack of Wheat**, 1890-1. Opposite page: Edgar Hilaire Germain Degas, **On the Stage**, 1876-7.*

mer, of purchasing paintings by artists of the Barbizon School, among them Corot, Millet, and Diaz. The American success of the Barbizon School was largely due to William Morris Hunt, the New England painter and brother of architect Richard Morris Hunt, who studied in Europe and identified closely with the Barbizon painters, especially Millet. Back in the United States, Hunt, a "dominating personality," published controversial works of art theory and encouraged American collectors throughout New England (especially in Boston) to purchase Barbizon paintings. Bertha Honoré Palmer was drawn to these studies of the simple life in pastoral landscapes. According to her biographer, Ishbel Ross, she also checked out the painters first-hand, driving out to Barbizon in the Fontainebleau Forest outside of Paris to see them at work.

She also bought American works by Mary Cassatt, James MacNeill Whistler, Eastman Johnson, George Hitchcock, and George Inness, and paintings by Delacroix, whose impressive use of color and highly gestural brushwork was not unlike the style of the new Impressionist painters.

Bertha used her visits to Paris in the early 1890s not only to stir up support for the Exposition but also to shop for Impressionist paintings which she hung in her gallery, brightening up the rooms and creating an atmosphere of picturesque French life. As the Impressionists were not popular with French collectors at the time and the influence of the Salon still ruled, those who bought their works—among them the Palmers, and the Havemeyers of New York—were considered pioneers. Her first Impressionist acquisition, purchased for $500 in 1889, was Degas' pastel, *On the Stage.* Her motivation and that of her husband was twofold: to exhibit art in their new gallery and to invest in paintings that they "wouldn't lose money on," as Potter Palmer I confided to American Impressionist painter Theodore Robinson. In her purchases, Bertha was helped

by two women: Sarah Hallowell, a Chicagoan who used her expert eye at the Salons to find art for rich clients—in late 1893 she even helped Bertha hang her paintings in the new gallery—and Mary Cassatt, a painter herself and an intimate friend of Degas.

Bertha Honoré Palmer was among the American collectors who had attended the exhibition of Monet's *Stacks of Wheat* at the Durand-Ruel Gallery in Paris in 1891. The exhibition was revolutionary because it was a one-man show, rarely seen at the time, and because only one theme was displayed. The series of stacks of wheat consisted of twenty-five slightly varying views of more or less the same scene, fifteen of which were displayed in 1891. It was the nuances in light, color, and composition that made the paintings powerful. In painting these stacks of wheat landscapes as he saw and felt them in the moment, Monet strove to express the ephemeral quality of nature. And by depicting a "series of instants" and focusing on his experience and the effect of his paintings rather than on their subject, Monet captured the spirit of Impressionism. Viewers were forced to focus on details and on the various effects of different light and color treatments. While not all who viewed the exhibition were able to understand the significance of these works, the enlightened among them participated in a sort of collaborative experience with the painter. The show resulted in a boost of enthusiasm for Monet, especially among Americans. The paintings from the exhibit were sold individually, to Monet's regret, as he had earlier stated that "their true worth only reside[d] in relation to each other and as part of the entire series." However, Bertha Honoré Palmer bought nine, and though she sold several—one to Louisine Havemeyer, which is now at the Metropolitan Museum, and others to fellow Chicagoans, including the Ryersons—it is largely due to her that six of them, the largest single collection, hang together today at the Art

*Opposite: Mary Cassatt, **Mother and Child**, 1888. Above: Pierre Auguste Renoir, **Acrobats at the Cirque Fernando**, 1879.*

Institute of Chicago.

Over the years Bertha enjoyed her Impressionist paintings in the Castle's enormous gallery. Later she took some to her apartment in Paris, where they were hung on white-and-gold walls, with complementary flower arrangements on low tables in front of them. These paintings exemplified some of the prime interests of the painters themselves. Her seascapes by Monet, Manet, and Whistler explored the themes in marine painting that so fascinated these painters; the *Stacks of Wheat* by Monet illustrated his studies of light falling on the same object. She owned examples of Degas' favorite subjects: dancers and bathers. As Suzanne McCullagh writes, "Approximately half of Degas' entire output of paintings and pastels concerns dancers." Degas' oil *Preparing for*

*Above: Camille Pissarro, **The Place du Havre, Paris**, 1893. Below: Pierre Cécile Puvis de Chavannes, **The Sacred Grove, Beloved of the Arts and the Muses**, 1884-9. Opposite: Edouard Manet, **The Races at Longchamps**, 1866, which captured the feeling of movement so popular with Impressionist painters.*

the Ballet (1872–6) deals with a favorite theme, "that of dancers adjusting their costumes off stage." Her pastel of the nude bather *In the Bath* (1887–90) shows the artist's way of articulating the female form in an unconventional composition. The foreground is given over to an unmade bed while the main interest—the colorful nude figure—occupies the background.

Several of the paintings pictured moments in which the artist caught an instant in time—an aim so characteristic of the Impressionist movement. As Richard Brettell writes, "Flux came to be perceived as the central condition of modernity and, like it or not, painters needed to find forms for it…sunsets, trains rushing over bridges, sailboats turning, carriages coming down a boulevard, horses rushing toward a finish line, gusts of wind, flowers just cut from a plant, people chatting intimately at a café, etc.—these were the subjects that the Impressionists chose to investigate." Two of Bertha's Manets gave the viewer this sense of recording a moment in the movement of forms: *Departure from Boulogne Harbor* (1864–65) and *The Races at Longchamps* (1866), in which "Manet's horses rush pell-mell at the viewer, their legs pounding the turf into fine dust"

and their jockeys "hanging on for dear life."

In 1892 the Palmers purchased a set of Cassatt's 1890–1891 color prints and her pastel *Young Mother*, now at the Art Institute. The same year Bertha also bought Renoir's *Dans le Cirque* for $1,750, valued in the 1960s at $200,000. (Paintings on which she spent only a thousand or so dollars, would now probably bring millions.) This painting of the two little circus girls became one of the prized pieces in Bertha's collection; she claimed it reminded her of herself and her sister, Ida Honoré Grant, when they were children. Bertha also made her way to Monet's studio and garden at Giverny, where one could see the scenes he painted over and over: the poplars, the water lilies, the brightly colored flowers in his garden. The story goes that she soon purchased enough Monet canvases—the number is usually put at thirty-two—to form a frieze around the top of one of her grand rooms.

Bertha used her winning personality in her art dealing. She became a familiar figure at Durand-Ruel's in Paris and at Sotheby's in Lon-

don. As Alice Saarinen writes, "Bertha got people to do what she wanted, with such tact, such cordiality, such charm and quiet self assurance that her foes fell painlessly." (The Durand-Ruel Gallery was asked to advise her on the lighting in her new gallery in 1893.)

In the exhibition of "Foreign Masterpieces Owned by Americans" at the World's Columbian Exposition in 1893, works from the Palmers hung in the Fine Arts Palace: a Corot, a Puvis de Chavannes, Cazin's *Judith and Elsinine*, three Rafaellis, and a Delacroix. Along with these hung a Manet, a Pissaro, a Sisley, and several canvases by Degas, called by a critic "of little value except as specimens of the Impressionist School, from a man who seldom completes a picture and yet is hailed by his brethren as one of the most talented and original artists of his day." For the most part, the lenders of these controversial pictures, often called "unfinished," were Alexander Cassatt (Mary's brother, who would soon be the president of the Pennsylvania Railroad,) and the Potter Palmers.

Bertha had dealt closely with Mary Cassatt in

Top: Eugene Delacroix, **Lion Hunt**, 1860-61.
Bottom: Jean Charles Cazin, **Theocritus**, 1890.
Opposite top: Jean Francois Millet, **Young Woman**,
1844-5. Below: Alfred Sisley, **Street in Moret**, 1890.
Preceding pages 296-297: Edgar Hilaire Germain
Degas, **Yellow Dancers**, 1874-6. Edgar Hilaire
Germain Degas, **The Morning Bath**, 1892-5.
Bertha H. Palmer owned paintings that dealt with
Degas' favorite subjects: dancers and bathers.

the planning stages of the Columbian Exposition. She was involved not only in selecting the architect for the Woman's Building, Sophia Hayden, but also the artists for the mural that was placed high upon its walls. The mural had two parts, representing on the one hand, "woman in her primitive condition as a bearer of burdens and doing drudgery. . . and, as a contrast, woman in the position she occupies today." Mary Cassatt executed the panel on the modern woman, and Mary Fairchild MacMonnies the one on the primitive woman. Primitive Woman was pictured crushing grapes and carrying water, burdened by a babe in

Above: Claude Monet, **The Departure of the Boats, Etretat**, *1885. Opposite Page: Claude Monet,* **Bordighera**, *1884*

arms. Modern Woman picked fruit, plucked a lyre, and gracefully pursued an Ideal. These two paintings, like the building in which they were placed, reflected what Mrs. Palmer called "the inspiration of woman's genius."

After 1893 Bertha's energy for buying paintings subsided somewhat, and following Potter Palmer's death in 1902, she bought no more paintings, but began to collect faience, statuary, medieval wood-carvings, and silver tankards. In addition to her paintings and decorative arts, she also owned Oriental works from the Tang and Sung dynasties. She continued to be an active

presence at the Art Institute of Chicago, attending openings, giving talks, and arranging for her sons to become involved.

In 1910 fifty-three of her paintings went on exhibit at the Art Institute. The exhibit showcased her artistic tastes, including as it did works by Monet and Delacroix, whose reputations have lasted, and minor painters like Cazin and Rafaelli, who are now considered less significant. There were eight works by one of her favorites, Jean Charles Cazin, as well as Pierre Puvis de Chavannes's now highly prized *The Sacred Wood*, which hangs in the Institute today and is often

300

loaned to exhibitions. Other works were by French Academy painters Jules Bastien-Lepage, Paul Albert Besnard, and Charles Francois Daubigny. The Realist Jean-Francois Raffaelli was represented by five canvasses, while the Hungarian Realist, Mihaly Munkacsy and the Swedish Anders Zorn had one each on display. Also shown were Bertha's American paintings and her Barbizon School paintings by Corot and Millet. The Impressionist works included one by Pissaro, the early *Rowers' Lunch* by Renoir, *Village Street* by Sisley, six works by Degas, eleven by Monet, as well as Delacroix's *Lion Hunt*.

In 1922, four years after Bertha's death, her sons carried out their mother's intention to make a massive contribution of Palmer art works to form a gallery at the Art Institute. Fifty canvasses had been on exhibit the year before. Pauline, who often played down the family's celebrity status, wrote to her mother on May 11, 1921: "The paintings from 1350 [the Castle] are hung and have attracted a crowd. A prime psychological fact is that everyone who goes to see them puts on their best clothes! Isn't that funny?"

The will required the art works to be valued and allocated to two bequests, one of $100,000

maximum. The second bequest, indirectly by way of $400,000, enabled her sons to designate for charitable purposes a further group of paintings. Beyond that Honoré and Potter II gave an additional collection of thirty-two paintings bequeathed to them by their mother and valued at $343,500. The donated artworks included many that had been exhibited before and most of the choice Impressionist masterpieces: Monet's *On the Bank of the Seine at Bennecourt, Bordighera, Stacks of Wheat (Sunset Snow Effect)*, and *The Departure of the Boats*; Renoir's *The Rowers'*

Lunch; Pissarro's *The Place du Havre, Paris*; and Degas' *On the Stage*. The Institute thereby received exciting Impressionist pieces plus many good Barbizon School works such as Corot's *Interrupted Reading*, the important Puvis de Chavannes, and paintings by Delacroix. This gift, joined by the Martin Ryerson collection in 1932 and the collection of Annie Swan Coburn in 1933, helped to establish the Institute as a leader in the French Impressionists.

Like Bertha Palmer, Pauline and Potter II ("Min") were also serious and sensitive collec-

Opposite page: Pierre Auguste Renoir, **Lunch at the Restaurant Fournaise (The Rowers' Lunch)**, *1875.*
Above: Edouard Manet, **Streamboat Leaving Boulogne**, *1864.*

tors, although they were more likely to purchase decorative art objects and prints and drawings. Pauline, president of the Antiquarian Society between 1919 and 1927, and again between 1931 and 1934, made numerous gifts through her involvement. From 1941 until her death in 1956, she gave money and works, including a large number of prints, textiles, and decorative arts pieces. Although she enjoyed her Art Institute efforts, she preferred not being in charge, telling her mother in November of 1925: "Well, my awful meeting is over! and I feel weak after such a strain…for I no longer want to be president, but to have some pleasant job at the Institute like getting up exhibitions or looking for things to add to the collections. One can have a great deal of fun that way, and much less responsibility."

Min had become president of the Art Institute in 1925, a post he kept until his death in 1943. He succeeded Charles L. Hutchinson, founder, passionate art enthusiast, and the Art Institute's first president, who had died the previous October. Min's background qualified him for the post: he had grown up in the opulent interior

*Opposite page: Martin Schongauer, **St. Anthony Tormented by Demons**, 1480-90. Above: Upper Part of a Tabernacle from Santa Maria Maggiore, Rome.*

of the Castle, surrounded by his parents' ground-breaking paintings, and he had constantly traveled abroad with his mother and later with Pauline and the children. Min had an interest in early Chinese art, which, as C. J. Bulliet notes, allowed him to develop an insight into "Modernism." He also enthusiastically collected Old Master prints and engravings. After the First World War, important abstract art was appearing and was not always appealing to a museum board that was still largely conservative. With his appreciation of both the avant-garde and the traditional forms of art, Min could understand the points of view of board members who were conservative, and others who welcomed the new post-Impressionist and Modernist art.

After the death of the director Robert B. Harshe, Potter briefly became director pro-tem in 1938, a position which allowed him to manage even more aspects of the Institute, including the controversy between "modernism" and "conservatism." Harshe had succeeded in installing the thoroughly modern—even revolutionary —Birch-Bartlett Collection, allowing the Art Institute to take the lead among American museums as an advocate of modern works. After Harshe's death the Institute's more conservative members wanted to return to the ways of the 1893 World's Fair, and, as one article stated, "there were plenty of people who wanted to send the Birch-Bartlett Collection, including Seurat's *Grand Jatte*, greatest of 'modern' paintings, to the basement." Stepping in as pro-tem director, Potter Palmer, in his diplomatic way, handled the situation with tact and wisdom, remembering that even his mother's once-revolutionary interest in Impressionism was by this time regarded as "conservative." When the conflict subsided, Potter relinquished his position to Daniel Catton Rich, Harshe's young protégé.

During Min's years as president, the Art Institute continued to develop into one of the world's great art centers. While he was president, the Mather Addition, the Allerton Wings, the Industrial Art School, the Worcester Collection, and the Birch-Bartlett Gallery were added. In addition, great expansions to the Prints and Drawings Department and the Department of Decorative Arts took place. He oversaw many notable exhibitions, including two "Century of Progress" exhibits and "Masterpieces of French Art." He was known for his cool and genial manner—"self effacing to pretty near the vanishing point"—and generosity with praise for those he worked with.

In her letters Pauline mentions Min's talking with experts in different fields of art and furniture. On one trip to Europe he purchased part of a mid-fifteenth-century Italian marble tabernacle from the Church of Santa Maria Maggiore in Rome, which he later gave to the Institute. His real interests, however, were prints and drawings, furniture, and Chinese art. His collection of prints was enormous. Pauline had written her mother in April 1921 that "Min's engravings of early Italian, French, and German masters are to be hung in the A. I. during the first week in May, to be the summer exhibit. And he wants to be there then." And in May: " Our etchings are up at the A. I. and look very well. We've never seen them hung before, and I had no idea that we had so many. They stay up all summer." Min had been elected a member of the Prints and Drawings Committee the year before, in 1920, and became its chairman in 1922.

According to Martha Tedeschi, curator of the Institute's Prints and Drawings Department, the importance of Min's Old Master print collection is its great range. There was an attempt to be, "if not actually encyclopedic, at least broadly focused on major printmaking endeavors across the centuries." His collection not only includes late fifteenth century and sixteenth century prints, but also prints by Jacques Callot of the seventeenth century and some eighteenth-century works of the French color printmaker Jean Francois Janinet and the English engraver Richard Earlom. Particularly indicative of Min's seriousness as a collector was his acquisition of complete matching sets of the fifteenth-century Italian playing cards known as the *Tarrochi*, the work of an anonymous engraver now called the Master of the E-Series Tarrochi.

He collected works of both the Italian and Northern Renaissance; the latter included many fine impressions by the great printmakers of Germany: Martin Schongauer (c. 1450–1491) and Albrecht Dürer (1471–1528). Schongauer's *Saint Anthony Tormented by Demons*, one of his most famous works, combines, as H. W. Janson writes, "savage expressiveness and formal precision, violent movement and ornamental stability," and a great "range of tonal values." Schongauer was represented in Potter's collection by some sixty prints, and Dürer is represented by more than forty. By amassing such large numbers of prints by particular artists, it would seem that Potter was seeking to have representative collections of entire careers.

The fact that Min collected the jewel-like works of the Little Masters—Aldegrever, the Beham brothers (particularly Hans Sebald Beham), and Altdorfer—also reveals him as a very knowledgeable collector. These small, refined images would not have been of interest to everyone. His prints by Jacques Callot (1592–1635) number around forty. The French artist worked for the Medici court, recording in

The Library in the Palmer's Castle with Min's Chinese figures in the glass case in the left background.

his etchings and drawings fairs, festivals, and *commedia dell'arte* characters. Later, in his native Nancy, France, he also produced religious subjects and landscape drawings. Potter also collected works by important Italian printmakers such as Tommaso Finiguerra, Marcantonio Raimondi, and the school of engravers under Andrea Mantegna. With its breadth, depth, and the fine quality of the impressions, his was one of the most important print collections formed in the early twentieth century.

Potter later made many gifts to the Institute's Asian Department, showing his eye for Chinese masterpieces. His interest in Chinese art started when, as a young man in Paris, his mother began acquiring some outstanding pieces of Ming porcelain. These would later be at the center of his collection. Potter preferred the austerity of early Chinese art; Tang Dynasty sculptural pottery, dating from 618–907 AD, was his special favorite. As Charles Kelley has noted, "the glazed horses, camels, and attendants in his own home and the female musicians in the galleries of the Art Institute are the best that have come from China. But perhaps his most highly prized pieces were the Han dragon tiles." Under Potter Palmer II, the

*Above: Raoul Dufy, **Venus with Seashell**, 1925. Opposite: Paul Cezanne, **Man Wearing a Straw Hat**, 1905-6.*

Buckingham and Tyson Collections were formed and installed in the Asian Department.

After Potter's death, Chauncey McCormick, Joseph T. Ryerson, and Russell Tyson wrote that "his breadth of art interests is evidenced by his many generous gifts to different departments of the museum. He gave, as well, constantly of himself, unsparingly and tirelessly." He was frugal and practical with the Institute's money, preferring to repair a roof before buying new paintings.

Min and Pauline's taste could also be seen when they moved into the Castle in 1922, after buying out Honoré Palmer's share. The placement of Pauline's portrait above the fireplace symbol-ized the beginning of the junior Palmers' new reign, which would only last till the end of the decade. They asked David Adler, architect and friend—his wife was a family relation of Grace Palmer—to make alterations to some rooms, including the gallery. The cluttered Baroque style of Bertha's drawing room was gone, replaced by lighter walls, beautiful Chippendale furniture, chairs placed in appealing conversation groups, and an understated elegance overall.

Pauline's keen visual sense and awareness of color is evident in her letters, in descriptions of Italian towns and other European destinations, and in comments on people's clothing and

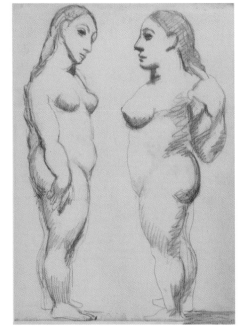

*Above: Henry Spencer Moore, **Group of Draped Standing Figures**, 1942. At right: Pablo Picasso, **Two Nudes, Standing**, 1906. We can see Pauline Palmer's distinct taste in art collecting and compare it to that of her mother-in-law. While Bertha favored rooms in the Moorish, French and Flemish Renaissance Revival styles, Pauline reorganized the somewhat cluttered rooms of the Castle with the help of her friend and architect, David Adler, to create an elegant and simpler ambience. While Bertha loved the Impressionist and Barbizon school paintings, Pauline preferred the post-Impressionist works shown here and on the previous two pages.*

The taste of the two Mrs. Palmers was contrasting and complementary. As Daniel Catton Rich noted: "If Bertha Honoré Palmer stopped at the post-Impressionists, Pauline Palmer supplied Cézanne."

*Opposite page: James MacNeill Whistler, **The Fan**, 1879.*

appearance. In 1908, she tells her mother how she witnessed the end of a mass at the Salute in Venice: "...all the people were streaming out. Men in red gowns carrying huge lighted candles and priests in white with different coloured banners. In the twilight it was a marvelous sight." This same visual sense is displayed in her collecting, which was both an offshoot of the Palmer family's enthusiasm and a display of her own interests. Pauline enjoyed many of the works that she and Min had inherited from Bertha, and she added to these collections either with her husband or on her own. For example, it is known that Bertha owned Whistler etchings and hung them in her rooms in Paris. Min followed suit in a birthday gift to his wife. As Pauline wrote to her mother on June 11, 1912: "Min gave me some beautiful etchings—four Whistlers and a Schongauer—so I managed to do very nicely."

One of Pauline's most elegant Whistler prints is *The Fan*, his fourth transfer lithograph, in which his model and mistress, Maud Franklin, sits on a chair holding a fan. In 1878 when Whistler was first experimenting with lithography, Maud Franklin became an important collaborator, posing tirelessly and encouraging him to continue his efforts to master the medium. Despite the simplicity of the drawing style, Whistler carefully rendered details of the model's dress, demonstrating his "fascination with costume." Among Whistler's most frequent themes were beautiful, fashionable women. As Pamela Robertson points out, these depictions seemed to conform to the Victorian convention of displaying "women as beautiful objects and homemakers." But she also notes that Whistler was revolutionary in his intentions, which lay in his theory of *"l'art pour l'art."* His primary concern was aesthetics and creating images of delicate and fashionable women rather than any underlying political message.

Whistler's portraits and depictions of women were probably among Pauline's favorites, as she herself was enamored with beautiful clothing and fashion, and the proper way women should appear. As she said when her daughter Bertha returned from boarding school amidst a group of sloppy-looking girls: "I could hardly wait for Bertha to come to see if she looked as awful. Fortunately she didn't, but on the contrary, very smart and English, with tweed suit, scarf inside her collar, and plain felt hat, all soft tones of brown. I was proud of her."

The Palmer collection of Whistler prints included substantial holdings of both his etchings and lithographs. Many of the subjects are city or river scenes. The collection favors the early realist etchings in the "Thames Set" and the "French Set," rather than the much-coveted, highly regarded Venice plates. The Venetian scenes were misunderstood by critics at the time, as they were unusually abstract and minimal. Among the Thames Set etchings in the Palmer collection are *Old West-*

Above: A panel showing The Crystal Palace c. 1851, given by Pauline to the Antiquarian Society.
At left and opposite page: Two examples of Pauline's **Verre de Nevers: The Crucifixion**, *late eighteenth century and* **The May Dance***.*
Page 315: A portrait of Pauline Palmer hangs in the gallery after she and Min made the Castle their own.

minster Bridge, Chelsea Bridge and Church, Black Lion Wharf, The Forge, Eagle Wharf, and the "superb portrait" *Becquet*. The beauty of these impressions demonstrates the Palmers' good eye when it came to collecting fine prints.

Pauline also showed finesse in her taste for modern art. Former Art Institute director Daniel Catton Rich was a close observer of Pauline's passion for collecting. He described how when they were together in Paris on a group scouting trip, he and Pauline "used to leave the others poring over print portfolios to sneak off and gaze at pictures and drawings." He admitted that there were not too many people with whom he enjoyed looking at things, but she was one of them. She bought prints, paintings, and drawings of modern painters including Dufy, Cézanne, Picasso, Seurat, and Henry Moore. He described the art in Pauline's apartment: "A distinguished Matisse drawing hung near a vigorous Picasso oil of the Blue period, *Woman and Child at the Fountain* (1901), and a dark brush drawing of Picasso's war years, *Two Pigeons* (1942)." He remembered how happy she was when she found one of Toulouse-Lautrec's circus series drawings—perhaps it reminded her of the evenings spent with Min at the Moulin Rouge in their early trips to Paris. Rich also observed "her quiet appreciation of Seurat's *Lady with a Parasol* (1882–84)." Although Pauline had her own strong opinions, she was also advised by specialists: Alice Roullier, a dealer in French modernism, and Carl O. Schniewind, the Institute's curator of Prints and Drawings.

In addition to collecting prints, Pauline collected many items through her association with the Antiquarian Society. Following in her mother-in-law's footsteps, Pauline had become president of the Society for the first time in 1919 and served two terms. Her main interests within the Society were needlework and textiles. As Celia Hilliard notes: "During and after WWI, she hosted frequent sales of fine handiwork in her Lake Shore mansion to benefit French widows and orphans." Her exquisite taste and generosity led to an important Society purchase. In 1923 a member of the Russian nobility offered her a veil of Brussels lace carrying the imperial Russian coat of arms and reported to have been worn by the last two czarinas. When Pauline showed the veil to members of the Antiquarian board, they were greatly impressed, but refused to pay the high fee. Pauline then purchased it herself and presented it as a gift to them, adding to the list of important textiles she gave over the years.

Pauline also had an interest in glass figures, especially the glass and enamel figures from Nevers, France, known as *verre de Nevers*. As noted in the Art Institute's European Decorative Arts catalogue, "*Verre de Nevers* figures and groups have long held a reputation for providing an insight into the taste and humor of their period." Pauline's collection included works of both secular and religious subjects, including an intricate reliquary known as *The Crucifixion*, comprised of a glass figure of the crucified Christ, along with elaborately "quilled" gilded paper and an encased piece of bone. Pauline's gifts of these figures make up a large part of the Art Institute's French glass collection and are on regular display.

The Palmer taste for art collecting was passed down from generation to generation. While Bertha Honoré Palmer began in grandeur with her revolutionary and stately collection, Pauline Palmer continued the legacy with, as Daniel Catton Rich writes, her "intimate, tender and more elusive moderns. If Bertha Honoré Palmer stopped at the post-Impressionists, Pauline Palmer supplied Cézanne." The next generation—Gordon Palmer, Bertha Thorne, Rose Movius Palmer, and Pauline Wood—were also generous donors, making Rich's point that "it is reassuring to see the sons and daughters and granddaughters continuing to admire and to collect."

CHRONOLOGY

MAY 20, 1826—Potter Palmer I, son of Benjamin and Rebecca (Potter) Palmer, is born in Albany County, New York.

MAY 22, 1849—Bertha Honoré, daughter of Henry Hamilton and Eliza Jane (Carr) Honoré, is born in Louisville, Kentucky.

MARCH 22, 1853—Herman H. Kohlsaat, future newspaper owner and father of Pauline, is born.

NOVEMBER 12, 1861—Mabel Blake Kohlsaat is born.

JULY 1870—Bertha Honoré marries Potter Palmer, twenty-three years her senior, after a two-month engagement. Their vows are exchanged at her parents' home at 157 Michigan Avenue in Chicago. Her father, Henry Honoré, is a real estate associate of Palmer's.

1871—Potter Palmer builds the Palmer House Hotel on State Street in Chicago; it succumbs in the Great Fire of October, 1871, just thirteen days after its opening. Rebuilding begins immediately after.

NOVEMBER 1873—The new Palmer House Hotel opens, much larger and statelier than the first.

FEBRUARY 1, 1874—Honoré Palmer, first son of Potter and Bertha Honoré Palmer, is born.

OCTOBER 8, 1875—Potter Palmer II, younger son of Potter and Bertha Honoré Palmer, is born.

JUNE 1876—Julia Grant, daughter of Frederick Dent Grant (son of President Ulysses S. Grant) and Ida M. Honoré (Bertha H. Palmer's sister), is born.

1877—The Antiquarian Society of the Art Institute of Chicago is founded as the Chicago Society of Decorative Art. The Society would officially become affiliated with the Art Institute in 1891.

1879—The Art Institute of Chicago is founded as the Chicago Academy of Fine Arts.

JUNE 10, 1882—Pauline Kohlsaat, daughter of Herman H. and Mabel (Blake) Kohlsaat, is born.

1882–1885—The Palmers construct their mansion, "the Castle," on Lake Shore Drive, the drive overlooking the lake that Potter Palmer himself had designed with the purpose of expanding Chicago. Lake Shore Drive would become one of the most fashionable residential sites in the city.

MAY 1893—The World's Columbian Exposition opens in Chicago, which draws people from all over America and other countries. Bertha Honoré Palmer is president of the Board of Lady Managers, and Potter Palmer is the Exposition's vice-president and director.

1893—The Art Institute of Chicago moves to its current location in its Beaux-Arts-style building on Michigan Avenue.

1899—Julia Grant marries Prince Michael Cantacuzène, whom she met while travelling with her aunt Bertha in Rome.

MAY 4, 1902—Potter Palmer I dies, leaving his estate to his wife and sons.

1903—Honoré Palmer marries Grace Greenway Brown.

JULY 27, 1908—Pauline Kohlsaat marries Potter Palmer II ("Min") at a small ceremony in Chicago.

1908—Pauline and Min visit Europe on their honeymoon.

MAY 1909—Potter Palmer III is born.

1910—On their second trip to Europe, the Palmers travel to London and attend Edward VII's funeral with Bertha Honoré Palmer.

1910–1911—Bertha Honoré Palmer buys land in Sarasota, Florida. Her uncle Benjamin Lockwood and his wife, Laura (Carr) Honoré, also own land there. With her brother Adrian C. Honoré, Bertha forms the Venice-Sarasota Company with early Sarasota developer J. H. Lord. Potter II and Honoré Palmer begin building their Sarasota house, Immokalee.

APRIL 1911—Bertha Palmer, Pauline and Min's first daughter, is born.

1912—Pauline and Min spend time in Europe with their two children.

WINTER 1912 AND SPRING 1913—Pauline and Min visit Sarasota, staying at the newly-completed Immokalee.

JUNE 1914—Gordon Palmer, Pauline and Min's third child, is born.

AUGUST 1914—The Great War begins.

SEPTEMBER 1914—Pauline writes from the Palmers' summer place in Biddeford Pool, Maine.

JANUARY 1917—Pauline Palmer, Min and Pauline's fourth child, is born.

1917—Julia and Michael Cantacuzène leave Russia as a result of the Bolshevik Revolution. She would later write *Revolutionary Days*.

1918—Min and Pauline spend winter months again in Sarasota.

MAY 5, 1918—Bertha Honoré Palmer dies, days before her sixty-ninth birthday, leaving her sons close to $20 million in assets, including the Palmer House Hotel, the Castle, and other property.

1919–1927—Pauline serves her first tenure as president of the Antiquarian Society.

1920—Min and Pauline are in Europe again, for the first time after the war. They stay in Paris to divide up Bertha's belongings there.

FALL 1920—The family travels to Sarasota again, staying at the Oaks in Osprey until the following April.

1922—Min and Pauline move into the Castle; their three older children go off to boarding school.

OCTOBER 17, 1924—Herman H. Kohlsaat dies in Washington, age 71, in the house of then Secretary of Commerce, Herbert Hoover, after paying a visit to President Coolidge in the White House, and just before a World Series game he had planned to attend. President and Mrs. Coolidge lead the mourners, which include a delegation of leading city newspaper publishers including Colonel McCormick and Arthur Hays Sulzberger.

1925—The Palmer House Hotel is torn down and rebuilt on the same site. Potter II becomes president of the Art Institute.

1925–January 1926—Pauline writes the last set of letters to her mother, describing the Christmas holidays.

1929—Honoré Palmer, Min, and Prince Michael Cantacuzène found the Palmer National Bank and Trust Company, which later becomes Palmer First National Bank.

SEPTEMBER 3, 1943—Potter Palmer II dies, age 67.

1945—The Palmer House Hotel is sold to Hilton Hotels.

FEBRUARY 12, 1950—"The Castle" is demolished.

JULY 7, 1956—Pauline Kohlsaat Palmer dies, age 74.

1959—Mabel Blake Kohlsaat dies, age 98.

1976—Palmer First National Bank merges with Southeast Bank.

NOTES

The sources for Chapters 1–12 were consulted for the Introductions to the chapters. For authors' complete names and publication information, see the Bibliography.

INTRODUCTION

On Chicago history and the World's Columbian Exposition: Miller, *City of the Century: The Epic of Chicago and the Making of America*; Weimann, *The Fair Women*; Lowe, *Lost Chicago*; Larson, *Devil in the White City*.

On the Kohlsaat–Palmer wedding: newspaper clippings in the family's collection.

On Bertha Honoré Palmer and Palmer family background: Ross, *Silhouette in Diamonds*.

CHAPTER ONE

On ocean travel: Maxtone-Graham, *The Only Way to Cross*.

CHAPTER TWO

On Worth fashions: Milbank, *Couture: the Great Designers*.

On Bertha's London entertaining: "Phyllis," "Is Mrs. Potter Palmer the Only American Woman Who Knows How to Spend a Fortune?" *Chicago Sunday Tribune*, September 22, 1907.

On women's self-development: Matthews and Mansperger, *Bertha Honoré Palmer: Legendary Lady of Sarasota*.

On Bertha Palmer's London and Paris homes: Ross, *Silhouette in Diamonds*.

CHAPTER THREE

On Sarasota: Ross, *Silhouette in Diamonds*; Matthews and Mansperger, *Bertha Honoré Palmer: Legendary Lady of Sarasota*; Blanchard, "Queen of a Europeanized World: Mrs. Potter Palmer and the Woman's Building in Chicago 1893;" and interviews with Palmer family members.

CHAPTER FOUR

On Rosa Lewis: Masters, *Rosa Lewis: An Exceptional Edwardian*.

CHAPTER FIVE

On the Oaks: Matthews and Mansperger, *Bertha Honoré Palmer: Legendary Lady of Sarasota* and Ross, *Silhouette in Diamonds*.

On Bertha Palmer, ibid.

CHAPTER SIX

On Biddeford Pool: Locke, *Shores of Sacco Bay*, quoted in William B. Jordan, Jr.'s Introduction to *Gleanings from the Sea* by Joseph W. Smith.

CHAPTER SEVEN

On Julia Cantacuzène: Ross, *Silhouette in Diamonds* and Cantacuzène, *My Life Here and There*.

On Bertha's death: Ross, *Silhouette in Diamonds*.

On Bertha's will: The will of Bertha Honoré Palmer in *Chicago Evening Post*, May 17, 1918.

CHAPTER EIGHT

On Bertha and her Paris collections: Ross, *Silhouette in Diamonds*.

On the Republican convention: Kohlsaat, *From McKinley to Harding: Personal Recollections of Our Presidents*. H. H.'s loyalty and wise advice had earned him a respectful intimacy with political leaders and presidents, including Republicans William McKinley, Theodore Roosevelt, and Mark Hanna, and Democrats Woodrow Wilson and Colonel Edward House.

CHAPTER TEN

On Pauline and the Antiquarian Society, and Robert Allerton: Hilliard, "'Higher Things': Remembering the Early Antiquarians," and Tvrdik, *The Antiquarian Society of the Art Institute of Chicago: The First One Hundred Years*.

On decorations of the Castle: Lowe, *Chicago Interiors*, and interview with Pauline Metcalf on David Adler.

CHAPTER TWELVE

Quotation from F. Scott Fitzgerald's *The Great Gatsby*.

On the Antiquarian Society: Hilliard, "'Higher Things': Remembering the Early Antiquarians," in *Museum Studies*, Gifts Beyond Measure: The Antiquarian Society and the European Decorative Arts, 1987-2002.

EPILOGUE

On Potter Palmer II: Obituaries in the *Chicago Tribune*, *New York Times* and *Sarasota Herald Tribune*, September 1943.

On Pauline Palmer: Obituaries in the *Chicago Daily News*, *Chicago Tribune*, *The News* (Sarasota), *Sarasota Herald Tribune*, July 1956, and interviews with family members.

On Honoré Palmer: Obituaries in the *Chicago Tribune*, *The News* (Sarasota), *Sarasota Herald Tribune*, March 1964.

On the Palmer National Bank and Trust Co.: *Sarasota Herald Tribune*, June 2, 1999.

On D'orsay Palmer: *Tampa Tribune*, May 1939, and obituary from an unknown publication, May 15, 1939.

On Honoré Palmer, Jr.: *Sarasota Herald Tribune*, February 1938.

On Potter Palmer III: *Sarasota Herald Tribune*, *Chicago Tribune*, October 1946.

On Grace Greenway Brown Palmer: *Chicago Tribune*, April 1966.

On Gordon Palmer: *Sarasota Herald Tribune*, February 1964.

On Julia Grant Cantacuzène: Obituaries in *Time* and *Sarasota Herald Tribune*, October 1975.

On the Palmer Castle: Mary W. Blanchard, "Mrs. Potter Palmer's Castle." *Nest*, Winter 2002-2003.

On "The Oaks": Matthews and Mansperger, *Mrs. Potter Palmer: Legendary Lady of Sarasota*. Gulf Coast Heritage Association, Inc.

THE PALMER ART COLLECTION

p. 283: Mary Cassatt on Bertha Palmer: Mary Cassatt to Sara T. Hallowell, *Cassatt and Her Circle, Selected Letters*, edited by Nancy M. Mathews, New York: Abbeville, 1984.

James Wood on Palmer Collection: James N. Wood, *Treasures from the Art Institute of Chicago*, Preface, The Art Institute of Chicago, 2000, p.14.

pp. 283–288: Information on the Palmers' "Castle": Ishbel Ross, *Silhouette in Diamonds*, p. 53; Mary Blanchard, "Mrs. Potter Palmer's Castle," *Nest, A Quarterly Magazine of Interiors*, Winter 2002-2003; David Lowe, *Chicago Interiors*, pp. 57-61; and articles of agreement between Potter Palmer and Herter Brothers, April 3, 1893 in

Chicago Historical Society, Potter Palmer Collection, Box 4, pp. 1-3.

p. 288: On Herter Brothers: Howe, et al., ed. *Herter Brothers: Furniture and Interiors for a Gilded Age*, Houston: Harry N. Abrams, Inc. and the Museum of Fine Arts, 1994.

pp. 288–290: On collecting Barbizon paintings: W.G. Constable, *Art Collecting in the United States*. London: Thomas Nelson and Sons, Ltd., 1964, pp. 72-73.

p. 290: On visiting Barbizon: Ishbel Ross, *Silhouette in Diamonds*, p. 149.

p. 290: Potter Palmer's letter to Theodore Robinson: *Treasures from the Art Institute of Chicago* by James N. Wood with commentaries by Debra N. Mancoff. The Art Institute of Chicago, distributed by Hudson Hills Press, New York, 2000.

pp. 291–293: Hallowell helping Bertha Honoré Palmer: Sara Hallowell, letter to Mrs. Palmer, December 20, 1893.

p. 293: On Monet exhibit, and his statement about his *Stacks of Wheat*: *Monet*, Carla Rachman. London: Phaidon Press, 1997, p. 251.

p. 293: On Bertha Honoré Palmer's acquisition of Monet's grainstacks, and selling one to Louisine Havemeyer, now at the Metropolitan Museum: Frelinghuysen, et al., *Splendid Legacy: The Havemeyer Collection*. New York: The Metropolitan Museum of Art, 1993.

p. 293: Largest collection of Monet's grainstacks are at the AIC due to Bertha Honoré Palmer: "Monet" by Andrew Forge, *Artists in Focus*. Chicago: Art Institute of Chicago, 1995, p. 44.

pp. 293–294: On Degas: Brettell and McCullagh, *Degas in The Art Institute of Chicago*, pp. 56-57.

pp. 294–295: Brettell on Impressionists: Brettell, *Impression: Painting Quickly in France 1860-1890*, pp. 17-18; on Manet, pp. 74-77.

p. 295: On the Palmers' set of Cassatt's 1890-1891 color prints and the pastel *Young Mother: Treasures from the Art Institute of Chicago* by James N. Wood with commentaries by Debra N. Mancoff. The Art Institute of Chicago, distributed by Hudson Hills Press, New York, 2000, p. 21.

p. 295: On Bertha traveling to Monet's studio and garden at Giverny: Ishbel Ross, *Silhouette in Diamonds*, p. 149.

p. 295: On Bertha as a natural leader: Alice Saarinen, *The Proud Possessors*. New York: Random House, 1955, pp. 3-24.

p. 295: On Foreign Masterpieces Owned by Americans exhibition: Alice Saarinen, ibid.

p. 295: On what the murals represented in the 1892 Columbian Exposition: Bertha's letter to Hallowell, of February 24, 1892, quoted in Weimann, *Fair Women*, p. 191.

pp. 295–299: Description of Mary Cassatt's panel on the modern woman, and MacMonnies' on the primitive woman: Weimann, p. 214.

p. 300: On what Bertha collected after Potter Palmer's death in 1902: Ishbel Ross, *Silhouette in Diamonds* and Mary Blanchard, *Nest* article.

pp. 300–301: On 1910 Art Institute of Chicago show exhibiting Bertha's paintings: *Art Institute of Chicago Exhibitions Catalogue: Paintings from the Collection of Mrs. Potter Palmer*. Publications 1910-1911, vol. 1.

pp. 301–302: Bertha's will required the art works to be valued and allocated to two bequests, one of $100,000 maximum. The second bequest, indirectly by way of $400,000, enabled her sons to designate for charitable purposes a further group of paintings. Beyond that they gave an additional collection of thirty-two paintings valued at $343,500 from their mother's collection, which she had bequeathed to them. Source—The will of Bertha Honoré Palmer and article in *Chicago Evening Post*, May 17, 1918.

pp. 302–305: On Potter Palmer II's roles at the Art Institute: *Bulletin of the Art Institute of Chicago*, Potter Palmer Memorial edition, November 1943.

p. 305: On the controversy between "modernism" and "conservatism" in the Art Institute, and Potter's insight into Modernism stemming from his interest in Asian Art: extract from C. J. Bulliet's column from the *Chicago Daily News*, as printed *in Picture and Gift Journal*, September 1943.

pp. 306–307: On importance of Potter Palmer's print collection: Interview with Martha Tedeschi, curator of Prints and Drawings at the Art Institute of Chicago, and J.W. Janson, *History of Art*, p. 12.

p. 307: Description of gifts from Potter Palmer's Oriental collection: Charles Fabens Kelley—Assistant Director, 1943 *Bulletin of the AIC*: "Potter Palmer and the Oriental Department."

p. 308: On what Min meant to the AIC and his lasting mark on the institution: Chauncey McCormick, Joseph T. Ryerson and Russell Tyson, 1943 *Bulletin of the AIC* "Committee of Resolutions on Potter Palmer."

p. 311: On Whistler's *The Fan*: Martha Tedeschi, "Songs on Stone: James McNeill Whistler and the Art of Lithography," Art Institute of Chicago Exhibition Catalogue, 6/6/98-8/30/98, in Museum Studies, 24, no. 1.

p. 311: On Whistler's depictions of women as fashionable: Pamela Robertson, *Beauty and the Butterfly: Whistler's Depictions of Women, Pastels, Etchings and Lithographs*. Glasgow: Hunterian Art Gallery, 2003, p. 20.

p. 311: On the comparison of Whistler's landscape "sets" and evaluation of his other works: Frederick Wedmore, *Whistler and Others*. New York: Charles Scribner's Sons, 1906, p. 7.

p. 314: On Pauline's modern art collecting: Introduction by Daniel Catton Rich for catalogue of *Palmer Family Collections*, Ringling Museum of Art, Sarasota, Florida, 1963.

p. 314: On Pauline's work with the Antiquarian Society: "'Higher Things': Remembering the Early Antiquarians," Celia Hilliard. Published in *Gifts Beyond Measure*, p.18-19.

p. 314: On the "verre de Nevers" figures: Art Institute of Chicago's European Decorative Arts catalogue.

BIBLIOGRAPHY

BOOKS:

Bach, Ira J. and Susan Wolfson. *Chicago on Foot: Walking Tours of Chicago's Architecture*. Chicago: Chicago Review Press, 1987.

Barter, Judith A., Kimberly Rhodes, and Seth A. Thayer, with contributions by Andrew Walker. *American Arts at the Art Institute of Chicago: From Colonial Times to World War I*. Chicago: The Art Institute of Chicago, 1998.

Brettell, Richard R. *French Impressionists*. New York: The Art Institute of Chicago and Harry N. Abrams, Inc., Publishers, 1987.

———. *Impression: Painting Quickly in France 1860-1890*. Williamstown, Mass.: Yale University Press and Sterling and Francine Clark Art Institute, 2000.

———. and Suzanne Folds McCullagh. *Degas in The Art Institute of Chicago*. New York: The Art Institute of Chicago and Harry N. Abrams, Inc., Publishers, 1984.

Cantacuzène, Princess Julia. *My Life Here and There*. New York: Charles Scribner's Sons, 1921.

———. *Revolutionary Days*. Chicago: The Lakeside Classics, R. R. Donnelley & Sons Company, 1999.

Constable, W. G. *Art Collecting in the United States of America*. London: Thomas Nelson and Sons Ltd., 1964.

Forge, Andrew. *Artists in Focus*. Chicago: The Art Institute of Chicago, 1995.

Frelinghuysen, Alice Cooney, Gary Tinterow, Susan Alyson Stein, Gretchen Wold and Julia Meech. *Splendid Legacy: The Havemeyer Collection*. New York: The Metropolitan Museum of Art, 1993.

Gere, Charlotte and Marina Vaizey. *Great Women Collectors*. Philip Wilson Publishers, 1999.

Harris, Neil. *Chicago Apartments: A Century of Lakefront Luxury*. New York: Acanthus Press, 2004.

Heise, Kenan & Mark Frazel. *Hands on Chicago: Getting Hold of the City*. Chicago: Bonus Books, Inc., 1987.

Herbert, Robert L. *Seurat and the Making of La Grande Jatte*. Chicago: The Art Institute of Chicago, 2004.

Howe, Katherine S., Alice Cooney Frelinghuysen, et al. *Herter Brothers: Furniture and Interiors for a Gilded Age*. Houston: Harry N. Abrams, Inc. and the Museum of Fine Arts, 1994.

Kohlsaat, H. H. *From McKinley to Harding: Personal Recollections of Our Presidents*. New York: Scribners, 1923.

Landau, David and Peter Parshall. *The Renaissance Print, 1470-1550*. New Haven: Yale University Press, 1994.

Larson, Erik. *The Devil in the White City: Murder, Magic, and Madness at the Fair that Changed America*. New York: Vintage Books, 2003.

Lowe, David Garrard. *Lost Chicago*. Boston: Houghton Mifflin, 1975.

———. *Chicago Interiors*. Chicago: Contemporary Books, 1979.

Mansperger, Linda W. and Janet Synder Matthews. *Mrs. Potter Palmer: Legendary Lady of Sarasota*. Sarasota, Fl.: Gulf Coast Heritage Association, Inc., 1999.

Matthews, Nancy Mowll, ed. *Cassatt and Her Circle, Selected Letters*. New York: Abbeville Press Publishers, 1984.

Maxtone-Graham, John. *The Only Way to Cross*. New York: Collier Books, 1978.

Masters, Anthony. *Rosa Lewis: An Exceptional Edwardian*. New York: St. Martin's Press, 1977.

Milbank, Caroline Reynolds. *Couture: The Great Designers*. New York: Stewart, Tabori & Chang, 1985.

Miller, Donald. *City of the Century: The Epic of Chicago and the Making of America*. New York: Simon & Schuster, 1996.

Naylor, Maria, ed. *Etchings of James MacNeill Whistler*. New York: Dover Publications, 1975.

Rachman, Carla. *Monet*. London: Phaidon Press Limited, 1997.

Robertson, Pamela. *Beauty and the Butterfly: Whistler's Depictions of Women, Pastels, Etchings and Lithographs*. Glasgow: Hunterian Art Gallery, 2003.

Ross, Ishbel. *Silhouette in Diamonds: The Life of Mrs. Potter Palmer*. New York: Harper & Brothers, 1960.

Saarinen, Alice B. *The Proud Possessors*. New York: Random House, 1955.

Salny, Stephen M. *The Country Houses of David Adler with a Catalogue Raisonné*. New York: Norton, 2001.

Smith, Joseph. W. *Gleanings from the Sea*. Wells: Harding Publishing Co., 1987 (1887).

Smith, Richard Norton. *The Colonel: The Life and Legend of Robert R. McCormick 1880-1955*. Evanston: Northwestern University Press, 2003.

Spink, Nesta R., Harriet K. Stratis and Martha Tedeschi. *The Lithographs of James McNeill Whistler: Catalogue Raisonné*. Chicago: The Art Institute of Chicago, and New York: Hudson Hills Press, 1998.

Taussig, Meredith. *Seven Houses on Lake Shore Drive*. Chicago: Commission, 1989.

Thorne, Martha, ed. *David Adler, Architect: The Elements of Style*. The Art Institute of Chicago and Yale University Press: New Haven and London, 2002.

Tvrdik, Valerie, ed. *The Antiquarian Society of the Art Institute of Chicago: The First One Hundred Years*. Chicago: The Art Institute of Chicago, 1977.

Wedmore, Frederick. *Whistler and Others*. New York: Charles Scribner's Sons, 1906.

Weimann, Jeanne Madeline. *The Fair Women*. Chicago: Academy, 1981.

Wood, James N. and Debra Mancoff. *Treasures from The Art Institute of Chicago*. Chicago: The Art Institute of Chicago, 2000.

———. and Teri J. Edelstein. *The Art Institute of Chicago: The Essential Guide*. The Art Institute of Chicago, 1993.

McCormick-Hamilton Lord-Day. *Ancestral Lines*. Privately Printed, 1957.

Oasis in the City: A History of The Casino. Privately Printed, 1997.

Palmer Family Collections. Introduction by Daniel Catton Rich. Ringling Museum of Art: Sarasota, Florida, 1963.

Palmer, Honoré, Grant and Allied Families. New York: The American Historical Society, Inc., 1929.

ARTICLES:

Art Institute of Chicago Archives, Paintings from the Collection of Mrs. Potter Palmer. Bulletin vol. 4, no. 1, 1910–1911.

Art Institute of Chicago Archives, 1943 Bulletin of the Art Institute of Chicago on Potter Palmer.

"Art Institute of Chicago's Architectural History," *Art Institute of Chicago Museum Studies*, vol. 14, no. 1.

Blanchard, Mary W. "Queen of a Europeanized World: Mrs. Potter Palmer and the Woman's Building in Chicago, 1893."

———. "Mrs. Potter Palmer's Castle," *Nest, A Quarterly Magazine of Interiors*, Winter 2002–03.

Hilliard, Celia. "'Higher Things': Remembering the Early Antiquarians," in *Museum Studies*, vol. 28, no. 2, *Gifts Beyond Measure: The Antiquarian Society and the European Decorative Arts, 1987-2002.* The Art Institute of Chicago, 2002.

McKinney, Megan, Dennis Rodkin, Judy York, Amber Holst, Geoffrey Johnson, and Bryan Smith. "What Ever Happened to the Great Chicago Families?" *Chicago*, February 2005.

"Noted Art Patron Dies—A Comment." Extract from C. J. Bulliet's column in *Chicago Daily News*, printed in *Picture & Gift Journal*, September 1943.

"Phyllis." "Is Mrs. Potter Palmer the Only American Woman Who Knows How to Spend a Fortune?" *Chicago Sunday Tribune*, September 22, 1907.

Rotzoll, Brenda Warner. "The *Other* Bertha Palmer: Socialite also a shrewd businesswoman, social activist." *Sun Times*, March 16, 2003.

Tedeschi, Martha. "Songs on Stone: James McNeill Whistler and the Art of Lithography," *Art Institute of Chicago Exhibition Catalog*, June-August 1998.

"Text of Mrs. Palmer's Will." *The Chicago Evening Post*, May 17, 1918.

First of all I would like to thank Charlotte Bordeaux, granddaughter of Pauline Palmer. Together we had the idea of using her grandmother's appealing letters to her great grandmother to tell this story. Charlotte backed the book from the beginning. She was continually generous in giving me family stories, answering my questions, and supplying photographs. As our families had been friends in the earlier generations, it was a pleasure for me to relive in my imagination the lives and worlds of our mothers and grandmothers. Other Palmer family members provided me with memories and helpful information: Potter Palmer IV, Oakleigh Blakeman Thorne, his son, Oakleigh Thorne, the late Honoré Wamsler, Arthur MacDougall Wood, Sr., and his son, Arthur MacDougall Wood, Jr. Constance Shepard Otis, niece of Pauline Palmer, spoke with me often, giving details of her aunt and mother and times past, and lending me books on family history.

I wish to thank those at the Chicago Historical Society who made the book possible: Russell Lewis, in particular, for his generosity and help, and his enthusiasm for the project. I wish to thank those there who aided in the research and picture-selection process, particularly Rob Medina, and also Colleen Beckett, Anne Marie Chase, Lesley Martin, Debbie Vaughn, Justin Huyck, Tom Guerra, and Amy Marshall.

I could not have completed my research or talked of the Palmers' involvement at the Art Institute of Chicago without the help of many there. Suzanne McCullagh was generous in talking with me, and putting me in touch with others; Martha Tedeschi advised me on describing Potter Palmer's print collecting; and Bart Ryckbosch aided in the research into Art Institute history and discussed the Palmers' collecting with me. Vanessa Le Fort made an enormous contribution in investigating all aspects of the Palmers' interest in art. I would also like to thank Amy Berman, Amy Babinec, and Mary Woolever, who kindly aided us in securing images.

At the Museum of Fine Arts in Boston, Tiffany Webber Hanchett helped me, as did Debbie Dyer at the Bar Harbor Historical Society, Linda Mansperger of the Gulf Coast Heritage Association and Ann Shank of the Sarasota County History Center.

I am grateful to historian Mary Blanchard, an authority on Bertha Honoré Palmer, for answers to many of my questions; to Pauline Metcalf, architectural historian, for discussing the interior of "the Castle" with me, and to others who helped me in various ways, including reading parts of the manuscript and discussing Chicago history: Andy Austin Cohen, Ted Cohen, Jane Brandes, Viola Winner, and Mary Yost Crowley.

I want to thank my assistants: April Marks for her excellent help and advice; Matthew Rotman for his hard work and contributions; Ali Bujnowski, who was so enthusiastic and organized the material beautifully; Lisa Dorfman for her hard work; and particularly Sandra Roldan for her expert handling of the pictures, her enthusiasm about all aspects of the project, and her contributions and insights into the Palmers' art collecting.

I owe thanks to those who worked so hard and brilliantly in actually making the book—working with the illustrations and smoothing out the bumps in the text: my superb designer Elizabeth Avedon and her associate Laura White, my publisher Maria Teresa Train, the index maker Judy Lyon Davis, and my excellent editor Ruth Greenstein.

Finally, I am grateful for the continual support and enthusiasm of my family: my sons Sargent Gardiner and Willard Gardiner, my daughter Daphne Trotter, my daughters-in-law Aimee Gardiner and Beth Dulik, and my son-in-law and fellow writer Andrew Trotter. And once again, my husband, George H. P. Dwight, continually cheered me on and offered amusing comments and good ideas to add energy, vitality, and irony to our subject.

PHOTOGRAPH AND ILLUSTRATION CREDITS

Every reasonable attempt has been made to identify owners of copyright. Errors or omissions will be corrected in subsequent editions.

OPENING PAGES:

Image of Palmer Castle—Photograph by J. W. Taylor. Architecture by Cobb and Frost. Potter Palmer Residence. Historic Architecture and Landscape Image Collection, Ryerson and Burnham Libraries. Reproduction © Art Institute of Chicago.

Opposite title page—Portrait of Pauline Kohlsaat, Chicago Historical Society.

Following pages (pp. viii–ix)—Photograph by Kaufmann and Fabry Co. Architecture by Cobb and Frost. Potter Palmer Residence. Historic Architecture and Landscape Image Collection, Ryerson and Burnham Libraries. Reproduction © Art Institute of Chicago.

p. xiii—Portrait of Bertha Honoré Palmer, Chicago Historical Society.

INTRODUCTION:

p. 15, 16—Collection of Charlotte Bordeaux.

p. 17—Portrait of Potter Palmer, Chicago Historical Society.

p. 18—Top (Palmer House Hotel): Photographer and artist unknown. Chicago Historical Society. Center and bottom (Chicago cityscapes): Photographs by Barnes-Crosby. Chicago Historical Society.

p. 19—Advertisement for Reaper Broadside, McCormick Farming, Chicago Historical Society.

p. 22—Color reproduction of poster, artist unknown. Chicago Historical Society.

p. 23—Photographers unknown, Chicago Historical Society.

p. 24—Top left: Collection of Charlotte Bordeaux. Top right: "Those Palmer Boys" newspaper clipping. Photographers: J. H. Schultz and Matzene. Chicago Historical Society. Bottom: Photographer unknown, Chicago Historical Society.

p. 25—All from the collection of Charlotte Bordeaux.

CHAPTER 1:

p. 28—Collection of Charlotte Bordeaux.

p. 31—The Mauretania, by Alfred Stieglitz © Hulton Archive/Getty Images.

p. 32, 33—Chicago Historical Society.

p. 37, 45—Collection of Charlotte Bordeaux.

CHAPTER 2:

p. 46—Collection of Charlotte Bordeaux.

p. 49—Funeral Procession of Edward VII © Hulton-Deutsch Collection/CORBIS.

p. 50—Collection of Charlotte Bordeaux.

p. 60—Photographer unknown, Chicago Historical Society.

p. 61, 67—Collection of Charlotte Bordeaux.

CHAPTER 3:

p. 68, 70, 71—Collection of Charlotte Bordeaux.

p. 77—© Gulf Coast Heritage Association, Inc.

p. 84, 85—Collection of Charlotte Bordeaux.

p. 86—Photographer unknown, Chicago Historical Society.

CHAPTER 4:

p. 90, 92—Collection of Charlotte Bordeaux.

p. 100–101—"Le drapage du corsage chez Worth" © Boyer/Roger Viollet.

p. 102, 104, 111—Collection of Charlotte Bordeaux.

CHAPTER 5:

p. 112—Collection of Charlotte Bordeaux.

p. 114—Top: © Gulf Coast Heritage Association, Inc. Bottom: Photographer Unknown, Chicago Historical Society.

p. 115—Photographer Unknown, Chicago Historical Society.

CHAPTER 6:

All images in this chapter are from the collection of Charlotte Bordeaux.

CHAPTER 7:

p. 136—Collection of Charlotte Bordeaux.

p. 138—Photographers Unknown, Chicago Historical Society.

p. 139,140—Chicago Historical Society.

p. 144—© Gulf Coast Heritage Association, Inc.

p. 147—Collection of Charlotte Bordeaux.

p. 148—Photo print by A. Pafetti, 1902. Library of Congress, Prints and Photographs Division, LC-USZ62-76219.

p. 149—Photograph by Underwood and Underwood, 1924. Library of Congress, Prints and Photographs Division, LC-USZ62-115611.

p. 151—© Gulf Coast Heritage Association, Inc.

CHAPTER 8:

All images in this chapter are from the collection of Charlotte Bordeaux.

CHAPTER 9:

All images in this chapter are from the collection of Charlotte Bordeaux.

CHAPTER 10:

p. 212—Collection of Charlotte Bordeaux.

p. 214–215—Photographers unknown, Chicago Historical Society.

p. 216–217—Images are from the Antiquarian Society Scrapbooks, Institutional Archives, The Art Institute of Chicago.

p. 221—Photographer Unknown, Chicago Historical Society.

p. 227, 229—From a family scrapbook in the collection of Charlotte Bordeaux.

CHAPTER 11:

p. 230—Collection of Charlotte Bordeaux.

p. 233—Illustration by Cde Fomaro, Color reproduction © Chicago Historical Society.

p. 234—Photographer Unknown, Chicago Historical Society.

p. 236, 237—Photographs © Bar Harbor Historical Society. Letter is from the collection of Charlotte Bordeaux.

p. 251—Postcard of Ralph Waldo Emerson house in Concord, Mass., from the collection of Charlotte Bordeaux.

CHAPTER 12:

canvas, 73.6 x 92.6 cm, Potter Palmer Collection, 1922.425 Reproduction, The Art Institute of Chicago.

Jean François Millet, French, 1814-1875, *In the Auvergne*, 1866-69, oil on canvas, 81.5 x 99.9 cm, Potter Palmer Collection, 1922.414 Reproduction, The Art Institute of Chicago.

Jean François Millet, French, 1814-1875, *Young Woman*, c.1844/45, oil on canvas, 52.1 x 62.4 cm, Mr. and Mrs. Potter Palmer Collection, 1922.415 Reproduction, The Art Institute of Chicago.

Claude Monet, French, 1840-1926, *Bordighera*, 1884, oil on canvas, 25 1/2 x 32 in. (64.8 x 81.3 cm), Potter Palmer Collection, 1922.426 Reproduction, The Art Institute of Chicago.

Claude Monet, French, 1840-1926, *The Departure of the Boats, Etretat*, 1885, oil on canvas, 73.5 x 93 cm, Mr. and Mrs. Potter Palmer Collection, 1922.428 Reproduction, The Art Institute of Chicago.

Claude Monet, French, 1840-1926, *Stack of Wheat*, 1890-91, Oil on canvas, 25 13/16 x 36 1/4 in. (65.6 x 92 cm). Restricted gift of the Searle Family Trust; Major Acquisitions Centennial Endowment; through prior acquisitions of the Mr. and Mrs. Martin A. Ryerson and Potter Palmer collections; through prior bequest of Jerome Friedman, 1983.29 Reproduction, The Art Institute of Chicago.

Claude Monet, French, 1840-1926, *Stacks of Wheat (End of Summer)*, 1890/91, oil on canvas, 60 x 100 cm, Gift of Arthur M. Wood, Sr. in memory of Pauline Palmer Wood, 1985.1103 Reproduction, The Art Institute of Chicago.

Henry Spencer Moore, British, 1898-1986, *Group of Draped Standing Figures*, 1942. Pen and black ink and black crayon, with

brush and gray wash, graphite and touches of red conte crayon, heightened with white gouache, on cream wove paper. Height: 391 mm, Width: 565 mm. Mrs. Potter Palmer Sundry, 1945.2. Reproduction, The Art Institute of Chicago.

Pablo Picasso, Spanish, 1881-1973, *Two Nudes, Standing*, c. 1906. Graphite on cream laid paper (soft pencil drawing). 63 x 46.9 cm, Gift of Mrs. Potter Palmer, 1944.575. Reproduction, The Art Institute of Chicago.

Camille Pissarro, French, 1830-1903, *The Place du Havre*, Paris (Place du Havre, Paris), 1893, oil on canvas, 60.1 x 73.5 cm, Mr. and Mrs. Potter Palmer Collection, 1922.434 Reproduction, The Art Institute of Chicago.

Pierre Cécile Puvis de Chavannes, French, 1824-1898, *The Sacred Grove, Beloved of the Arts and Muses*, 1884-89, Oil on canvas, 93 x 231 cm, Potter Palmer Collection, 1922.445 Reproduction, The Art Institute of Chicago.

Pierre Auguste Renoir, French, 1841-1919, *Acrobats at the Cirque Fernando* (Francisca and Angelina Wartenberg), 1879, oil on canvas, 131.5 x 99.5 cm, Potter Palmer Collection, 1922.440 Reproduction, The Art Institute of Chicago.

Pierre Auguste Renoir, French, 1841-1919, *Lunch at the Restaurant Fournaise (The Rowers' Lunch)*, 1875, Oil on canvas, 21 11/16 x 25 15/16 in. (55.1 x 65.9 cm), Potter Palmer Collection, 1922.437 Photograph by Robert Hashimoto. Reproduction, The Art Institute of Chicago.

Alfred Sisley, French, 1839-1899, *Street in Moret*, c.1890, oil on canvas, 23 7/8 x 28 7/8", Potter Palmer Collection, 1922.441 Reproduction, The Art Institute of Chicago.

Martin Schongauer, German, c.1450-1491, *St. Anthony Tormented by Demons*, 1470-1475, Engraving on paper, 320 x 235 mm (sheet), Gift of Mrs. Potter Palmer, Jr. to the Mr. and Mrs. Potter Palmer Collection, 1955.1227 Reproduction, The Art Institute of Chicago.

Unknown Artist, *The May Dance*, 18th-19th century, *Verre de Nevers*, Gift of Mrs. Potter Palmer II through the Antiquarian Society, 1942.607 Reproduction, The Art Institute of Chicago.

James McNeill Whistler, American, 1834-1903, *The Fan*, 1879, Transfer lithograph in black on cream chine, laid down on off-white plate paper, 205 x 160 mm; primary support: 264 x 188 mm; secondary support: 381 x 275 mm. On loan from the estate of Pauline K. Palmer, RX20769/1702 Photograph by Robert Lifson. Reproduction, The Art Institute of Chicago.

James McNeill Whistler, American, 1834-1903, *Gray and Silver: Old Battersea Reach*, 1863, oil on canvas, 50.9 x 68.6 cm, Potter Palmer Collection, 1922.449 Reproduction, The Art Institute of Chicago.

Wright & Lee, England, probably Manchester, *Panel showing The Crystal Palace*, c. 1851. Cotton, plain weave; engraved roller printed; glazed. 14.5 x 71.5 cm, warp repeat: 37.4 cm. Gift of Mrs. Potter Palmer II to The Antiquarian Society of the Art Institute of Chicago, 1928.464. Reproduction, The Art Institute of Chicago.

Anders Leonard Zorn, Swedish, 1860-1920, *Mrs. Potter Palmer*, 1893, oil on canvas, 258 x 141.2 cm, Potter Palmer Collection, 1922.450 Reproduction, The Art Institute of Chicago.